DESTINATION
FREEDOM

DESTINATION FREEDOM

A Time-Travel Adventure

Stage II: Arrival Instruction

RAMTHA®
and
DOUGLAS MAHR

BASED UPON THE WRITINGS OF J. Z. KNIGHT

PRENTICE HALL PRESS

NEW YORK LONDON TORONTO SYDNEY TOKYO

This work is based, in part, upon *Ramtha Dialogues*®, a series of magnetic recordings authored by J.Z. Knight with her permission. Ramtha® is a trademark registered with the U.S. Patent and Trademark office.

The fictional composite characters Ogg, Grogg, and Mrs. Grogg were created by Douglas Mahr and are registered with the U.S. Patent and Trademark office. The fictional composite character, James Summerlund, was created by Douglas Mahr. Any resemblance to persons (living or dead), organizations, institutions, or corporations is entirely coincidental.

 Prentice Hall Press
Gulf + Western Building
One Gulf + Western Plaza
New York, New York 10023

Copyright © 1989 by Private Thoughts, Inc.

PRENTICE HALL PRESS and colophon are registered trademarks
of Simon & Schuster, Inc.

Library of Congress Cataloging-in-Publication Data
Ramtha, the enlightened one (Spirit)

 Destination freedom.

 "Based upon the writings of J.Z. Knight"—V. 2, t.p.
 Contents: Stage 1. Departure instruction—Stage 2. Arrival instruction.
 1. Spirit writings. I. Mahr, Douglas James,
1946–   . II. Knight, J. Z. (Judy Zebra),
1946–   . III. Title.
BF1301.R233   1988   133.9'3   88-17816
ISBN 0-13-202219-2 (pbk. : v. 1)
ISBN 0-13-202227-3 (pbk. : v. 2)

Manufactured in the United States of America

10 9 8 7 6 5 4 3 2 1

First Edition

YOUR DESTINATIONS
Stage II: Arrival Instruction

—❦—

Let's Roll

Let's Roll

You're sitting in the left seat of 174 tons of machine, waiting for takeoff clearance. You key the mike button. "Clearance, Flight 972, IFR to Los Angeles, requesting departure clearance."

A mysterious voice bathed in red and amber light hidden in a darkened room responds, "Flight 972, IFR to Los Angeles, Suma II departure route, maintain 13,000 feet, 250 knots until advised, departure frequency 119.2, squawk 3534, cleared as filed."

You read back this mysterious code to the voice hidden in the cavern. You switch to departure frequency. A voice in the control tower staccatos, "Flight 972, you're cleared for takeoff. Blue Angel 7, continue to hold for clearance."

You glance over to your copilot, "Let's roll."

The whine of the engines begins its crescendo in your headset. The power of your bird is unleashed as you push the throttles forward with a sensitive movement gained from thousands of hours in the left seat. Your gear breaks loose from its captive stance. "Power's set . . . airspeed's alive."

The rush hits you as you feel the acceleration, as the giant machine you control begins its charge down the runway. The whine of power reminds you, the thrust of energy focuses you, as you glance continually at the airspeed indicator display.

". . . 80 knots."

You're focused on thousands of bits of information as you control your bird, as it begins to hurtle down the center line, seemingly out of control, yet fully in control. All your senses are active. Your sight is jutting right, left, center; scanning, looking, watching. Your peripheral vision is sending you input as familiar markers begin to speed by. You're sensing, *feeling* the performance of your engines as they begin to fill your ears above the chatter of the other airport traffic. Your first officer inputs data as the takeoff roll speeds onward. You feel and hear the *thud, thud, click click, clickity click,* as the gear crosses over the separations in the runway, faster and faster, *clickity click, clickity click, clickity click.*

"V-one . . . ," you've reached takeoff decision speed. You're crossing a threshold. You've made the decision to separate from the ground and rise into the air. If you lose an engine now, your craft has enough performance to fly out of it, into the future sunrise. If you can handle the emergency.

"V-one, Rotate," is the callout.

You squeeze the yoke toward you. Your nose wheel begins to lift off the ground, pointing you upward into the sky. In a few seconds, the rest of you will follow. You're airborne.

"Positive rate." You've established a positive rate of climb. There's nothing holding you back now; you're climbing into the sky.

"Gear up, flaps five . . . flaps two . . . flaps up." Your ship is clean, trimmed for maximum climb performance. It's almost like you've been here a thousand times before.

"Climb power," is the call.

You're airborne, rising into a new understanding, traveling into Superconsciousness, into *Flightlevel: Freedom.*

Destination 6

CLEARED FOR
TAKEOFF

The Wild Blue Yonder
Disembark from Illusion
Embark into Amusement

Welcome to Stage II of your flight training. We promise to make your Arrival Instruction as exciting and freewheeling as your Departure Instruction was in Stage I. We realize we left you hanging in a holding pattern, a little bit like those soapie de-operas leave millions glued to their TV sets. Did you notice anyone's eyes glued to a copy of Stage I? Well, since it's okay to leave you glued to the TV, we figured it would be okay to leave you stranded in mid-air. Ready to get on with it?

You've heard much about the mysterious, unseen personality Ramtha. Who am I, you ask? Well, I've been called a lot of things, but unto my reckoning and unto yours I am Ramtha, called The Enlightened One. I salute you this hour as you continue your climb-out from mundane Social Consciousness to an elusive dimension called Superconsciousness into Destination Freedom. I salute you this hour as my brothers and sisters in equality—not as something more grand than you but equal to you.

Those of you who are reading this flightlog are reading it for quite a few reasons. Some of you sincerely want to know—no, you're not sure what it is you're going to know, but you want to know anyway! That's a very good reason to be here; puttering around inside the feelings created by these words. And then there are those of you who are deadheading this flight, looking in on it out of ominously curious motives. For you, the curiosity will go on, and on, and on, and on . . . and on!

To those of you who were coerced, threatened, and shoved into reading this, I am pleased you're here! What you experience in the flight of these words will manifest blatantly in your life. No matter what you think I am, it is what *you* are that is important.

Where Do You Think You're Headed?

Flightlevel: Superconsciousness—what are you climbing out into? In this Age of Gossip you know all about words, aye? Words, communication, that which is termed *common* speech. Well, the more you have evolved common speech, the more you've become limited in your mind. Your mind shuts down just for the purpose of running the motor system within the body for communication; your speech patterns are on continuous autopilot! The one grand thing you do without speech is, you nod or shake your head. That is a noble gesture—it didn't take anything to open your mouth to do that, it just was.

Many of you, to fulfill your desire to communicate, have lost the ability to know; you've lost the touch within your brain. How important is the ability to know? When you're in knowledge of, you're enlightened because you've stepped out of the realm of fear.

Everyone is equal in their brain masses, but you've lost the knowingness ability. You've shut your brain down to leave yourself with absolute *un*knowingness. And when you shut it down, you begin to become gabbrellas; you're climbing out on one engine and you aren't very proficient in engine out-procedures. You're unfamiliar with the term, *gabbrellas?* Gab gab, gab, gab. Talk talk, talk talk—well, you know, you just can't talk *enough*. (Do you know one of those?)

Knowingness appears, not as a speech pattern, but with a spark to the mind that sends an electrical current to the central nervous system from the pineal system at the base of the brain. And that whole electrical shock, if you will, uplifts every cellular mass within the body. Your autopilot-Soul then records that feeling as a new feeling, and that new feeling is without words. To superlove, you don't ever have to utter the words, "I love you."

Words are the means of communication to those who are working with the less than 33 percent of their brain-power, which all of you are. Whatever happened to the other 67 percent of your brain-power? Where is it, what's it doing besides filling up your noggin? It's asleep; it's called the dormant knowingness.

4

You've heard the words, *spiritual* truth as differentiated from the words, *truth* truth? Mark this in your logbook: *everything* is spiritual—what isn't?—because everything is the Godfire. When we refer to spiritual truth, it's for the purpose for you to understand an *accelerated* knowingness. Spiritual truth is that which is hidden in the 67 percent of your brain that is dormant mind. Because you're operating at the 33 percent mind-flightlevel, you've closed down the ability to know, to be in the flow of absolute knowingness.

There are many who think spiritualism is something separate from physicalism. (Is that a proper word?) The body cannot exist without the light that is around it, which holds it in place. Without that light there is no mass. Haven't you ever wondered what keeps your knees together, what keeps the flesh from just floating away? You are *loved* into being by the Great Light.

Engine-Out Operations

Spiritual truth in metaphysical dogma is separate from *reality* reality, that which is unseen; the movement *behind* the action, the wind behind the swaying of the trees. Any dogma is separate from reality reality. I desire you to reason this scientifically: why isn't your brain *completely* operational? Did you ever wonder why you had that rather large slab of flesh occupying your head, and why you only use a little bit of it? It's a bit like using only one leg to walk even though you have two!

You're only operating on 33 percent brain-power because that's all you need to operate on to survive; that's all you need to communicate, that's all you need to be sociably acceptable. Therefore, how can you, with only 33 percent of your brain-slab in operation, contemplate the exotic destinations that await you in the other 67 percent of your brain-slab? You can't at this checkpoint. Therefore, what I'm attempting is to instruct you about a flightplan that has no limit, with words that are limited.

In other words, I'm instructing *around* a knowingness that

there are no words for, to leave you with a *feeling* that begins to open up your slab-work. The technique is to instruct you in a circle around your *Super*knowingness, and everything that lies within that circle we will manifest. How? Because it is pure emotion that opens up the 67 percent! Simple? *Simple.*

Where does the emotion evolve from? The runners—experience. From the experiences you'll gain the wisdom to understand; *"Ah ha"* becomes more prevalent in your vocabulary than curse words. All of these words in this flightlog are just circling around the great truth that lies within. It's not so much what I say to you, but what I *don't* say to you that you're going to realize.

The Think That Holds Your Hairdo Up

Let's get a little physical. How *does* your brain operate? Perhaps you think your brain creates thought, it doesn't; it's a facilitator or a receiver of light propellants, which constantly lowers frequencies from the Godsource, Thought. You all know where your brain sits; it's the thing that holds your hairdo up. What is spiritual about your brain? That which sits in the cavity under your thick skull used to be *fully* open. Everyone knows about the left half and right half of your brain; different hemispheres. How do you activate them, what turns them on? A different thought-frequency.

Your brain-flab is governed by a great gland. It's called the seventh seal; it sits in the center of both sides of your brain. It's called the pituitary system. You've heard of it; everyone thinks it's the third eyeball, correct? It has eyelashes, correct? It doesn't—it resembles a little pear and at the smallest end of that pear is the mouth that opens.

What is it that triggers the pituitary to begin to open up? Want! It's a *feeling,* that's the key. *Desire*—that's the key that begins to open you up. When the Seventh Seal, the crowning seal of the whole body, begins to open, it sends out a hormone flow into the pineal system. Through that flow, another part of your latent mind is awakened—you're pushing your throttles forward, rolling down the runway to liftoff.

What happens to the latent mind when it begins to receive the flow? Let's say you begin to increase your mind activity only 10 percent—through want. This great light that's around your body—remember the light whose Blue Corona has been eloquently photographed—it begins to widen and it begins to pick up a greater thought impulse. You've activated your receiver; you're starting to tune into other frequencies!

Are you aware what thought is? What do you think holds up your universe? What do you think holds your world up, aye? Nothingness? Something grand holds it all together—deep space is *deep thought.* And the *thought* is what feeds your light. When you shove your throttles forward, your light becomes more sensitive to the thought. As it becomes more sensitive, there is a higher frequency light propellant that begins to emerge within your brain-slab nurtured from the higher frequencies you've allowed yourself to receive. Then a little part of your brain will open to facilitate the *new* knowingness, the exotic destinations; your brain is a little less slab and flab and a little more vibrant energy!

The knowingness is not in words—it's a natural *high,* it *is* an emotional feeling, it is seeing lights, it is feeling lifted. As those exotic destinations flood into your open mind, that feeling is rushed throughout the entire central nervous system; every cell is awakening to a new truth. Your autopilot-Soul *records* that emotion as perpetual memory and holds it for all time.

The Liftoff

That's the beginning of Superconsciousness, the liftoff, so to speak. That *is* absolute knowingness. How would you react if you were in the flow of nature, if you were *in* the flow of life and knew all things that that window provided for you? You wouldn't be destitute, would you? You wouldn't be unhappy, would you? You wouldn't be ill because, you see, you would be seeing a new life. Whenever you see the new vision, you're not ill any longer; you're *revitalized* into a new understanding.

Presently, almost everyone you see is living on 33 percent mind-power; it's called, appropriately, Social Consciousness. Everyone is coasting in *FL: SocialC,* limited mind. You're limited by its boundaries and borders; it boxes you into its canyons. What is Social Consciousness?

SOCIAL CONSCIOUSNESS CHECKLIST

Prior to takeoff, check the following emotional switches, buttons, and programs. Place them in their make-ready positions for *Flight-level: Superconsciousness.* Any time you're switched ON to these feelings, you are living in limited mind.

1. Check your *Doubt* switch; turn OFF your doubt of everything, everyone, and self.
2. Is your *Limitedness* switch on? Turn OFF everything that you think you are not.
3. Check your *Hate* button; flip it from standby to OFF.
4. Set your *Bitterness* button to OFF; the past is the past.
5. *War* switch to OFF; war is simply war with self.
6. *Disease* switch to OFF; you don't need the identity any more.
7. *Unhappiness* switch to OFF; grab your joystick and prepare for takeoff to *Flightlevel: SuperC.*
8. *Misery* switch; flip it from standby to OFF—who needs misery?
9. *Judgment of Others* program; reprogram to *Love of Others* program for effortless flight.
10. Turn the *Living for Others* and *Dying for Others* program to OFF. This is the *living to please the whole of the world who shan't ever be pleased* program.

8

The liftoff into *FL: SuperC* is the jetroute into the unlimited truth of the Godfire essence. Social Consciousness is the *limited* truth of the Godfire essence—it is *survival,* that is all that it is. How many of you can cut your arm off and say, "grow," and it will grow anew? And how many of you can see the flow of nature and move in its direction? And how many of you can leave your body in a moment and travel somewhere else, in a moment? And how many of you have learned what it is to *own* joy? Very few.

Those realities lie in the latent mind of receivership. It's not that one becomes enlightened by plugging in his brain; it is that one becomes enlightened through *knowledge of,* and the mind begins to open up to receive the greater understanding.

Like Old Rubber Bands

If you function in Social Consciousness, no doubt about it, you'll have a lot of problems. The problems flutter all around you: you have a lot of hang-ups, a lot of hang-downs, you carry around a satchel of miseries, you have *multiple shame* emotional disturbances, your relationships are boxing matches instead of love-fests, and there are those of you who are in the midst of the slings and arrows of career changes. Well, *keep the faith,* as the saying goes. And wasn't it once said that the pioneers always ended up with the arrows in their butts!

Where is your fully operative mind? Did you leave it in some other time-travel dimension? Where is *your* ability to control, to change, and to have dominion over all of these things in *your* life? Where is your ability to own the answer? You just don't know, you're lost in your dreamfog because you only go within that part of your mind that you've always had available to you. And in there, you pull up the same old answers; you snap back to old soul memory like an old rubber band.

I know why you are perpetually looking for who you were yesterday, digging up old bones and the like. I know why you look for answers in yesterday. Because you haven't expanded your

9

knowingness of *today*. There are no answers in yesterday, only fleeting memories, often unrecognizable. Many in the pursuit of knowingness look back instead of living *now,* and through looking back, they never master the joy of *now.* They never grab the joystick because they have no mind to go forward into.

FL: SuperC is not the jetroute to *past* consciousness—it is *super*mind blatantly unfolding, the awakening of the Godforce in you. It is profound knowingness. It is the resurrection of the Master, individually.

Are you aware that that which lives in the unseen and in the seen are all equal? Perhaps you think that because you are alive that you are somehow condemned by the universe, owners of the *original* sin. Somehow you want to escape this and transcend into the next planes and levels and, of course, into heaven. Don't you know that right now who you are is the greatest adventure of all levels? Without being you, you shan't ever become the Godforce, for God is never fully realized within the self until it becomes the Godforce; and *only* through flesh and blood does this happen.

But look at you—you think that because you're living in a body that you're not powerful. You think that because you live in your social structures you are not divine. You think because someone else comes from another plane that they're so special and you're not—poppycock! All dogma, all-enslaving dogma.

I wish you to know that who you are, where you are, is the greatest you will ever be. And there is nothing in the unseen—nameless or named—that is any greater, any wiser or any more powerful than you are when you realize it. For we are all brothers unto the same mind. For you are all the Godforce. You think the Godsource spawned only one son? How absurd. For you are all sons and daughters of God *realized* in humankind.

This book is supposed to be an adventure in time-travel through unexplored dimensions. Would you like to explore the dimension of Manifesting? Manifesting is printed with a capital "M" because it's such an important word in today's world of illusionary lackings.

Focus back into your reality base for a moment. Remember back to the moment of your birth when somebody slapped you on the behind and you started crying wondering where you were? Remember those faces staring into yours making funny sounds? From that instant on, you've been conditioned to learn how we do things on planet Earth. You've been conditioned every step of the way since. Guess who were your prime conditioners? Unless you ran away from home when you were three, your parents were your prime conditioners. You see reality essentially as you were conditioned and trained to see it by your parents, and they, in turn, by theirs, etc., etc., etc. You are a product of tradition and superstition.

All that *stuff* that you heard, read, and learned over all those years and lifetimes is dredged up any time any new thought or idea comes along. You plop the new thought into the most convenient box of reality that you've experienced. In other words, the past allows you to relate to the new thought in the *now*. Without the boxes of the past, the new thought would be a *fearful* thought because it wouldn't fit anywhere; it would be *unknown*. Whatever is unknown is feared; fear doesn't sit too well with us, so we want to put it away somewhere to watch it cautiously.

Why are some people able to manifest anything they want? Because they don't need to put new thoughts into old boxes. They let new ideas create their *own* new reality bases that take them to new dimensions of excitement and adventure! Instead of a fear of the "ughknown," it's fun. Once you know how you function from your reality base, you see your limitations immediately. And remember you are only as limited as your last thought.

To manifest, focus the absolute love that the Supersource has for all things into the reality base that you function from. From there, create a reality curve that jumps off from your reality base into the new thought that you don't fear. Then ride that energy curve of your desire back into the Supersource—that's it! Let the new thought carry you where it will, outside of your boxes of illusion and fear, into new boxes without borders. That's all there is to it. Sort of like hitching a ride on a rainbow; ride a new thought right out of your fearbox. You wanted *complicated?* Simple. This also proves that you can teach old pilots new tricks.

Optimum Cruise Power-Settings

Cruising into *FL: SuperC* is the process called *waking up.* You're re-claiming your kingdom and your heritage. Have you ever wondered what the Kingdom of Heaven meant? Some place far out into space, as the old woman would say, a piece of real estate, *God knows where it's at?* It is the *within* that is omnipresent.

What would it be like if you had your full faculties at hand? What if in a moment you could go wherever you wanted to go? What if in a moment, what you are and who you are would stand still for eons without aging? What if there were no such thing as disease? And what if you were *totally* in knowingness and the thought was absolute? What if you could manifest your daily bread? Could you imagine what it would be like to live with a Fully Realized Godfire Being rating? Contemplate how your social structure would change if a majority of you were FRGB rated!

It's not a fable, it's a great truth—what *would* your brain feel like if it were turned on, awake? How much more of you could there be? Most of you keep shut down because of your insecurities. You know all about your insecurities, so I don't have to define them, to *reveal* them to you. You know them well; you maintain a desperate clutch on them because they give you an identity. You know the ones: *I am sick, I am unhappy, I'm a failure, I'm a success! I have marital problems, I have sexual problems, I have mental problems, I have working problems, I am, . . . I am, . . . I am. . . .*

Don't you know that every moment you speak about yourself,

you're creating an infallible identity that is arduous to let go of? There are many who hold on to limited mind *earnestly*, because it means they can say, "That's what I am!"

First Runners, Get Ready

Are you prepared for the first runners of this leg of your journey? I will send back to you, via express delivery, all that you identify yourself with—you know, the *I am's*. I will send them back to you as runners; the experiences will arrive in the reflection of others.

However many *I am's* you're clutching, they will come forward straightaway. You're going to look into a mirror and realize all that you say you are; you're going to face that emotion for the first time. You'll pick them up on your radar before a fortnight; however many hang-ups you have determines how many runners will appear. Won't it be wonderful to know yourself as seen in others? You might encounter some turbulence, but you'll fly right through it.

To see yourself is very important for you. How else would you know what you are? When seen, if you embrace all that you see and say, "I *own* this reflection," that ownership allows you to move into a little more unlimited space. There you'll find a brilliant feeling that will begin to induce the soul into other dimensions, other realities.

In other words, you're going to wake up out of your dreamfog and climb out into another one. It took me sixty-three years to own up to who I was, *without* any runners. This is a short cut to realization! Remember, these are all words that you are hearing. The greatest adventure will begin and follow pell-mell when you finish this flightlog.

Final Departure Clearance

The legs of your flight into Superconsciousness are made up of various objectives—*wants*.

1. You want to *Become*, even though you are not quite sure what that is; the word is *chic*, don't you know.
2. You want to know Superconsciousness because, so far, it sounds pretty good to you.
3. And you want to live through the days to come, because what good is it to know all this stuff if you can't hang around and enjoy it?

The process of owning yourself is *imperative* before you slide into alignment with everything else. There is one remaining departure clearance you need before you can venture into *FL: SuperC*. Without it your growth is retarded, your mind is hindered from opening into the unlimited horizon of Superconsciousness; all of your systems are shut back down into their tightly knit little fearbox. Superconsciousness cannot be Superconsciousness without *Super*love.

I know you've heard all about the word *love*, no doubt from a myriad of sources: brotherly love, and sisterly love, and puppy love; infatuation love, lust love, and making love; marriage, separation, and divorce; fatherly love, motherly love, grandmotherly love, grandfatherly love; sensual love, sexual love, tough love, easy love, tender love; romance novels, soap operas, love songs; love lost, and love gained, and love gone, love earned and love yearned—on and on and on. After living through all of that, do you have any idea what love *is?*

Love—do you love what *you* are, *all* that you are? Sure you do, I know. Well, let's verify. Do you love your nose? Do you know that your nose is divine? Do you love your body? Fancy this; I've seen you look at your body and I watch all of the gnashing of teeth and cursing. Was that really you who loves your body doing all that gnashing?

Run the *Runner Program* on your autopilot—here we go again! I desire to send a mirror to you. The mirrors will reflect all of the *beauty* that you are; they'll reflect it double back to you. *Every* facet of who you are, every *thing* that you have doubted, that you have cursed, that you have thrown away, that you have misused— they'll all shimmer before you.

These polished facets, the lucent mirrors, will reflect what you will see one day beyond blind eyes. Then you'll begin to fathom an insight into the divine creature that you are. The mirrors will appear before your Summer is at an end, because it will take all Summer for you to break down the ugliness you feel about yourself to realize the beauty that you are. That's hard work!

A Long, Hot Summer (Whew!)

Let's get into it! Do you love all people? Can you allow all people to be what they are? Do you love your family? Of course, I see. Can you allow your family members to be what they are? I *see!* What about your lovers past and present? Do you love your in-laws and out-laws? Do you love your neighbors (not just the ones that moved away)? Do you love your, your—what are they called?—slave-driver *bosses,* that's what they're called. In other words, are you at peace with all peoples? Hardly.

Christianity flourishes in this nation and around the globe. Historically, do you know what the Christ was all about? Let me give you the inside scoop—he was a person who was amiable to all peoples. And once he found the treasure of God within himself, he endeavored to find it in *every*one, and he did. Do you know why he was resurrected from the dead? Because he was at peace with the *whole* of life. He *became* Superconsciousness just as you can! Blasphemy? Hardly.

May I venture to ask, what was different about Yeshua ben-Joseph from you? There are many of you, through your dogma, who feel *less than;* I believe it is called *sinner;* in other languages it is called karma or karmiacs. Why was it important to be at peace with all people, to *superlove* them? One who is in the process of becoming from Social Consciousness to Superconsciousness, becomes acutely aware that whatever he sees in others, so is he. (The previous sentence is one of the best-kept secrets of all time!)

You've listened to all sorts of definitions regarding the words love, love, *love*. But you don't understand love because you haven't become the *understanding* called love in order to *love*. You are hypocrites milling around. Christ—religious style; there is no such thing as a chosen people of God. There is only God and that is in all places, in the eyes of all people, in the embrace of all children, and in the color of skin of all creeds and races. (More blasphemy, I suppose.)

Well, the word is out about all the coming excitement. A lot of you want to survive and, indeed, you want to have it your own way and on your own terms, but you don't want to give of yourself in order to make it happen. You're never going to see it happen, for Superconsciousness *is* an emotion that is a humble, strengthening, unifying feeling that lifts the *whole* of the world, not just your Sunday school class.

How difficult is it to become so humble and so meek in your spirit that you become a genius in the mind, you become a Fully Realized Godfire Being like a Christ? You can become the magician, the philosopher, the teacher, and you can issue forth meaningless words, but if the Superlove isn't there, the power of the manifestation shan't ever occur. The words are a nothing without the love. You can get hung up on all the strides you're making, but it's all nothing until you have humbled yourself to become the *love* of yourself.

How do you love yourself? By simply realizing this—that you are the walking temple of an omnipresent God; and that within you, through you, by you, many things exist in your world. And that, in essence, you are a divine, enraptured creature who is stuck on not knowing it.

Soon, being the genius that you are, you begin to sense the truth, the consciousness, the *divinity,* that when you are angry and ugly with someone, it hurts *you* because you've hurt yourself when you hurt someone else. Are you aware of that or is that a revelation to you? Awakening is not simply a process of being so bloody enlightened that you can quote scriptures and do wondrous things— it is the awakening based on love, *Super*love.

A Nightmare of Lives

Think about everyone you judged this morning. (We'll wait, it's a long list!) Do you need a reminder? I can send them back to you. Judgment—why does one need to master judgment? Because one needs to master *good and evil* in order to come to the center focal point that is called *is*. The center focal point is without perfection and imperfection, it is without the good and evil, it is *wholly* without negative and positive—it just *is*. And in *is* there, is, alas, no judgment.

Do you know that every moment you judge another, you're judging yourself? Did you know you cannot see in another what you do not already possess in you? Hard truth, aye? Of course it is. That's called swallowing it and learning to be humble.

How can you *know* if someone is a certain way unless you've been that way? (See it now?) And every moment you see in another that which is less than the glory you possess in yourself, you are degrading and falling further away from that engaging, beloved, enlightening truth of what *you* are—*every* moment. In essence, what is in your reality is what you are. What you hang on your walls in your homes represents what you are. What you eat represents what you are. What you consider fashionable and *unfashionable* is what you are.

Let's have some amusement! I will send back to you all that you have judged this morning for a refresher look. During your refresher look, you can see whatever you want to see. What I desire for you to see is the truth that says, *"Whatever see I, so am I."* Look for it; you'll see all that you are. *Very* amusing!

And also, if you look close enough, you may find the *Godfire* in everyone, whether it is those wonderful rimmed eyelashes, or the clarity and depth of the eyes; or that beard, or that skin, or that hair, or just that sparkle in those orbs. If you look you'll find it. And every moment you begin to find it, you're finding *you;* and every moment you begin to love what you see, you're *loving* you. Then you're waking up out of your dreamfog, a nightmare of lives without end and, indeed, without beginning. The alarm clock is ringing . . . ringing . . . ringing. . . .

Well, this morning I woke up with a new working model of the universe. Since I had asked myself the question, "Isn't there anybody who can step out of this illusion?" as usual, the question created it's own challenge and then its own answer.

I'm a pilot, and flying airplanes is a profession that lives in truth, the truth of the science of aerodynamics. If you step out of those boundaries, that envelope, you end up crunched. Yet, within those boundaries, tomorrow is dictated by perfect logic. For example, if your dirty stall speed is 78 knots, that's where you'll stall with flaps and gear down. And if you add a thirty degree bank at that speed, expect simply to slide out of the air—you've lost all of your lift.

I saw a fellow on TV the other day who was saying he thought the New Age was pretty old, that it was transitioning into a Light Age, an age where everyone turns on to the grandeur of what they are. Of course I thought that was pretty corny and then he said, "Of course, you might think my statement is a bit airy-fairy, but we should think about loving each other before we blow ourselves up."

Man, he hit the nail on the head—I thought I was reliving my flower-child days in Berkeley. Then he doubled me over with "Sure, the peace movement of the '60s was the beginning of the awakening—I think of myself as a stoneground flower child; in fact, I suppose all of us are stoneground flower children trying to discover how we fit in with this crazy plane of living that the Church and State has us vibrating in.''

This guy was really an oddball—"vibrating in"—man, I sure would run from him if I saw him walking up to me in a bar! Still, he was on national TV so at least the host thought he was worth talking to. He had written a book that was selling like hotcakes. The book was all about this cosmic jargon of the New Age—you've heard it: You create your own reality; there are no victims; there is no right or wrong, there just *is;* you choose your parents; beings from other dimensions are communicating with us . . .

Well, that one stopped me in my tracks. I really never did believe that we were alone in the universe. Man, I fly—I've seen the vastness of it all; I've peered into telescopes and sent my thought beyond the stars, I've read about black holes and parallel universes, I think I've even seen a UFO—many high-time pilots who have clocked a lot of hours in the air will confide to you, most won't because it could mean the end of their careers. The question that I couldn't answer really began bugging me—how could there be no right or wrong, how could love and allowance be the keystones of the next age, whatever it will be called?

You see, it seemed to me in my limited mind that our universe was all there was, and within that universe there was a struggle transpiring, a struggle between good and evil. In fact as I had looked at the so called New Age thinkers, I found them to be as *old age* as the Old Age thinkers—they were claiming doom and gloom—"some will survive, most will die, only if you believe my way"—sounded just like another religion being born, just using some new verbs and adjectives.

That's why I liked that guy I saw on TV. He was talking about a Light Age, an age that allowed everyone to be anything they wanted. An age where they *ruled* themselves in love and compassion, a place where everyone was a part of everything, where the necessities of life were provided instead of monopolized—all brothers and sisters in the human family. The host asked him how that could come about. He said just two things will trigger it: when you see yourself in all people and when you love what you see.

19

It was so simple, and *that* was what I had always thought Christ was all about. You see, God to me was an all-allowing Father—I never saw Him or It or Her as something that was going to sentence me to an eternity in hell, or some such thing. What kind of a Father would that be? So, to emulate *that* God, to become like that, all you need to be is loving and allowing. Sounds too simple, but that to me was the example of the Christ Consciousness.

It was beginning to appear to me that there was a great illusion running amok; this illusion that calls us bastards of the universe, that creates separation between all peoples based upon the brand of religion they believe in, that has us fooled into believing that the *only* God is a God who purports love yet is ready to blast you if you don't do it *His* way. It seemed to me that the whole premise of religion was set up to enslave us to their thought, *their* way. The question for me became, "How could I escape from this illusion without creating another illusion that elevated me to the office Guru-in-Command?"

This morning I woke up with a new model of the universe. I'll tell you all about it when we meet again.

Love Gauge Registers Empty

Awakening the Godfire, the God-essence in you, *is* awakening the love of self. Love—you think it is the love of your husband, your wife, your relationships, in and out. Oh, and you have them— they're passing fantasies every moment of the day. You're desperate one moment and in ecstasy the next. Or you feel it is the love of your children, of your parents, of your friends, your teachers, whatever. That's just a reflection of an insecure self. It isn't a *profound* knowingness that true love is, because you can only love yourself before you can ever love anyone else.

If that's a truth, here's an interesting hypocrisy for you to consider: How can you say you love God and then despise yourself in the same breath by saying you are less than, *sinner?* How can that be? How can you march off every Sunday, kneel down and beg to be forgiven? How can you say you love your children and despise yourself, *thick thighs* and all of that? Where could the love come from if that which it is coming from is despised? In other words, you're leading them on (is that the proper terminology) leading them on with empty love. You can't possibly love another until you love yourself!

Empty love is quite all right, for there are those who have lived for eons who don't know what topped-off love feels like; they've destroyed their lives searching for it. They've always looked outside of their countenance and never into the unseen glory that perhaps *this* is them. Can you guess why? For eons your dogma and your rulers, your religions, have taught that it is a *selfish* thing to love what you are—it is a *sin. Appalling!* May I candidly ask, how does one love God if he has not unified himself within to know what love is?

Superconsciousness cannot be ushered in by turning on a master switch and shouting, *Clear prop! I'm on, let's fly!* It's something that must be *felt* into being, and the more humble one becomes, the more splendid one becomes in his mind. Why are the meek inheriting the earth? Because they are simple enough to be in the flow of genius. Those complexities, your hang-ups, your dogmas, your dependencies of spiritual truth, they'll only carry you to *FL: Nowhere.*

The simple in mind are the simple in spirit, for they are the salt of the earth that just love you and allow you your truth. They are *un*complex beings who shan't ever argue with you, who shall never compete with you, who shall not try to destroy you or exalt you—they just are. They are embarking upon the awakening of the Godfire within, because they are humble enough to begin to love themselves enough. Now they can allow everyone else their own truth.

Wind Tunnel Tests

By now you should know what *Super*love is. It's called *freedom*. What is it to love another without the chains, without the possessiveness, without the mistrust, the wonder, the lies? That's not love, that's *in*security. When you enchain another you only ensnarl yourself. Superlove *allows*. And only when one loves that which one is, *deeply* within one's Soul, does it become profoundly erect with the knowingness, can it love the whole of the world and *allow* the whole of the world.

Would you like to know where your insecurities lie? No, yes, maybe? I will send back to you an emotional vision that will be spurred by your dependency on others. You will know the difference between true love that allows and insecurity that enslaves. Bargain? So it shall be. That will even happen this evening in your time.

Why go through all this wind tunnel testing? Why not? Since you want an FRGB rating and you're desiring to see Superconsciousness, to *know* what that feels like, it's important to put your priorities in order. How monumental is it when that hour comes, when you realize that you're not loving, you're holding onto? Then you can remove the chain, and in humbleness and accepted frailty you can free the bird from the cage.

That may seem humble and frail, but that is magnificent strength that builds the Superlove that is earnest in your entire being. How many are you holding onto? Holding on for security because you need them? When you don't need anyone any longer save the Godfire within termed your *own* truth, when you can open the cage and let them go and allow, allow, allow, then you're waking up.

These emotional traumas that will begin to visit you—it's not that I am laying a *heavy* on you—you know what heavies are? Nor am I laying a trip to China on you—that's not why I do this. And I'm not laying it on you to upset you, even though that's what you need. The purpose—for you to begin to start looking at where your dependency lies, to see how much of it lies *outside* you rather than *in* you.

The unspeakable we're speaking about is called Supermind. Your brain can only be a Superbrain when it is embraced emotionally. The more sovereign one becomes in his autopilot-Soul, the more awake your brain becomes. As long as you have your little groupies outside you—your teachers, your guides, your rituals, your dogmas, your children, your husbands, your wives, etc., etc., which means the goings-on of forever—as long as you have that, you will never own sovereignty and this slab of flesh under your haircut is not going to wake up.

How far, fast, and furious do you desire to go? You call it. And if you discover to your amazement that you are dependent upon everyone around you, and you feel utterly like collapsing in the center—collapse, it's all right! And if you feel you need to hold on, continue to hold on; there will come an hour when you will have to reach out and discover your *own profound self.*

This little heavy that I'm putting on you, for all of your emotional beinghood, *needs* to be put there. Now, if you don't like what you're feeling and you're getting a little testy and you begin to curse me, and you're mad and regretful that you ever opened the pages of this flightlog, have your tizzy! Get it all out—I will just blow you away in the wind and allow you because it is all right. And if the ride gets too hot, wild, and furious, you can always punch out screaming, *"I don't want anymore,"* and it will stop. Roger that?

Well, we've chattered about reality bases and we've touched on manifesting skills. Let's take a look at the most typical reality base and how its baseline thought-systems manifest its desires. Almost everyone that you talk to or bump into starts off from a reality base of fear. Fear is the great illusion that works in concert with guilt.

Fear is the emotion that keeps you from moving out into a different reality base. Fear also doesn't exist, except when guilt is ingrained into your reality base. The second you're born you're placed in fear of death—your parents hover over you incessantly checking to see if you are still breathing. This overlord relationship continues until you sneak the car out of the garage on a Friday night.

Reality bases based in fear are perfectly all right, if you want to live there. This type of reality base, however, automatically forces you to live a life in the negative—all of your fears will manifest, basically because anything you fear you secretly worship. That's right! When you try to bury a fear you end up hiding it under the carpet—it's still there, but you don't dare bring it up for *fear* of the consequences. Anything with that much power over you, you have no choice but to worship it.

Since the fears are never resolved, they always keep coming up. Then you live a life of unresolved guilt—you feel guilt because you know intrinsically that there is "nothing to fear except fear itself" and all of that, so you're guilty about feeling fear. Am I right? This brings up the question, how do pilots become *pilots;* how do they break through *their* fear of flight? Through knowledge.

How do you move away from *your* fear-oriented reality base? By bringing all the fears up, facing them, *owning* them. Lay in a comfortable space alone and go deep inside; call forth all your fears. Don't lose yourself in the emotion of the fears, just watch them as you time-travel through the layers of your mind. As they all come up, you'll be in communication with the conscious and subconscious aspects of your mind.

After *all* of your fears have paraded before you, you'll hear a little voice say, "Are those all of your fears?" and you will answer, "yes" or explore further to other layers. When you finally answer, "Yes" you will hear, "Let them go," and the relief will be remarkable as they float away into eternity.

That's it! You are fearless, until you start loading yourself up with a new set of fears.

Set Your Altitude Bug for FL: SuperC

When do you know you're flying in *FL: SuperC?* When you can look at all people and realize that the Godfire lies within them, and that they are doing precisely what they *want* to do so you can allow it. *That* is the Superlove of an FRGB-rated Pilot-in-Command. And what really could be more simple? I can hear you saying that we can't say that! Why won't *you* allow it? What could be *wrong* with that? And what is *right* about that? It simply is *the law.*

Have you ever cast your gaze at another, not approving of what they're doing because it isn't what *you're* doing? You know that old scenario. Well, did you know you're an enslaver? If someone is running amok and not doing a civil thing at all, does that mean they're wrong? Perhaps to *civil* understandings they're causing a fervor, but what about their divine right to do that?

Have you ever looked at the whole of the world? The beggar on the street—have you ever looked at one who is beautiful and one who is not so beautiful, seen someone who is erratic, witnessed the peace of someone who is quiet, seen them all and realized they are doing exactly what they want to do? Through the Superlove of the Godsource He is allowing them.

Pull out your flight computer and think about this one: Why didn't God, whatever that may be, do away with those murderers, those rulers, those entities who were mean and devilish? Why didn't He do away with them before they did what they did?

Fatalists know that life is very temporary; unlimited mind knows it's forever. One never dies, one only *excels* one's life into grander levels of understanding—one doesn't die. And they were doing what they wanted to do. How can you say they are right or wrong? How can you impute a divine law that loves and through Superlove allows *you* to have your fantasies? For although you think that no one knows they are there, they are alive and well. Whatever you dream and feel emotionally, you have created a reality and it is all known.

So the real question is, why are you allowed, you wretched, hypocritical, narrow-minded person you? Why—you should have been cut down long ago. But look at you; you're still here, so it must not have been such a biggie after all. Everyone has made biggies—*everyone*.

The Godsource, the *Is* factor, allows. Are you aware that God has never judged you or anyone? There is a great difference between religion and *God*. Religion is the law of man; the Godsource is *without* that law. The Godsource is a lawless, allowing, feeling called *life*. You have never been judged, *never*—you have only judged yourself! (That's a revelation.)

You've been allowed to be your crazy, unsuccessful, manic-depressive self, and you pray for help and nothing happens. Why? Because you're superloved and allowed. The Godsource does not see that you are wrong and it does not see that you are right; it just *sees* and loves.

The point here is that SuperLove has allowed you to *be*. The divine inspiration that is within you all, is working every moment of every day, of life, of forever. The counterpoint here is, you've hidden Superlove in limitations; you only love on conditions! If someone does you a *wrong,* you despise them forever, don't you? You don't even care about them any longer because they have been put upon you, and in your divine arrogance you do away with them—the term is, *writing them off.*

What would you be if you had been written off? Not one of you would be here; not *one* of you. Superconsciousness is the understanding and the imitation of the *is* called God, in unlimited, allowing love—*allowing*.

Certainly you have your truth. Did you know everyone who is wrong, is right? There is no such thing as being wrong, for everyone is correct in what they think, what they believe, what they are. How can you say they are wrong? Are you a tyrant that impurges upon another your own truth? Are you a dogmatic who says, "I must have safety in numbers," and you convince every-one, and if they don't go along with the program, you do away with them, banishing them to *hell,* and all of that? *Allowing* is the nature of the Godself. In order to fly from here to there, it must be imitated to the finest harmonious string.

Strap on your shoulder harness; snug down your vertical re-straints! I'll send you a dream, a vision. Do you know what a vision is? Some do, others have just had too much to drink. I'll send it anyway; you can figure out which is which. The vision from me will arrive unexpected; it will assail you in the least ex-pected of all places. In the vision you're going to see with the mind of God what God is. (Pretty exciting, I'd say!)

The vision will take place in a kaleidoscope of the human drama—in one flash you will *be* the omnipresent mind. And what you're going to see, you're going to feel; it will be as if you are enraptured in light, for when one is in the wholeness of light and wholly aware, there is nothing *except* love in its simplest form. What is love's simplest form? Read the word backwards, *love.* Sound familiar? Evol . . . evolu . . . evolution! I do believe you've got it!

With this brief kaleidoscopic glimpse into that wonderful win-dow, perhaps you're going to reassess all the elements and all the people that are around you—how could you not? If you think you have an enemy, I beseech you to resolve that feeling; to come to terms with it and embrace that understanding within your own soul, to forgive yourself and allow the love to flow. For in that humble-ness, one is exalted to the *zenith* of his understanding of the Godfire realized. Bargain? So be it! That is what we call a goodie.

Love in its Simplest Form

Well, so here we are, climbing out to *FL: SuperC.* Where's all the activity; where's all the action, where's it *happening?* Where's the party! Why don't you know what's going to happen? Because you don't have the mind to know it yet. Your receiver just isn't tuned in yet.

When you can know without ever asking a question, you're in the flow. This autopilot system of yours, your soul and your brain, operates on programs that are patterns of experience. The patterns are inputted by you to open up your mind so you begin to *feel* what is just under the horizon. The parlance is, understanding through *emotion*.

Love. Love, love; love, Superlove, *love* . . . *feel*—the glimpse of eternity. There are many who have never seen such a vision of love, because they could not; they were not equipped mentally, they were not equipped emotionally to be allowed to look into a window and see it.

Have you ever been dogmatized? Many are enchained to the dogma that if they chant, chant, *chant*, if they breathe, breathe, *breathe*, if they thin, thin, *thin*; if they ash, ash, abstain, abstain, become celibate, become nonpeople, they're going to experience the kundalini energy, the legendary serpent, rising up the spine to open up the whole of the mind!

Let's reason this. There *is* an energy there. The energy that activates alignment-of-flightlevel-seven understanding, flows from the first through the seventh seal. It's not a snake and you don't chant it into being and you don't drug it into being! I have seen some of you who, what is the term, stoke it to get high—proper word? Smoke it, stoke it? You think by aciding the brain, smoking the weed, drinking the drink, that it is going to engage enlightenment—it is going to kill you.

Nothing wakes up the kundalini except the simplicity of the spirit that is love. *That* is no serpent—that is the glory of the God-force realized in you. Think about it like a glideslope, gliding you in for a touchdown. You don't force it; you *glide* down, gently, in love—evolve.

Dogma holds you off your glideslope. Show you? All right. How can you say on the one hand, *"to love someone is to love yourself,"* and say on the other hand, "the way you *love* yourself is to starve yourself into oblivion, to chant yourself into insanity, to breathe yourself into the depths of your crater''!? (Got ya!)

Dogma is a nonthing—well, look at the word, *dog ma.* What does it mean? Dogma is a practice *outside* that creates nothing on the inside except *practice,* and a little discipline along the way. Well, ask yourself; what *has* it done for you? *Life* appears when you no longer need the obstacles or instruments that hold you off your glideslope. Life appears when you just time-travel from here to there.

NOTAM (Notice to Airmen): IFR-hood Training Is Completed

My flight instruction has been labeled outrageous. Why? Because it's so simple, swirling outside the realm of dogma. Remember: the simplicity of the line becomes the genius of knowingness. The more simple it is, the more quickly one begins to realize. Those of you who want the snake, the viper to rise up, and *blam*—you know everything—it's not going to happen.

One day soon you'll know that ritual is only *ritual.* You'll understand that knowingness is an emotional embrace that radiates from the simplicity of the love of self. The *love* of self is the love of the Godsource inside that allows that feeling outside, for the whole of the world, in grace. How do you define *grace?* To *allow* someone—no matter how absurd their truth, no matter how they feel about you—to allow them their truth and Superlove them for it. Then there is peace. Then the serpent is alive with fire, and only through that act.

Superconsciousness is a state of mind that is in essence the state of God. It is the Godforce realized—God *realized* in Man/Woman. You are state-of-the-art Godfire. You *are* capable of that all-loving, all-allowing attitude—just *turn it on!* In other words, the becoming process, which everyone is lallygagging with, is something that is taken to the zenith of it's knowingness and then *reversed* and brought forward in self; in your very own self. Once you visualize it, emotionalize it, wisdomize it, you own it, you *are* it.

What is the *something* that you visualize, emotionalize, wisdomize to own and become? I can't define it for you. Your *something* fits into no dogmatic premises, into no religious fervor, into no social acceptance, into no *words*. Your *something* sits on the horizon of your fearbox, which your autopilot-Soul is trying to fly you out of. Except you keep disengaging it! Notice this: only through love does one begin to realize. Love allows you to look back upon self to see what you are. Love allows you to fly out of your fearboxes.

Flip off your hood and stop flying blind! What is the definition of love, *Super*love, I'm referring to? The love of *self*. Become aware that you are loved more than you can comprehend, through all the mundane meanings of the word *love,* you are loved into life. And when you *know* you are superloved, you can love. Become aware that what you are affects all flightlevels of the Supermind, the mind that is all things. Let it be known that you *are* the sleeping Gods. Wake up! Know that it is *that* love which has allowed you to be in this dream unrealized.

Into the Light

In a place that is called alone, where you are not bombarded by Social Consciousness, when you least expect it, there shall come forth what is termed a magnificent Light. That Light will surround you, and in surrounding you, it will lift you in a state called pure love—*pure* Superlove. In that state, which will seemingly be for all eternity, you will realize, not in words but in emotion, the *value* of yourself in relation to the Godsource.

One caveat—I know how you think. This does not mean you will now be endowed to teach the world all of your illustrious understandings. That is not where this visitation is coming from. It is to show you for a moment, only a moment, how valuable you are to the whole. And seemingly all of nature around you will be watching in a divine astute silence. Just for a moment.

Now, you say, "But if this is going to happen, why can't I keep it and forget about all of these things that I have to do?" Wrongo-congo! Remember when I told you that you are divine will, and through *your* will your Godsource acts or reacts? In other words, *it's all in your hands,* correct? If anyone else held you there, that would remove from you the joy of extricating yourself from what you have created for yourself. Jolly good amusement, aye? This sidetrip is for you to reach into a knowingness that has no words, to begin to assimilate what a feeling *feels* like, what *love* feels like.

You see, I know how you work. You can rationalize away the most brilliant of thoughts; why, you do it all the time. You rationalize away genius; I've watched you have splendid ideas and then you talk yourself out of them. That is shutting down. You know what it feels like; you sort of *forget about it, it wasn't that impor-tant, somebody else will do it.* Sound familiar?

This light experience? I *know* that you're going to doubt your-self about having this experience, you're going to talk yourself out of this experience, and then you're going to weep a lot after this experience because nobody is going to *believe* you about this ex-perience. And because they don't believe you, you'll talk yourself out of it! Well, that won't work this time. For every moment you rationalize *it is not so,* I'm going to remind you that it *is* so. What keeps you from waking up is not being strong enough to embrace an emotion and, indeed, own it.

You have had glorious moments. I've seen you become a humanitarian and it is the grandest of feelings. I have seen you become humble and love someone who didn't love you—for mo-ments. But after that glory fades, you've become your old self again. You do this to yourself simply because you do not *love* yourself, so you don't *hold* that love within. Social Consciousness and social acceptance still have you in their bombsights; they bom-bard you out of your feeling. When the *glory* fades, it's because you have allowed it to fade.

This feeling that will arrive in your reality base, this blip that will appear on your radar screen; it's to remind you that you *are* worth it, that is all. And if you cannot ascertain that feeling within your own self, then you have a lot to think about. I keep telling you this, because you're waiting for a magic elixir to be handed to you that does the trick. There is no such thing. Every FRGB candidate who began to wake up from the dream of the human drama, began to embrace the whole, knowing that there must be something more, and there was. Very few embrace that concept, and thus *very* few of those who dream the humanoid dream have ever awakened to skyrocket into *FL: SuperC.* You think your reality is *reality* when in reality it is the *illusion.*

Realities, reality! How does a pilot break through the F-barrier? The awarenesses that you manifest from a fear-oriented reality base are called negative. When you fly into a non–fear-based reality base you begin manifesting what is called the positive. This is, as you've heard, when "everything keeps coming up roses" and all of that. Well, that's what happens—you can't strike out, all of your landings are three pointers, and life is just a bowl of cherries.

Why don't we live there all the time? It's a matter of choice— which reality base do you *want* to live in? The only reality base that you know is what you've been taught by your parents, who have learned from their parents, etc., etc., etc. You've been educated in reality-base understanding—you are an American or a Russian, a Jew or a Christian—you've been educated to be what you are. To fly out of your fear-oriented reality base into another base takes great courage, conviction, drive, and deep, deep, absolute emotional love for the explorer—that's *you.*

To fly out of it means you will leave behind all that you think you are and travel into what you really are. You'll delve deep into the corners of your mind and pick the sweet spot you wish to hang out with a bit. Then the adventure begins—a guided tour into the amazing reality of you. Snug down your shoulder harness, fasten your helmet—the thrill is about to begin!

One and the Same, Pure and Simple

Let's break you out of a reality box. Supermind has nothing to do with how many books you read. Superconsciousness has nothing to do with how many rituals you do, it has nothing to do with what you drink, it has *nothing* to do with what you eat; has nothing to do with what you wear, has nothing to do with how successful or *unsuccessful* you are (are you following this?—it sounds outrageous) it has nothing to do with belief systems. Supermind has *everything* to do with realization of the simplicity of *self,* that you and the Godsource are one and the same. *That* is the reality that wakes you up.

Do you think that in order to become the Godfire you must become austere? Do you think you must turn your back and live in caves, wandering around in the wilderness eating locusts? Do you think you cannot be *successful* because being successful is blasphemous to God's kingdom, when everything is God's kingdom?

These conceptions of what you *think* you must be are rigid barriers to break down in your reality. Many still believe that sin is equal and proportionate to the amount of money you possess, that poverty is equal to grandness of spirit—*that* is an atrocity.

And let's really face it head-on! It's not your social dogmas that are restraining you from knowing the grandness of yourself—it's not that at all. It's what *you* have contrived in your mind that relates to what FRGB-rated pilots *must* be; how they must look, how they must walk, what they must wear (of course, it should always be long and white and flowing), how they do their hair, what they wear on their fingers and on their foreheads, how they paint their nails, where they live and what they live on. Think about it—that's the barrier that you've locked yourself into, by thinking you could never be that.

At this very moment there is an FRGB candidate who is awakening, who is in the seat of power of this your country—very close—who is awakening to a great truth, has been for a long time, in your time. And yet, it is not the power of the people but the power of the Godfire within that he has always hungered for. And he would be the *last* one you would think would do it.

And even at this moment there is a woman, get this, a *woman*—do you know there has never been a woman who ascended or became the Godfire essence, because, since women were *less than* men forever, how could *they* become? But even at this hour there are women who are awakening to their understanding. Their greatest block was that they could not become the Godfire, they could not become *loved* by the Godsource; they could not *love* themselves, nor could they aspire to a divine truth because they were *women*.

To the great surprise of many, there are women who are waking up, who *own* the whole of their past, who own their unequal selves in grand equalness, and they are becoming loved of themselves and of the whole world. There are FRGB candidates waking up in the female gender—that's *never* occurred before, so it is long overdue.

It isn't that it is hard for you to overcome what others think; it is hard to overcome what *you* think. Just what truly are your ideals of a divine personage? Picture them for me. Is it a *he,* or a *she,* or an *is?! And could the is be you?*

What Does This Creature Look Like?

What is your image of an FRGB? What do you think of when you hear the words "Fully Realized Godfire Being?" Can you separate the essence of a Christ from the dogma that has formed *around* that essence?

34

An FRGB is simply one who *imitates* to the most pristine degree the essence of the Godsource. What is the essence of the Godsource? Surely you know by now, I'm not even going to state it again. (*Love* and *allow,* just in case you forgot!)

Funny enough, your religious dogmas would label the imitation of the Source *blasphemy!* That's why your ideal of FRGB status has always been so different from what you really are—you've been indoctrinated out of you; what you really are has been plastered over by the Ages of Indoctrination. Consequently, you've shut down your knowingness, you've shut down the feasibility of being the Godfire essence, so you've wallowed and grappled in your limited selves. In other words, you're failing to *live.*

Hold onto your hat for this one: there is not *one* person all over your world who is *not* divine. Be it man or woman or child it does not matter, for the love of the Godsource manifested into the consciousness of the human drama is both male and female. The latent Godfire that lies within is *everyone.*

You are *very* aware that the prophets have spoken of the second coming of Christ. You've heard of that? Do you have an inkling of what it is? It is not Yeshua ben-Joseph (Christ's full Hebrew name), fluttering down from the heavens to collect you. It is the *Super*knowingness that all things are—unmolested, un–put upon, unlimited—arising in *all* people. Those who hear this truth are the meek within themselves, who can allow that profound truth without feeling as if they were blasphemous and heretical—they just *are.*

You are very chic and cosmopolitan in your attitudes; why *don't* you know it all? Why aren't you open? Why don't you love? Because you have never matched up to the ideal you have imagined the Godsource to be. You, to yourself, are always a failure—difficult to accept, but a reality for hundreds and hundreds of millions. Why else would they tread off to the churches and temples every week to repent for what they are? They have accepted in their attitude the miserableness that they are. Appalling! And they call religious gods lovers of your being?

The paramount mastery on one's flight into freedom is the

mastery of *oneself.* It is not to master the fear of dying, it is to master oneself. What is the end result of the flight? Look at you. You're afraid to look at yourself; you're afraid that what you're going to find underneath is some nasty, vile, and evil thing. No, that's only an illusion that you've created. That isn't what exists underneath your limited mind. What is there in shimmering splendor is pure God, pure Godfire essence, waiting to wake up, stirring inside. The greatest mastery is the mystery of oneself.

Flight into Forever

Let's begin to uncover the mystery with the next set of runners, your copilots, remember? Your right seat will be filled up straightaway because it is imperative that you experience this—be very observant. I send to you, via *express* shipment in runner form, all that you ever thought your ideal of an evolved Godbeing would be. It will arrive in the form of three entities. Oh, what fun! We shall have a jolly good time, after you've recognized what they are and then begin to see what they aren't. Straightaway!

The purpose of these runners is for you to identify what you thought was so. Once you identify it, you can own that truth that you thought was truth. Then you can own the wisdom; you've released whatever ideal you thought existed out there and seen the ideal within you. And in that pure, virgin void of feeling, the impression of *Super*knowingness is seen on the horizon—the Godfire essence begins to arise in you just as it is.

How grand it is to walk the path of undiscernment! How grand it is not to have an idol at the end of the path that you must look like, but just to walk the path, and however you form, to accept that as divine. Sweet revelations. Take a long look in the mirror. In that reflection you will receive a very clear ideal of what the Godsource is. Look into the mirror without winking, smiling, blinking, or turning sideways for a profile shot—can you do it?

Look into your eyes, because only through your own reality can you connect to divine, omnipresent mind. And if you take a long hard look, you'll begin to see why you are loved so much. To describe the all-loving Godsource, well, there just aren't any words, for all *is* and *is* is the all—you can take it from there. On a personal basis, you summed the adventure of this dream up quite nicely. Take a look at how wonderful you are.

See You at the Airshows!

During the first leg of your flight into Superconsciousness, runners will rapidly appear. They will spur the emotion that allows your brainmass to begin to wake up. Only through that knowingness, that superb, clean, brilliant light, do you begin to have a functional Supermind that can be in harmonious flow with the changes that are coming forth.

The runners teach you emotionally what these words cannot describe. Your unfoldment can never be taught with philosophy, but must be experienced. That is the profound heritage of everyone who reads this flightlog.

The opening begins, straightaway; and the runners appear walking on the wings of biplanes, they are glistening with challenge. And your heart pounds and your soul responds—you'll know by the measuring stick of truth that you own. Your mind has opened when you can look into the eyes of your most outraged enemies and find no reason to despise them. That's how simple it is. And when you can look naked into the mirror at yourself and see *not* a sexual thing, but a divine thing that no longer repulses you, which you just love because it is divine. Then you *know* you're opening up.

You're opening up when you can look at others regardless of their faith and their creed, without fear and without intimidation; you can look at them and love them for *their* truth no matter how outrageous it is—even the worshiping of a worm. If you can look at them and love them and allow them their truth without feeling threatened by it, you are opening up, *way* up. Even before these pages are closed, surprises will appear on your horizon. You, wondrous Godfire being, *need* them to happen.

From the sound of it, you're in store for a very busy summer. I'll see you at the airshows, flying aerobatics, no doubt! This is your opportunity to know what you think you are; to meet your runners head-on, inverted, in a barrel roll, opposing solo, and all that. The prize? To do away with the worshiping of an idol that is an empty ideal, to return back to the virgin self of becoming without any limitations. I salute you . . . thumbs up. *Go for it!*

Waypoint to Destination 7
Flat Out!

"Clearance, Blue Angel 7, request clearance as filed."

"All aircraft listening. Please copy Blue Angel 7 departure clearance. Blue 7, you're cleared from your takeoff roll to a high performance climb. Clearance approved from the end of the runway up to 6,000 feet. Time out and up, 62 seconds. Climb-rate, 10,000 feet per minute: angle of attack, 70 degrees nose up. You're cleared for rapid-rate aileron rolls and a split-*S*"

"Blue 7 readback, cleared as filed, except you left out the inverted pass at 50 feet over the runway."

"Sorry Blue 7, you're cleared as filed. Go for it!"

You're in the back seat of a blue jet. The canopy's coming down. You snug down the harness, pulling tight the vertical restraints on the straps over each shoulder. You wiggle around in your seat, testing your lap belt. You pull the visor down over your eyes, *helmet feels perfect.* You know where the airsick bag is. The rudder pedals have been adjusted for you: yet, you won't dare touch them. You pull the boom mike down over your mouth.

The front seat driver asks, "Let me know how you're feeling; we'll do as much or as little as you want." You smile, a little uneasy, "Roger."

The whine begins to build in your ears; the bird quivers during the run-up, brakes locking it stationary—it wants to fly! You feel it won't stand still for another second . . . release . . . the forward movement begins. The acceleration is rapid, pinning you back against the seat . . . *whoosh.*

In seconds you're off the deck, holding 35 feet off the runway . . . *gear up,* building airspeed . . . . *flaps up* . . . 100 knots . . . 125 knots . . . 150 knots, 200 knots. *Oh man* . . . you're laying on your back, nose high, climbing for the sky . . . 250 knots, 300 knots . . . you're flying out of the illusion of grounded reality, into the sky, straight up to 6,000 feet . . . higher and higher. You feel your body lift up against your restraints, you're over the top diving straight down, 450 knots . . . 5,000 feet, 3,500 . . . 500 knots, 2,500. . . . Will she hold together? *Has anyone been here before me,* you wonder?

Well, We'll See . . .

Okay, you're airborne now. Let's check into your piloting abilities. Sometimes you're scared to touch the stick; other times, you feel you invented flight! At least you have the courage to slip into the cockpit.

You've been putting yourself through all sorts of maneuvers in order to acquire your ticket to travel into multidimensions. You know all about straight and level flight, takeoff procedures, climb-out. What about navigation, aerobatics, traffic patterns, and landing procedures? All of these procedures measure your ability to fly an airplane. But what about your unknown abilities? Shall we delve further into the unknown? Shall we break out of the dreamfog of the illusion?

Everywhere you look today you see criers in the street proclaiming that they are psychics. They even carry little cards, created at considerable expense, that say, "Psychic at Large." Many say in embossed lettering "Astrologists" or "Teachers" of some sort. To be talented, to be sure, is a sensitive subject for you. During this important communiqué, you will decide whether you've got it or you don't have it. Prepare for a bit of turbulence as you open up into Superconsciousness knowing.

The word, *psychic,* would have to mean extraordinary abilities to know, wouldn't you say? You know, about *anything.* Well, big deal! Everyone is a psychic—did you know that? Everyone is, everyone *knows*. There are those who culture and nurture that fine knowingness into a great science, and they are splendid at what they do. And there are those of you who know sometimes, and other times you have to run amok asking everybody what you should do, as if it's up to them to know what *you* should do.

So what is it—do you know or don't you know? I'd like to know! *Lazy knowingness* will navigate you to nowhere in these days to come. Everyone has the capacity to know all things—*all* things. In fact, *you* could have written this flightlog if you devoted the time and focused the energy patterns. Yet, you just don't know!

Do you know why you don't know? It's one of those little ideals that you've put into your mind, one of those little things that you must be *before* you can do the *Godlaunch*—catapulting yourself into Superconsciousness. Is it? *Yes,* you nod—I can see you smiling. Let's discuss what it means to have a talent, to be gifted— oh, the word is nauseating!

Life in the Slow Lane

Those who are gifted seem to aspire to loftier heights, don't they? Those poor, miserable, wretched commoners who only wish they could be gifted, all they're left with is to worship the gifted. That's a separation of Gods; one gifted, one a little less. *Gifted*—if you're *alive* you're gifted! Tap yourself on the knee—feel it? You're alive! Well, that's the greatest gift of all because—guess what? If you weren't alive, you wouldn't have all these troubles, would you? You wouldn't have all these illusions, all these dreams. And you wouldn't be sitting complaining about how rotten you've got it because, after all, you wouldn't have *got it;* you just would not be.

Life is the grandest gift there is. You take it for granted every moment of your existence. That's why you live in an illusion—you live in an illusionary world of emotional blockage and *you* are the jailer of your self. You're traveling in the slow lane; you jail your mind, you continue your knowingness. Let's say, all of a sudden, you had to struggle for your daily bread. This evening, would you be concerned about your relationship problems, or would you be wondering how you're going to eat tomorrow morning?

Life puts everything into proper reality. You're jailed by your own sense of inadequacies—*that* inhibits you from becoming. *Becoming*—I watch you walk very piously; I've seen you smile that smile of an FRGB candidate. I've seen you unload a few bucks here and there to prove it. I've seen you read all the right books and tell people how they should live, and then I've seen you so fervently hunting down a teacher just to ask him a question; and you cop out by saying it was just fun to do.

What dream are you dreaming? What game are you playing?— and you do. The only one who has ever lived who knows everything about you, who could form the question and then answer it, because it is the game, is you—wake up! And you insist that *you* don't know. And so you run amok—I watch you; you run amok and you play the game of question and answer. You try to find the truth, the teacher, *the* knowingness—someone to tell you you're quite spiffy. Someone to tell you about your relationship, your business adventure, and you believe it lock, stock, and barrel roll— no wonder you manifest *their* truth.

Now, this is rough flying, a tough sector of *FL: SuperC;* but if you're going to wake up into the clarity of an all-powerful mind and an all-embracing soul, you'd better understand where your difficult areas lie. This is very important because, not only do you not love yourself when you reach out and ask someone else, it means you don't trust yourself either. You are an age of seekers.

Do you recall when I said to you that you're a confused lot? You are. Did you know that if you lived everyone's truth according to their gospel, you would be in a mell of a hess? You don't know what is real and what is unreal. Do you know that you don't even know how to *know?* You are the jailer of your mind and your Godfire. This powerful notion that you are hung up on—*I couldn't possibly have the answer, the insight, the wisdom*—has kept you from Superconsciousness.

I have told you, and it is a great truth, that everyone is quite

42

equal. There is not *one* being in all of the universe who is grander than the next, nor is there one less grand. There just *is*—the equality of spiritlove, of knowingness. So what makes you so different that you don't know? Because you have an image of lack in your ability to know—some are simply convinced that they *can't* fly, a lack-of-confidence situation; we've seen it before.

You've received many communiqués about sovereignty, and of your contemporary resurrections of the Godfire, of Buddha, of Mohammed, of Yeshua ben-Joseph, of Ra-Ta-Bin. Why were they different from you? Because they listened to their *own* truth, their own knowingness; and everything they did, did not depend upon the planetary celestial movements—how boring! Nor did everything they did depend upon a prophet, an oracle, a seer, a teacher. Nor did they do anything to *open their minds*—they just *were* simple beings with profound sovereignty.

Have You Lost Your Marbles?

Let me impart to you a secret—listen carefully. You're still engaged in what is termed a superstitious mind. You're still *engaged* with the probing and all the hocus-pocus. You like to entertain yourselves with different truths—you stop on one when you like it for a bit, and then when you're bored with it you move your marble until you find another truth you want to stop on for a while, and then you roll your marble on the gameboard until it plops into another hole and you sit on *that* truth for a while.

Well, keep laughing. Soon it's not going to be so funny. The truths of all those who know more than you are not going to be there—you're going to have to make your *own* decisions. And what will you do? What *will* you do? How are you going to know? Let's explore some alternatives to rolling your marbles.

In your social system, there are a lot of folks who are the teachers of truth. You read their columns every day in your newsprint, you listen to their talking-shows, you bump into them at the super-super, you meet them at the bank that guards your money.

Everyone that you meet is *very* interesting and *very* knowledgeable and *very* polite—well, so are *you!* And, of course, they're all right, all of them, except for this *minor* area—none of them should have the answer to your life; you should already know that.

Sovereignty, the ability to pilot yourself out of your dive, emerges from a simple, profound knowingness that says, *I know, I am, I own, it is.* It's that simple. The simplicity of an electrifying FRGB surfaces from holding the entire power that he is intact, and very soon he finds that every question he asks, he can answer. Very soon you begin to realize there are no more questions, because you hold the power, and now it is a process of knowing, and you *know.*

There are no questions when you know, are there? But you're riddled with them because that's how you've fogged yourself in. There is no teacher *anywhere* who is going to save you from yourself—it just isn't going to happen. They will play with you if you want to be played with; they'll roll your marbles with you. Ask any of them to die for you—I don't care if they've never been here before, the experience will do them good! Ask them if they will, see what their answer is. If they won't do that, you'd best take heed and seek succor from your own truth and your own knowingness.

The Godfire self is born of the spirit of the Godsource within. That means simply, your Superself is launched from the Godsource within you—that is *you!* The more you seek its council and its knowingness, the more you answer your own questions, the more powerful you become. And every moment that you compute the answer, your brain receiver begins to open up and your systems begin to bloom. The explanation? Any moment that you have the answer and then you desire to know, that desire *electrifies* the seventh seal and it begins to bloom, the mind begins to open up.

Life in the Fast Lane

Take a guess how close genius is to you. As close as the nose on your face. (That's why I asked you if you loved your nose!) Take a guess how close forever health is—as close as the skin on your flesh. The more you know that you are the panacea, the greater you become. If you're crippled in mind, running amok and seeking succor from everyone else's advice, *their* truth, guess what happens to your mind? You won't know anything, you can't manifest a toad, let alone make a happy day happen. You just won't have it.

Turn on the seventh seal—open her up, flat out! To open it means to gather the strength to be humble in one's sovereignty, to be strong enough to know that you're right, and to be grand enough to execute that righteous use of your own truth. In other words, living what you are, for what is the light within becomes the light outside.

There are many of you who cannot launch yourselves, because you are crippled in mind and you are crippled in the Godfire spirit—you can't know anything unless somebody tells you. And *anyone* who tells you speaks the gospel, *anything* you read is the verbatim truth, and gossip is the most tantalizing of creeds. Where is your reality base? You have't even taken off yet—you're still tied up in the dust of your ground loops. You're wrapped up in your petty bitterness, judgments, angers, doubts, suspicions, and you've done it all to yourself to such an extent that you can't manifest beans. Literally!

Do you even *want* to open the seventh seal? Remember *want?* It's in the love of oneself, which means to *trust* your own know-ingness, that you begin to be close-mouthed about your own God-self; you begin to allow that truth to work for you. It's sort of like stretching your knowingness into strength—maybe a bit like your first carrier landing. You know the carrier is there, you know you'll hook the cable, you *know* you're the only person who can land it, and you know your fuel is low. You stretch your knowingness into strength, into courage, call the ball and hit it—*on deck!*

To open the seventh seal, love yourself to know you've got

the answer. Love yourself to know that the Godsource loves you, and that that which you are is called life, and the Godsource is the endowment of that life. And then to embrace that Father within you, that takes the exceptional courage. Are you aware how much strength it takes for one to embrace their own knowingness without running amok and asking someone else's sideshow opinion?

It takes a classic, *powerful* Godfire being; sovereign, a thirty-thousand-hour pilot—like a great oak tree in the face of a blue northern wind. It takes a magnificent one. Not everyone of you owns that, because you don't love yourselves enough yet to listen to your own truth, to embrace your own knowingness; you don't love yourselves enough to allow it to happen.

But Yeshua ben-Joseph did, and Buddha did, and Ra-Ta-Bin did. They abstained from asking the question—they *knew*—which began to open the mind; the pituitary began to be activated, the hormones of life began to flow into the mind, and it became open so that the answer of unlimited truth, called divine knowingness, could then occur within the body. And the more they knew, the more powerful they became. And when they spoke to the wind, it obeyed. And when they manifested the bread, it became. And these acts were called miracles, but in knowingness it just *is*. It is not a miracle, it is a way of life.

But you, you are idol worshippers—you worship stars that are not in heaven, you worship stars that are rocks, you worship everything but you. And for that you have given all of your power away, you have found your teachers—your new ones, the old ones—you have had your cards read, your teas read, your hands read, your toes read, your mouth read, your eye lashes—how many fall out means something—and you don't even know how to live. Can you hear this?

Let's Go for It, Somebody. Break the Knowingness Barrier!

When *superknowingness* is desired in sovereignty, that is when the power is awakened, that is when the truth awakens *for* you. Why *can't* you manifest anything? You don't have the power to do it—someone else owns that, certainly not *you*. Why can't you manifest your own health? Because you're too busy being unhappy, diseased, and therefore crippled. You're your own jailer, you've grounded yourself; you don't *want* to fly.

In sovereignty, piloting your own life, *superknowing,* you begin to collect back your power and begin to do all of those so-called wondrous things; *making miracles happen,* I do believe it is called. And the more you fly this jetroute of manifesting, the more *powerful* you become, the easier your carrier landings become.

Remember the day in the left seat when your instructor handed it over to you and smiled, "Land it!" Do you remember the wave of fear that swept over your being, followed almost as suddenly by a grander and stronger wave of confidence that switched you into a whole new level of consciousness? That was the, *I can't!* consciousness switched into the, *I can!* consciousness. Well, you could and you did.

And this is what you *can* become. Superconsciousness—the Godfire: a being who sees the window of the world. A being who can see the window of the human drama and where it's moving; someone who is in flow with the universal element, life, nature; you who are the Godfire that is the light to the world.

At this hour on your Earth-gameplane, there is no one that is a Fully Realized Godfire Being, therefore the truth of this message still is mythical; it hasn't been proven yet. But when the whole of consciousness begins to arise, and what you think and how you are begins to arise, that attitude *feeds* the whole of the world. Very shortly many are going to be feeding off your attitude, which is called sovereignty, and they will begin to *light up* everywhere.

It is not that you fly off into Superconsciousness in order to be a light to the world. Do you think that you should go out and save the world? From what? It is progressing, it is evolving, it is in the process of divine evolution. And what are you to save everyone from, their own truth? That is an enslaver. You don't fly into *FL: SuperC* in order to ignite the world—you'll never even break away from the ground with the *savior* attitude locked in your autopilot; the world will only take relish in destroying you.

Fly into Superconsciousness for the glory of the Godsource, the Father, that is within *you*. The residue of that light will be seen by others who wish to see, and then they will know that Super-consciousness is surely not a myth, but indeed is a grand reality. So, in spite of the world and for the world, one comes home to one's own truth. And so it shall be.

Back to Groundschool

As your flight instructor I charge you for a fortnight to abstain— now, don't *panic*. I charge you to abstain from asking a question! (Funny, aye, how you react to words?) But perhaps not so funny— this could be the most impossible thing I have asked you to do yet. Abstain and ask *yourself* the question, and speak it from the Godsource of your being. Ask it and then just allow, and see if you start to kick in that sweet little element called knowingness, that delicious premonition of truth. Bargain?

Now, many have tried to abstain from asking a question. On the average they last about three hours—can you imagine, they're right back into sentences with question marks in about three hours! The best way to achieve abstinence from questioning is to zip it shut—your mouth, that is. And that may be *altogether* impossible. But I do suggest that what you will hear after you've zipped your mouth may be extremely intriguing to you.

The voice of the Godsource that is the splendor within does not come from what has been termed rolling thunder. And it doesn't arrive via a FAX machine from some mountaintop stating conclusively, "Hello, I'm your God." It doesn't speak to you, sing to you, rock to you, lift you, exalt you—it doesn't talk to you that way. All those verbs still represent limited mind communicating with you.

*Super*knowingness comes from an emotion; and it's a feeling that doesn't say, 'Yes, I know,'' it just is an *is factor* that becomes very clear emotionally. And you'll know, you will *super*know. So if you're waiting for heaven to open up and kick in your afterburners, or for your guides, teachers, and whoever to speak with you, they shan't—it is a feeling that happens. For a fortnight ask no questions, but just *know*.

What happens if you backslide and you ask a question? Well, you've asked a question. You've sort of lost out on your ability to know; in other words you've said *uncle* and given in. That's all right, you may do whatever you want to do. But the bargain is, in accelerated rate and speed, for you to realize how much you can know when you answer your own questions, and how powerful that superknowingness is. It only takes a fortnight to understand.

Now, how long does it take for the answers to come—what's the response time? There is no time involved in level-seven knowingness—did you know that? Time is only related to your dream state and, of course, to this reality. It isn't going to come to you at precisely 3:10 in the afternoon over at so and so's place. It doesn't happen that way.

*Super*knowingness touches into your reality when you release the question. By releasing the question you are allowing the emotion to come forward—you *own* its truth. And you will know it when it touches in—so profound will the feeling be, it will be unmistakable. And everything you decide from your own knowingness will work in splendid harmony for your progress.

Secret Splendor

This should be a white-knuckle adventure for you because I know you; you shall be bursting at the seams to ask somebody something, biting your lips—*oh, hot misery*—and perhaps for the first moment in your life you will understand that flying into Superconsciousness is an alone process. In that aloneness, it is secret splendor when one embraces the truth of oneself, but keep biting your lip. You're going to touch into it, and once you do, know that you have touched level-seven mind.

This should be an interesting adventure, to be a part of and to watch. Now, this *not asking questions* goes for everything, even the price of a pair of those favorite shoes you've wanted for so long that might be on sale . . . I can feel you moaning and groaning right in front of these pages! Do you think that Superknowingness is only saved for *spiritual* truths? Perhaps that's why it is locked up in temples and caves, aye?

What do you think Superknowingness is? Wouldn't you say that it involves the price of oil, how much bread is, the price of gold, what time your appointment is, what the stockmarket did today, what time it is now—don't look at your watch—and what's for dinner? Superknowingness involves *everything* because it *is* life, correct?

In moments of deep contemplation, I sometimes am startled by an image of you entering a new age of consciousness blubbering and asking, *"Which way do you get there from here?"* And I suppose if you asked a crowd gathered on a street corner the way home, they would all point in different directions. Which way would you go? The way to go is to shove your throttles to the wall and dive into that understanding of your Supermind, which is coming forthwith; the mind that is the know-all understanding for *you*.

This is a weaning process for you. After all, how can you be finished with dogma, how can you be finished with creed, how can you love *all* of the whole of the world, how can you be at peace, until you have embraced the concepts that make these *miracles* possible? Indeed, how *are* you going to survive without asking someone how to? It's pure knowingness that will teach you—Superknowingness.

You *need* to be weaned, did you know that? You are a following, motley bunch. And in your *following* you are idol worshippers, song worshippers, book worshippers—you worship worshippers—you haven't found yourselves yet. These two weeks, this fortnight of being honorable to the God within you, should help wean you from the understanding that everyone else knows best, when you do, of course. Understood?

Check Your Parts for Commitment and Integrity

There is a word—*expectancies.* Do you know all about this tonal vibration? Well, you should, it's been vibrating about for some time now. Are you expected to make anyone happy, that you perhaps might know of? Think hard. Are you expected to heal, take care of, *soothe* someone you know? Are you expected to service someone you know, sort of like a filling station? Are you expected to fulfill what has been called your *obligations* to others? Why? Because someone told you you should?

Expectancy is your own creation. How's that for a flood of Superknowingness? And all from just five words—I can feel you heave a sigh of relief. Have you ever felt that you've been bought and sold? How can you own Superconsciousness when you're expected to be so many things for so many people, get it? In other words, you don't have enough of super *super* to go around. When most Godfire candidates desire their omnipresent self, they do not take into consideration just how many parts of themselves they have committed to others, correct? But how can you live without being committed to others—happy!

In the superfine realm of Superconsciousness, one shan't ever make it through as long as he is tied to the obligations of others. This is a very difficult understanding for you because others make your world go around, others give you the importance that you feel you so need, because *you* don't have it yourself.

You have signed your lives away—you have signed contractual agreements that are binding you to unhappy situations. You are answerable from the opening *gong* of your alarm clock to the closing *click* of your electric blanket (never had such things 35,000 years ago!). You are *owned,* you don't own it. Do you want some more runners, to understand how that works? You're thinking, *No, yes, you understand,* aye?

Let's rap about ownership—I'm learning all these *chic* terms. There are *very* few of you who are clear of being owned. Those are sovereign within themselves, they are bountiful in their families, but they are not owned by anyone save themselves. In other words, if they desire to take flight tomorrow morning at approximately 8:15, they could do so and in complete freedom—*freedom!* (They wouldn't even have to turn off their electric blankets.) Your mind cannot possibly expand into Supermind, nor can your soul swell into Godfire, if you feel you cannot go forward without offending someone. Do you comprehend this? Say you do.

What is worth one's freedom? What contract was ever worth it? What vow in the moment of lusty passion was ever worth it? (You know that one well, do you?) You cannot go forward and evolve because you may intimidate someone or threaten a situation, so you've become bought and sold by others by your own design—*you* did it, in other words. Adventure in the realms of Superconsciousness is activated when you are in full ownership of the whole of your faculties and your life.

I would be the first to say that there is nothing like the great strength of the family. The family—its roots and your heritage, its belonging feelings, *your* choosing of your family—it is wonderful. But what facades do you live behind in order to maintain the family happiness? Where have the family feelings gone then? Haven't the feelings become an imprisonment of your own self?

There are many who are reading these words who do not know themselves because they are busy living the image of their family heritage. Therefore, they can never touch base or become that part of a self-created inner vision, because it doesn't belong to them. It's not that I say to you to leave your family—they are your brotheren, they are the roots of your primeval heritage—but to realize who you have allowed yourself to be owned by, and for what reason.

Shooting Straight

Let's dive deeper into Superknowingness. Why *aren't* you *you?* Look at you men. Your fantasies are absurd—they are decadent, *decadent* because they decay the spirit of your own vital divineness. And you women, what are your daydreams? You dream of fanciful things, of unrequited romances—you dream of a fairytale vision only because you are not happy where you are, because you don't know what you're supposed to be. And every moment that you are reaching out *beyond* the plausible self of self, you are giving it away.

Listen, if you have to have a fantasy to excite your passion, it's better not to have the passion. If you have to have a fantasy to pretend you are engaging in it with joy, it is better to walk away and live a truth. In other words, there are many of you who live illusions for the appeasement of others. How can you go into a quality of Supermind, which is outrageous and free and all consuming of its love, when you are in fear of being yourself.

This is called straight shooting, I do believe. There are many of you who are kept people—do you know what kept people are? You are bought and paid for! You have married for money or comfort, and you are not happy in your Godspirit—you are *owned* by your past decision and you have jailed yourself because of it.

Where is your Superconsciousness going to come from? If it will emanate from the love of the Godfire within you, then that Godfire must be speaking to you of living honorably. Do you know what that is? To live in what it called noble virtue, in an honor that bespeaks the *quality* of the individual who you are. Are you aware that the realized being who lives in Superconsciousness is an uncompromising, beautiful thing? It is staunch in its truth, it is unwavering, because if it is strong it has the power to love all.

You are aware of the New Age that is upon the horizon. You have thoughts about being a part of that Superfun. But how are you going to get there from here when you can't make a decision on your own, because you have not lived in alignment with your own truth—you live a hypocrisy. I mean, the New Age will appear and mother won't let you out of the house!

There are many of you who think secretly that you are one thing, when really you have nothing to do with that *one* thing—you have lived in the fantasy of that thing, so you think it is you, yet it is not. It is an escape from the reality of what you truly are, you who are afraid to become what you are. Why would you be afraid to be what you are? Look deep and you'll discover why.

You have heard the term, *to live your truth.* The term does not just apply to the nonjudgment of others. To live your truth is to be *impeccable,* to be one who *is* what he is. In impeccability there are no shadows of yesterday—there are no shadows of limitation that creep into the omnipresence and cause the doom. Look at you. You want to be happy; you don't even know what it is! You think happiness is your fantasy, something you will never attain. And when happiness appears in moments you haven't planned, you discount it as something else, so you create other illusions to bury your head in.

The Breath of Freedom

Joy is the breath of freedom of being who and what you are; you've learned to love yourself enough to give you the strength to be impeccable. Joy, not *super* joy—just *joy.* It's so little understood on your gameplane that the word could never be overworked, not even by my scribe here who has *super* on his brain—*super* this and *super* that. Well, there is reason for all these *supers.*

It's to get you out of the fearbox that you're in, when you see an *un*super word. For instance, if we just said *"know,"* you would say, "I know all about knowing." But when we say, *super*knowing, you pause for a moment to think about it, and in that moment the word vibration has bypassed your altered ego, a *new* vibration has been felt by your Supersoul, and a little bit more of your *Super*mind is awakened. Thank you, superscribe!

Back to joy. It is far greater to walk away and have not one

54

drachma, not one ruby, to leave all the gold behind and walk away with none into a state of emotional glory, than it is to stay with all the rubies in the universe, for there is not enough to buy your freedom; there never would be. Even if your rooms were filled with gold, how would that change all of your hypocrisies? What are you living? Where are your values? What *truth* are you living, and why aren't you happy?

Well, shall we venture an answer, a nonhypocritical answer? There are many of you who are prostitutes in life. You have prostituted your Godfire and your truth while you sing songs and quote poetry of joy and unconditional love—I've *seen* this. These moments of bliss are only myths that belong to the fairy realm, because you are prostitutes of the truth which engages that fundamental, exalting, feeling.

You can spell the word, you can blow a kiss, you can embrace and say, "I love you," but *big deal*. Where is the well of emotion which that word comes from, if what you have done to yourself is to lie and betray happiness for the sake of gold, for the sake of comfort, for the sake of peerage, prestige, family, creed, religion, country? You see—squirming in your seat . . . uncomfortable, aye? The dive continues.

You Can't Cheat Yourself

I am not a stroker—you've opened these pages because you want to know about Superconsciousness and I want to make sure you receive your money's worth. I will not patronize you, because you have made all your choices freely—*you* have created this dream *and* this jail, and it is you who will escape beyond the bars or stay locked up; and it is all right either way. But how *do* you open the mind? Not because you *say* you want to—it is a process of being impeccably faithful to the truth within you, so you are clear in your autopilot-Soul.

This is the portion that many of you don't want to hear because it means you might have to ruffle the bed feathers—know you what those are? Downy geese—you may have to make a change, you may make someone angry with you, you may *disappoint* or fail, so you're afraid to make your own move. How could you ever become a light even to those you profess to love, if you live in the hypocrisy and in the *shadow* of love?

It's all about becoming into Superconsciousness, superknowing. Your mind cannot open up to purity, it cannot open up to love the whole of the world, until you have loved yourself to *love* the whole of *your* world; until you have found it a happy place to exist in—*all* of it, *even* the bill collectors. There are those who profess to be very enlightened—*very*—you know, you don't even smell, you're so enlightened. But just around the corner is a bitter, angry person who is waiting to get you if you don't live up to his expectations—that's how great they are.

Impeccable mind is impeccable life. *Impeccable*—'tis a grand word, because that is how you feel about you. And what is it to look another in the eye and say, "Yes, I love you greatly," and mean it because that is how you feel about you. To embrace your family in spite of how they feel about you and love them for their truth, love them and allow them—that is being impeccable. And it is being impeccable, if you don't like sleeping in the same bed, to say so. Get it? You can't cheat your way into Superconsciousness— you must *allow* yourself into Superconsciousness, and this is a part of it. Ready for some aerobatics?

Destination 7
TURN RIGHT BASE

Aerobatics
Disembark from Fear
Embark into Joy

Are you flying in a passenger jet, just sitting back and sipping your tea, reading the newspaper or one of those magazines they provide for you? Or are you in the back of that blue jet that was climbing at over 10,000 feet per minute, almost straight up? Or perhaps you're in both aircraft at the same time. Well, whatever the case, prepare for positive G-forces.

"Would you care for some tea?"
"Why yes, thank you."
"Relaxing flight, isn't it?"
"Why yes, it is, thank you."
"Will we arrive on time?"
"Yes, possibly."
"Oh, good."
"Yes, good."
"Thank you."
"Yes."
"Would you care for some juice?"
"Why yes, thank you."
"Relaxing flight, isn't it?"
"Why yes, it is, thank you."
"Will we arrive on time?"
"Yes, probably."
"Oh, good."
"Yes, good."
"Thank you."
"My pleasure."

Had enough of that? Good, let's fly!

You're over the top diving straight down in Blue 7, 450 knots . . . 5,000 feet, 3,500 . . . 500 knots, 2,500 feet. . . . Will she hold together? *Has anyone been here before me?* Yes, yes, he's pulling out of it. *Wait, I can see a crowd down there, what's going on?* Point one, point two, point three, point four . . . . we're inverted, screaming down the runway? *It's an airshow crowd watching us.* We're, we're upside down, 50 feet off the deck at 450 knots . . . point five, point six . . . *zip* . . . another jet just whipped by 20 feet away on knife edge. What's going on here?

Point seven, point eight . . . *Oh, here we go again,* pulling up, *straight* up. "You take the stick." Is he serious? I'm sure, what do I do with it? "Fly it." In the airshow—come on! "Try it, try a rapid roll sequence, just with a little stick deflection; that's it, there you go, see how she responds when you try . . . over and over and over again."

"Okay, here's the rest of the team . . . we're closing on them. I want you to snug her up behind Blue 1, into the Diamond Formation." Sure, no problem, just snug her up. "That's it, just ease her in the slot; I'm there with you if you need me. That's it." That's it, good, she's yours again. "No, you just hold her steady; you do what Blue Leader does, just keep focused on Number 1. Just follow him around, that's it, nice and easy." Nice and easy, and I'm 36 inches away from three jets moving along at 425 knots, and there's an airshow crowd down there 250,000 strong, and we're doing a 360-degree diamond roll over centerpoint, nice and easy he says.

"Great, great pass. Now watch Blue Leader. He'll roll into inverted position. He'll remain inverted while we fly the Diamond for this pass." *All right,* four Blues together, into a slow roll, wingtip to wingtip, 36 inches from each other in perfect harmony over centerpoint.

"Okay, you're doin' great. Now were going to link up with the solo and opposing solo jets. There'll be six Blues in Delta Formation, climbing to the stars, 90 degrees nose up."

I'll watch from the ground.

"Ready, break."

There they go, breaking away into their own directions, screaming like a 4th of July firecracker, each rolling to the thrill of the hearts down there, watching them touch the sky. What *would* it be like to reach up and touch the sky? And off we go, smoke streaming behind us. Hey, where are they going?

Ready to Experience Positive G-Forces, Roger!

Next runners. Every situation for which you have prostituted yourself and your truth, I will manifest one-hundredfold in front of you. So be it. (Do you want to read that sentence again?) Why a hundredfold? Because there are times when you are nearsighted—you have a way of not seeing what you really don't want to see. Positive Gs, coming right up!

In the past you could say, "Well, I left my glasses at home, so I can't see." You can't fly those blue jets if you can't see, so I'll magnify the view a little for you, just so you can earnestly look at who and what you are and learn to be impeccable in that truth. Impeccable—this is where the prime grind comes in; are you great enough and humble enough to be honest, or are you *small* and daring enough to be compromising? That we will see straightaway. And you want to touch the sky?

What are we doing here? Superconsciousness is only a word. In order for it to mean anything, it must begin to be an emotional feeling that expands the mind and challenges the soul, ferrying you into Supermind and Supersoul dimensions. You can back away and not look as long as you want to—it's all right, you're still loved. The assistance to you, to help you *emotionalize* your prime grind, is for those of you who want to become the *zenith* of the reason that you are here.

And conversely, being honorable will never haunt you. Every situation that you look at earnestly and to which you are impeccable, you will have just manifested one-thousandfold the generosity of your Supermind and spirit back to *you!* You'll find that your light is much brighter; you'll find that what you say begins to happen, and that's exciting news! The impeccable, simple Godfire being that you are is arising. Your days appearing over the horizon will be tantalizing and enthralling as you rush out on your wings to greet them.

Shooting to the Stars

In the days to come you will witness an all-out effort as evolution vibrates to it's zenith. You will see not only the earth and all the new land masses evolving, but the sun, that wonderful energy source that allows life to be through photosynthesis, will vibrate to a new understanding. And your dreams will be birthed in the echoes of space that is called forever, to return to you in peace.

It is *all* in synchronized evolution for the first time ever, and it is coming together in a most profound movement—it's called life, the great reality. Why blast off into *Super*consciousness? Because it takes superknowingness to be in that wondrous flow and in that change which is evolving. You expend all of your time trying to convert knowingness to money that you can exchange for so-called joy. In the days to come, you will expend your time converting superknowingness directly into joy.

What are you if you do not evolve? What are you if you do not change? You're only part of the stagnation of the flotsam and jetsam of the human drama that goes in and out with the tide. You're very fickle—you change with the tide of gossip. You were once in alignment, in an endowment of truth, with that which created the whole of the universe. Sadly, this knowingness has been talked out of you. You can see the conspiracy everywhere you look. You have to float back into that understanding to be a part of the flow that is no longer fickle or stagnated, but is volatile, ongoing evolution.

Evolution—it is the continuum of the Godsource experiencing the adventure of itself, and it is called the Forever Relativity. Do you think you have reached a state of perfection? If you do, you have reached a state of engrossed limitation, for there is no such element called perfection. There are only the limitations of the element called perfection.

To evolve means to change, and to evolve means to learn, and to learn means to be in knowledge of. Of course, in your world of relativity, the *fear* is attached to change. This is how deep your Soulwashing has been. What is there to fear when all is relative to you, as you are relative to all things—forever? That is not a question—it is an answer!

The Electric Understanding

There is an hour that is thus approached—it is already in movement. It is the fulfillment of the promise to the meek, the humble, the simple of mind; that they can move forward in the thrust of evolution, those who are going to inherit all the kingdoms. And knowingness, profound Superknowingness, like the fish and the birds—when you are that adept, that attuned to change, you're going to see a profoundly beautiful kingdom come forth, opening up right on your doorstep.

Why Superconsciousness? Superconsciousness is merely a word—it is a meaningless term that sounds wonderful, but if you have not the grasp of what it means, it is only a word. It represents expanded mind. It represents the flow of humankind into Godhood. You don't have to ask any questions when you *know* and it is absolute—wherever evolution is, you will be in the flow of that movement. It is inevitable; it *is* life.

I want you to know that knowingness, *owning* Superknowingness, will take you to a new age. If you don't possess it you will never see it, that is an even truth. To challenge and entice your mind to communicate the vibratory meaning of the word, one must live through profound expression—that is why all the runners are coming.

They arrive in your ready-room to challenge your integrity, to inquire about your common sense, to catapult you beyond the murk and the mire of your limited thoughts, to push you into a very electric understanding. It is the great sense of the Godsource, the all that is *you*. Without it you will continue to exist in blacked-out knowingness.

What is it like to have a blacked-out brain-slab? You have no idea if where you are living is the right place; all you know is that the schools are good and it's an easy commute. You have no idea if the water you drink and trust to be pure is in fact pure. You wouldn't even consider thinking that the fruits and vegetables, which are drenched in pesticides, might be poisonous to you. And they can't find the cure for cancer—bullarkey!

You have no knowingness of how long your food stores could keep their gleaming shelves stocked with all sorts of goodies when the days of the famine arrive in the land. You're a lazy people—you have given your power away and depend on everyone else to take care of you, including your remarkable government. What is that saying, "You can never be too rich or too thin." Well, some of you are so thin, a slight breeze would blow you over—you have hardly enough meat on your bones to last a day and a half!

You're wonderful, but your sovereignty of Superconsciousness extends to taking care of yourselves and infinitely knowing if you are prepared for everything that's going to happen. In the preparation, you have combated fear and are in ownership of your own destiny. The majority of you are tentative—you cannot say, "Whatever is there, come forth." Though you feel the need within yourself to prepare, you have filed it away in the back of your mind, because you didn't want to deal with it—that is your out, you did not want to deal with it.

I know, you would rather save and invest in stocks and bonds and mortgages and other pieces of paper that supposedly embellish your net worth. But if you had the famine that you're going to have, where are you going to find your food? You can't eat stocks and bonds—how are you going to make it, what nourishment can you derive from a net worth?

When you feel yourself slipping into the New Age, the feeling of sovereignty is absolute. It means being prepared and knowing acutely *when* to start putting up, when to start taking care of you.

Commerce and the movement of technology have been superb things—there is genius in those who are the inventors of industry, who are always rewarded by the sense of reaching out their minds to bring forth technological advancements in products, goods, and services that make life easier.

Let me inquire into your common sense—who is the beneficiary of this knowledge and this invention that has caused you to be lazy in your sovereignty? Look around you—they ride around in strrrrrrrretch limousines, fly around in fast business jets, float around in sleek yachts, sleep on satin sheets, and eat caviar and champagne for breakfast on *Monday,* fancy that! They are some of the stars that are not in the sky, and which you worship. The beneficiary of the creativity was the Godfire being who captured the genius of that thought and manifested it into a happening. These so-called creators are the beneficiary, and there is only a handful of them, worldwide. For all of the human race, there is only a handful of brilliant people who ever are doers.

When your country was birthed, it was born of the land—your prime industry was agriculture. There were no pesticides, there were no machines—you worked and your fingernails stayed dirty. Your water rose from a well; clear, deep, blue, and cold. Your grandmother made apple pie. Your neighbors were your friends— there *were* no fences.

There was no need for defense or representation, there was no taxation—have you forgotten these items of your history? There were no telephones, no magazines, no television, no computers, no credit cards, no automobiles, no gasoline, no pollution. You rode horses and courted in buggies that rocked down the merry lanes with the most fragrant of music.

At night, it was quiet—you could hear the night birds. In the morning you awoke with the sun—alarm clocks weren't invented yet. You didn't, "Hi ho, hi ho, it's off to work we go," because that song hadn't been invented yet. You worked hard, you ate well, you lived proud and long—you were happy, *happy!* Do you remember what that is, to be happy? To feel good about yourself, to feel those muscles ache after a day outdoors? Where did it go, those Sunday afternoons in the park at the bandstand, laughing with the trombones? Where did *you* go?

Let's Discover You All Over Again

Today, everything that you depend upon is solely outside you—how is that for a cold, hard fact. Yet, Superconsciousness is a knowingness—a feeling, an innate feeling—that attunes itself to nature, as you begin again to depend on you.

Have you given much thought to nature lately? Discover nature—what do you think it is? Just the molecules of life? Born, live, die, regenerate? It *is* life, it *is* the Godsource. And the thrust of nature? It is the sign, it is the handwriting on the wall. If you are not in the flow of its mind, that which evolves, then you are not engaging wholly in the enlightened self, because the enlightened self is the whole—nature.

Observe it—were you aware that nature does not possess an altered ego? It is the full and complete Godsource—it is not altered in any way. Could you conceive that nature, in the full thrust of it's evolution, listens to no man? *No* man!

Your earth is about to make a wonderful change—it's moving forward, it's evolving and expanding. Your sun is beginning its cycle of becoming larger. The whole of your universe and its balance will see a new orbit and a new planet. The whole of nature, which is the maturing Godsource, is moving forward into the dynamics of electrifying life. And where are you? Still spitting in the wind.

Superconsciousness is not only what is called the resurrection of the phoenix from the ashes; that is not what this is about. Superconsciousness is not entirely about the consensus that you are a God. Somewhere you can repeat that eloquently, but it doesn't hold any water.

Superconsciousness *is* the consciousness of the *whole*. You only hear what you want to hear now, you *think* according to the mass because you feed off one another's consciousness—your mood changes according to what you are fed. Superconsciousness is that involvement with nature that allows an unlimited point of view of life, and if you hook a ride with that you'll live forever. As your Supermind begins to open up, it will become attuned to nature, looking in awe at its infinite handwriting, its message of where it's going and what it's doing.

In the tomorrows of your days, you will see smiles on the faces of the ones who know, who can read the signs and the shadows cast before them of the days to come. Not smiles of contempt for those who don't know, and not smiles of *making fun,* but smiles that embrace it and know it is knowledge. Not smiles that read into the picture the dread of sorrow and doom, but smiles that *embrace* tomorrow, for they have the eye to see it. And he who has that which is termed the hand, let him create accordingly.

But for those of you who won't know, you will continue to live in these boxes—*your* little boxes. Your whole world revolves around two or three intimate companions; within your peer group you seek succor from fame; your moods fluctuate frantically around relationships, potency/impotency, beauty/unbeauty, money, prestige, status, wearing the right clothes—*looking good,* I believe is the term—and smelling like this month's fragrance, so as not to offend any of your two or three intimate companions.

Think it over—is there not truth to this? Outside your box, the world is fixing to quiver. Your earth is moving in spite of you who should know how to move in the flow with it.

Prognosis

Well, let's get into it! Go with the flow, aye? I want to expand on these days to come for I have heard all your curious questioning. I have gone into great depth about the window of the world, of nature, and of the shadow being cast forward in the natural evolution of ongoing life.

My communications are now recorded history that is available for you to see and read. If you do examine this information closely you will discover that the coming days are really quite wonderful, contrary to all of the doom and gloom gossip that has filled your ears. In gossip you do not receive the entire story, only the story of the one originating the gossip, be it a newspaper, magazine, a television set, or a telephone call. What follows is information for *you* straight from the source of all this *breathless* abandonment.

It doesn't take much *higher* intelligence to see vividly that your earth is polluted and riddled with filth. There may not be litter on your highways, but it is everywhere else. The earth's open sores of nuclear waste and yellowed waters *need* to be healed.

It doesn't take much *spiritual* vision to conclude that if you continue to decimate your forests and rain forests, there won't be enough oxygen to sustain life as you know it. Trees, after all, are the breath of life—you are aware that they convert carbon dioxide into oxygen? They don't just provide you with construction lumber, newspapers, and winter warmth, they also allow you to breathe. Quite accommodating of them, I would say. I know what happened to the dinosaurs! They ate the trees!

And what have you done with *their* bones? As you motor into your cities you can hear, smell, and see the pollution. Just twenty-five years ago the skies were vastly different. And you know all about the ozone layer being depleted by pollutants—even your television tells you about this, but not much is done about it. The ozone layer protects you from the sun's harmful rays, protects you from burning up and from skin cancers.

What is quite clear is that humankind does not have an interest in protecting mother earth. In fact, rather than conservationism and protectionism being an inborn part of everyone, they have become rare. Therefore, organizations of conservationism and protectionism, decidedly in the minority, must do battle with developers and industrialists who control all the money. We all know who wins these battles.

In its simplest terms, the earth, mother nature, is in a process of healing itself, since no one else seems to be interested. Just like you would do when you have scathed your skin, you heal yourself.

In that process there have been many prophets who have prophesied the end of the world. If the world were to end, where would it go? Seriously now, where would the waste go? Just plop it into a rather large trash can? Well, relax. There is no such thing as the end of the world. There is an end to Social Consciousness but *never* an end to the world. There will never be an end to life, no matter *who* predicts it! Your world shan't blow itself up—I've covered that topic extensively in *Voyage to the New World.* Your world is not going to pivot violently on its axis or rotate uncontrollably into oblivion—have you heard that one? Well, that's a fanciful fantasy. It shan't do that. It will change magnetic poles but it will not do it by rotating.

Of earthquakes—well, California is not going to fall off into the ocean. Where would it go? There are plates called crustal plates in the bottom of your Pacific Ocean that are creating a new environment this very moment. That environment is pressing toward the California shore. In other words, the new earth is rising up. If something is pressing towards you, how could you possibly fall *into* it? That can't possibly occur. You who are in California are taking a short journey north. And you thought you could buy beach property in Arizona!

Do you know all about fault lines? What a dreadful word—a *fault* line. It is only a zipper, it is the earth's zipper, so it can breathe and move—it needs that, it has always had them and always shall. Well, if you are living on the zipper, it would be best for you to consider what *super*knowingness led you there. If you want a lot of excitement in your life, you're in the right place, indeed.

What is an earthquake? It's the earth shifting to allow the new plasma of earth to come forward—shifting land masses. In my time, 35,000 years ago, your land masses looked very different in shape than they do now. Where you sit there once percolated an enormous swamp, filled with misty mornings and a variety of notorious creatures. All of your Americas, by the way, was a great swamp— oh, you know that.

Your continents have always been changing; that is wonderful, for the earth could not stand the assault of the human drama's devastating plagues upon it without rejuvenating itself. The release of energy through the zipper movement is the way the earth, in its ring of fire, can expand and heal.

The earth is beginning a magnificent healing process. The process is wonderful for it is a forward-moving understanding. If you are perched on a zipper or are perhaps living west of the zipper toward the ocean, perhaps you would not think this so wonderful. Those are areas that are on the march, so to speak. Superknowingness—if you know this and you live there anyway, how do you justify the fact that you haven't called the movers? You can find another wonderful school district. How do you justify being in harmony with life, realizing you are fixing to become mobile?

Take responsibility for what you justify. If you are perched upon an oceanside or on a zipper or on top of a volcano and you knew it was a volcano, you knew it was a zipper, you *knew* it was a vulnerable place, 'fess up—who is responsible for your actions? Only when you realize you did what you wanted to do, are you able to synchronize yourself with the flow that can allow you to see better and change, if you want to.

I Dare You!

Man has always dared nature. I notice it even today—because of his *invincible* attitude, or perhaps due to his karmic brownie points, *somehow* his divine self shall always be spared! Ignorance is one thing, stupidity is another. Pure reason is the checkpoint to look for. Superknowingness brings forward that consciousness.

Pure reason is the simplicity of common sense. Common sense is really not that common, because it is used so rarely. Yet the more Superconscious you become, the simpler and more reasonable you become. Being in that flow is going to be necessary in the days to come.

Your great sun is ready to give birth to a mammoth sunspot—the largest in recorded history. It is the thought; it is the knowingness giving forth expansion upon the sun. And the blast of the solar eruptions, followed by the solar winds that will occur from the eruption, will change your weather patterns drastically—it is already happening, for the least little shift in the sun's knowingness and in it's understanding makes a difference. What do you care about the weather? For the most part you only care if the sun is shining. But what if that is all it did? What if you become thirsty or hungry?

Superknowingness realizes that if there is a change in the sun, that change will be felt on earth, since the earth is like a child of the sun. Consequently, when the spot appears, the droughts reign. Man, working in harmony with others who see the way he sees, has already created a famine-like environment due to his carelessness and his greed.

If the sun displays it's glorious spot and the famine is rampant in the land, who is going to feed you? Those who you have depended upon for so long will be worried about feeding themselves. Your government has fed the world. What has it to do with you when there is no more?

What is the purposeful good of the sunspot and the famine? Every living creature that is in the throes of evolution is aware that this is coming. They all know it, even the birds you keep in cages know it. Your animals are beginning to take on fat and a lustre, and you want to keep them thin and glorious. They have a natural need to fatten up—they *know* it—it is putting away for hibernation. And what are you doing? Thinning down—you are oblivious to this preparation because you are not in a state of flow yet, but you will be.

Putting the Pieces Together

The sun is becoming larger, the knowingness is becoming grander. That sun and that great spot that is coming, this shift of your plates—of the North American Pacific and Atlantic Continental Shelves—all of these parts of the puzzle are in movement, motions, all happening in synchronized harmony. That dance is not horrible, it is wonderful!

And for the first time since time began, there is also a flow from the depths of thought into a new understanding that is pressing toward your consciousness—the rest of the parts of the puzzle. And only that which is attuned, that which hears by feeling, is going to know it. Of course you can run to your teachers and ask for advice. But if you don't superknow what's up, their answers are not going to last you very long when you are in an emergency state of survival.

Have you ever sunk your fingers into the fertile earth, thrusting a seed into the womb, nurturing it with water and love to watch it grow and bloom? And then plucked the fruit to nourish yourself at the highest moment of potency—do you know what that feels like? You think fresh vegetables come from the super super-duper? Fresh ones come from the earth right in front of you.

Can you name for me more than *one* seed company? What do you know about square-foot gardening? Can you freeze seeds? What can you plant that keeps insects away? What bountiful harvest will an eight-foot–by–eight-foot garden yield, all year? Do you know what it feels like to put up a pantry full of food? You have been tended to for so long you've forgotten how to survive. One day you will need to know again. Enlightenment is the preservation of life.

The Other End of the Dream Tunnel

These days to come, they are wonderful. Those who live through them, graciously living to see the other end of the dream tunnel and what is termed the kernel—the effect of the Superconsciousness that is in the land—will see what you have called the Kingdom of Heaven *realized,* for that is the *within* that allows you to sustain in the flow of life.

What is coming on the 'morrow doesn't make some of you

72

very happy. What would you rather have me tell you? That everything is hunky-dory? That you should just go on and *maintain* yourselves, continuing to live in the consciousness that you're living in? Well, it's always your choice. The information that I have communicated to you represents only a small segment of your adventure—there is more for you to know about, to be elaborately portrayed in my scribe's works.

The purpose of the current information delivered is to allow you to look into a window called life and allow you to understand its need to evolve. The complete extent of your adventure is only known by you. Yet, if your adventure were up to you, perhaps it would stand still because you don't want to be ruffled—it's bad for business, so you don't want to make a move because, after all, the status quo is just fine where you're at. You do not want to evolve, and that shows—you are not evolving.

This hour of Superconsciousness, how long will it last? Revolutions are coming in your world, freeing souls who were not free, who were enslaved to regimes of decay. There is an uprising coming, a revolution grander than you have ever seen. It will not strike terror into the hearts of the innocent—it is the rising up of the common people, *common,* whose dignity and honor and impeccable life enables them to understand their love for themselves in all the people of the world. They are coming forth, those who are marching at a very rapid pace.

The children of the Bear, before the end of your decade to come, will have freed themselves *totally* of what is called the reign of suppression—they will become more sovereign than even you in this day in your time. That is coming. Think of every warlord that you know of in the whole world. Only three will remain at the end of this decade, for their regimes, their enslavements, their atrocities of spirit, their will to play this dream to the fullest, are manifesting—they are coming forth at their zenith.

And in that, because they are of the Godfire, they must complete this dream in their sandbox. But their hour is at hand—it is becoming finished. It is the old age that is dying out and a grand one that is giving birth to itself; and all along the sun is evolving a spot, and all along the crustal plates within the canyons of your ocean floor are producing more land mass.

The Americas, the melting pot of the world. Are you interested to know why you are a grand people? Because the roots of every life are represented in your country, and every creed of religious fervor is allowed here. You represent the whole of the world—there are the Jews who are living next door to the Gentiles; there are, those who is termed, as it were, the Sumerians, living next to the Greeks; there are the children of the Bear having a cozy dinner with the Polish.

Your country is in a blessed movement because Gods from all walks of life are endowed here—Godfire souls who are striving to live together *harmoniously,* to love someone in spite of the color of his skin or the fervor of his religious beliefs, his creed. Your country has demonstrated its possibilities.

How will your country be affected by the change? The famine will hit your breadbasket, it is already suffering greatly. And there will be many changes, as it were, in your New England states because of the poisonous water there, because of your dying forests—and no more life for the rainbow fish that glimmer in the dappled brook.

But of your people and what is called your king, who will run your government, he is right on schedule. There is coming what is termed the one out of the three; an ending before the eclipse of this your century, a beginning like unto what is called Solon's Republic—a country no longer run by the professionals, but one that is run in turn by the common people who take their turn. It is called *absolute* freedom—*Super*freedom.

So what remains of the residue, of the change? After a famine *two* years in length, after the quaking of your cities and the poisoning of your water, what remains? Survival. Who survives? 'Tis not those who languish in the cities—the cities become the jailers. Those who survive will be those who nurture a small breadth of land, who are one with nature and the earth, and who can look around them every place and see that they have taken care of themselves—they are in the movement *with* nature. They will survive many things.

And before the end of your next decade to come, that which in the velocity of its perseverance, that which has acquired for itself a simple understanding, will live through what is called the eclipse of all human drama—you will be ascending into what is called the crowning glory or the return of Christhood in humankind—it is the new Kingdom.

And it makes no difference how powerful you are, how much gold you possess, how great your influence, or how long your arm of power is; that consciousness perished in the old age. What is in your soul, which allows it to be activated in your brain, which allows it to be borne in your consciousness, *that* will move you into a flow that will let you see a new age *grander* than you have ever thought possible.

The Kingdom of Heaven—it is not the creation of the holy city of Jerusalem that ascends and descends from the heavens with twelve gates of fire and gems. It is a consciousness, it is the resurrection of a knowingness within every person that glimmers like so many ascended masters, who work in whole unity and sovereignty, who are free of the limitations of space, distance, and time. And it is coming. If you could create it in a motion picture, it is coming. Rejoice, for the times that are coming are your times.

Greatest Natural Resource

I have sent quite a lot of runners scurrying your way—you're going to be busy for the rest of this your year. They are only intending to engage your autopilot-Soul in emotion, to open up that impeccable mind, the greatest natural resource that you own. They were also sent to trigger an understanding of Superconsciousness which could save your life—your life in this lifetime, your dream to finish this dream.

There are many who are confused by these statements, thinking they are just a bunch of bullarkey! They are presented for grand purpose. There are many issues that pertain to Superconsciousness and *where you're at* at the present time. They all need to be addressed. But if you look at them in a framework of understanding that *you* created those issues, that *you* manifested them, and then, with the same singlemindedness, if you can say, *I own it and I desire the change,* you can manifest the change—you are that powerful!

And what is the purpose of having a great Supermind if it isn't accompanied on your time-travel excursions by a great Supersoul? The great Supersoul is the bounty of emotion that exudes within you, that captivates and holds those electric thoughts of Superconsciousness, the bounty of emotion that holds all things. Why is loving yourself imperative? To understand what those electric thoughts are for all things, then to engage them in others, to realize the Superdivinity of self—to *realize* it, not just say it, to *own* it.

The ownership begins in the simplest of ways. In a flash you could realize that if you can ask a question, you already know the answer! Don't you know that the answer lies in the question? It is almost as if you were swimming in a sea of answers and one of them prompted your interest and you breached, leaping out of the water to explore that answer. The moment you breached, the answer disappeared beneath the surface. Superknowingness is that simple, just underneath your surface of consciousness. Strrrrrrrretch your consciousness into the *know.*

And when you do *know,* how do you own up to something that is called *brilliant* mind? I can see the advertisements now—*Be the first on your block to possess a brilliant mind!* I mean, who are you going to tell? Will this make you a better conversationalist at that dinner party Saturday night? I mean, what good is Supermind anyhow if it can't be converted into profit of some kind that you can relate to? The *good* that it is, is that it will catapult you into forever. Don't take my word for it, take yours. You know it just as well as I—you are as grand in the Godfire as I am.

What you are and what you are surfacing to be must be nurtured—being impeccable to self. You can take all of the verbiage in this adventure and throw it right out the cargo hatch—I'm sure some of you will, because it doesn't fit into your little fearbox. You just don't want to love yourself or to love everyone else under *any* circumstances—it's too big a deal, too much to ask. So you'll keep your personal vendettas and your vengeance—what else do you have to grunt and groan about! If that is where you find your happiness, go for it—you won't be remembered I assure you.

Plain, hard facts—was it *you* who hatched yourself into this fine kettle of fish? 'Fess up, you did, *own* it. You made every move in your life—you even chose your own parents, picked your own body, the whole works. If you can't accept this reasoning, you will just continue to blame, blame, *blame!* And what good does blame do other than wearing out your tongue? If you were so devout when you created your reality base, all you have to do is devoutly *uncreate* it. The creation came from the attitude—the *un*-creation comes from the attitude. It is not that you uncreate nature, but that you uncreate the blocks that keep you from moving in sync with it.

A *NOTAM* for those of you who *feel* the grand soul opening in your chest. You will actually feel it as it begins to expand. The warmth exudes from centerpoint center in your chest out through your central nervous system into all your cells, into your auric expression, back into thought—it is a response to the love of the Supersource, felt universe-wide.

For those of you who are beginning to feel this essence, who are beginning to live in the impeccable honesty, to live in the truth that shines forth, your smile tells me, *This is, oh, so simple! Why haven't I tried this before?* It is your understanding that is going to take you into tomorrow. I'm already there—I'll see you in the breeze.

What a Great Time to Be Alive—Never a Dull Moment!

You've selected to live in the times of the greatest change *ever*. Do you remember where you were when you made that decision? Time-travel back to where it was and look upon this shimmering emerald in the illusion that it lives.

When you conceived your flight to planet Earth, you didn't conclude it with someone else's fancy, their fantasy that the world should be destroyed just so *they* could prove a point. And you didn't see the atomic or hydrogen or whatever secret bomb exploding it all into bits and pieces eliminating all of your genetic offspring—that will never happen. But you did see that you are living in the times of *natural* evolution.

It is one thing to build a bomb shelter, but how do you survive once you build one? It is quite another thing to be out of snyc with nature and build your houses on zippers and then wonder why God doesn't love you because he rumbled your windows? Would you like to feel the trembling earth? Do you want to experience the awesome nature of life? For those of you who have not experienced it—you're going to experience it. You will live through it all, but the little demonstration is another runner to show you how insignificant your illusions are.

When the earth is trembling, you're really not worried about your present romantic state now, are you? Or what you're going to wear when it's all over with? See how quickly you can get into surviving, it doesn't take a lot! I'll manifest that runner for you, in order to know what it's like to have the questionable earth shimmer underneath, to wonder if you're going to make it through the tremor. Once you've had a little bit of that experience, then I dare say you are going to be Super*conscious* thereafter and be more in harmony.

Your Supermind doesn't open through words, it opens through experience and powerful emotion—that's why all the runners are going to visit your hangar. A goal for you to shoot for—a spot landing of a sort: If your mind opens up into the supermind state, you *are* in the flow of superknowingness.

What will it be like to wake up one morning, to walk out of your hovel and to feel a breeze, yet to find that there is something different about the breeze? Or to watch how the birds act as they fly overhead, to be *infinitely* aware of the stillness outside—to know that *they* know, and make a change? How acute is it going to be, in one moment, to drop what you're doing and in infinite know-ingness know exactly what to do in the next? And that is only less than a tenth of the mind of Superconsciousness.

In order to see how aware you are, how good your super-reflexes are, I intend to forward via nonstop delivery the next grand runner for a summing-up of this latest particular bit of intrigue that I have *laid on you,* as the saying goes. We're going to see just how aware you are. Now, hotshot pilots know all about reflexes, especially when they're chasing bogies or even on final approach for a normal landing. If their reflexes are shot, their flare will look like a template for a rollercoaster ride. So let's test your reflexes.

In the days to come where all of you live, a change will come about. I know what you're thinking already—it is not doom and gloom! It will have to do with *where you live* and it will be based on a water and weather condition. That no one can announce ahead of time, one morning it will just be there.

When it arrives I will press a feeling upon you. The feeling may arrive in the middle of one of your soapie de operas—you may have to turn them off. But the feeling will be heavy enough for you to pick up. And when that happens you will know exactly what to do. Why would I do this to you? What's the use of summing everything up if you don't have a little test—flight-test your flying ability, see how you score. After all, you bought this flightlog to join us in the adventure, didn't you?

Check your flightplan. We've already covered 10 percent of *FL: SuperC* on this leg of the hop. Let's time-travel onto the next. Ready? Thumbs up . . . salute . . . and off we go!

I made you a promise the last time we thought together—I offered to tell you my new model of the universe. I feel a bit like a little boy telling his best friend a new model airplane he has just built. Why construct a new model of the universe? Because the old model isn't working—it's too small and too limited, it doesn't allow all people to know that they are all things.

And then there's the *big* misunderstanding—God, the Father, The Source really *does* superlove everything and everyone unconditionally, would *never* think anyone was a sinner, would *never* find pleasure in condemning anyone or anything to a hellish place of torture for all eternity. How ridiculous! The Source that I've come to know only desires for *all* of its children to live in joy through loving themselves. The universe as we know it doesn't allow thinking of this sort—it's called blasphemy; they used to burn you at the stake for this, now they just banish you in forever, in *their* forever, that is.

My universe model, I'll call it Universe Model Doug, because everything has to have a name—there we go, limiting it already. See what I mean? You can call it what you want; see, I already wanted to *own* my universe model. I have another name for it— let's call it the Cube Universe Model; if you want you can name it after yourself.

The *Cube Universe Model* had to fit these criteria for it to work for me:

1. This universe could only exist if it allowed all things to exist in it.
2. This universe could only exist if it allowed all things not to exist in it.
3. This universe could only exist if it allowed all things to play out their games as they see them—if someone wanted to be a hero to a victim, they could be so. If someone needed to receive love and attention by being a victim, they could set the stage for that drama by creating a tragedy that they could experience.

4. The Cube Universe could only exist if it allowed all things to discuss all things—I believe it is called *gossip*.

5. This universe could only exist if it allowed all things to discover that when they judge or condemn another, since they *are* all things, they are really condemning themselves to whatever they wish to condemn the other to.

6. It could only exist if it allowed the first pain to be felt from mother to child and from child to mother.

7. The Cube Universe could only exist if it allowed love to be that all-pervasive energy that knows no other similar frequency vibration.

8. It could only exist if it allowed visitations from other beings from other dimensions, or simply put, this universe could only exist if it allowed all things to *think* all things—if someone believed they were visited by an other-dimensional being, so it would be.

9. The Cube Universe could only exist if it allowed all things to feel fear and guilt if they wanted to, although they didn't have to if they didn't want to.

10. It would only exist if it allowed me to be a visitor here, that allowed me to observe this as a playground filled with children playing, that allowed me to be free of the drama that everything must be *my* way—allowed me just to watch the children play.

11. This universe could only exist if it allowed the laughter of children and the romance of lovers.

12. It would only exist if it allowed all things to be rich or poor, depending upon their inclination, for I have been rich and poor and I *know* it is just a state of mind.

13. It could only exist if it allowed all things to feel bad if they wanted to feel bad, and to feel good if they wanted to feel good.

14. It could only exist if it allowed all things to worry about whatever they wanted to worry about, don't you think? But, of course, they need to know when they need to know that nothing needs to be worried about.

15. The Cube Universe could only exist if it allowed all things to war if they wanted to war, and to live in peace if they wanted to live in peace.
16. It would only exist if it allowed all things to *be* all things without affecting any other universe that was allowing *this* universe to be all things within it. (I can hear your thoughts now—you're starting to draw a picture in your mind about what the Cube Universe Model looks like.)
17. This Universe of All Universes could only exist if it allowed all other universes to exist within it and *without* it. (I gave it away; you guessed it.)

Does my description of the Cube Universe agree with your mind perception? Just imagining it made me feel good, to see all those endless playgrounds of adventure—suddenly time didn't matter, it was okay if I missed the boat, there would be another.

If you think about the model you'll understand that there is constraint around each universe cube—the lines of limitation that form the structure that your universe is in. You could create a universe in any shape or form—draw to your heart's content.

The lines that define the form are barriers that those who live in the universe create through thought. I call the lines the *backdrop of forever.* So now when you hear the term *light-years,* you can enter it into your consciousness as a no thing, because "hyper-thought" travels faster than light—therefore the Light Age premise, *If you can think it, it is,* has meaning.

Let's take a look at *our* universe, which has been called The Plane of Demonstration. What is it we demonstrate? Anything we want to demonstrate; that has certainly been proven throughout history—except the premise, *love is all there is*—that hasn't been proven yet. And we haven't proven that all that there is, is in us—we've only been taught what we aren't, not what we are.

Let's look into the little cube of our little universe. In this little universe of ours exists everything that we know, can see, can hear, and can conceive. Its borders are the edges of forever, beyond which we can't see, can't hear, can't know, and can't conceive.

One can make one of two assumptions about the edge of our known universe—there is an end or a border to it, or there isn't.

If you choose that there is a border, an *end*, then you have defined your universe—it's the little cube which is called the Plane of Demonstration, because you can demonstrate anything you want inside your cube. If you had selected the other choice, the choice of endless infinity filled with etceteras, then you have left yourself wide open for endless etceteras of adventures.

The next logical question then is, what is beyond our known universe? The answer can only be either nothing or everything. Let's take a moment here to present an analogy. You've been to a theater to watch a play. You were seated in the audience and looked toward the stage. On this stage was played out the infinity of the play; the script was played out in a little cube right before your eyes.

See if you can envision this cube now—can you see it? Within it are all the players in the play, the stage settings and the backdrops which set the scenes. Let's say one of the backdrops reproduced a magnificent sunset, the sky in all of its glory, with trees and clouds and the fiery crimson ball setting off in the horizon— you've seen one like that. The curtains were drawn and the stage hands set up another scene for you to view.

The curtains open and there it is, another backdrop that reproduces the evening stars in all their glory, you can almost see them twinkling now, way off yonder light-years away, you can smell the evening cold as it fills your senses, asking you to wonder about eternity.

And there you are, captivated and lost in the middle of this scene—you know it is only a stage but in a few moments you're swept off into the action of the play as you identify with the words of the actors, as they vibrate in your being. And then all of a sudden someone pulls the lever that raises the backdrop of forever, and there you sit staring at a brick wall realizing rather abruptly that you were in a cube whose backdrops convinced you you were staring out into forever, an illusion.

I wonder if someday the lever will be pulled on the backdrop of space. Will we be staring at a brick wall? What *will* we be staring at? Will we be peeking into other universes, universes beyond our understandings? Will we try to battle them? Will they play with us as if we were infants, or will they abruptly awaken us to our destinies?

Maybe we *are* in the Black Hole? Maybe this *is* the bottomless pit; perhaps our thoughts of hatred and anger and doubt and fear act like gravity on us, casting us further into the darkness of guilt, *deeper* into the murk and mire of our illusion? Could that be the G-force?

Maybe if we reversed our thoughts, we could reverse the law of electromagnetism; we could release our love into the universe and fill it with vivid, rainbow colors? Perhaps when our bubble of despisal and frustration is burst by these fresh, radiant thoughts, maybe we *will* see beyond the boundaries of the blackness of our universe cube?

And, quite possibly, we will see into the vastness of unlimited hyper-thought, into universes filled with rainbow colors of comfort and joy and a peace that passes all understanding. And it's my guess that those universes just might love us, *Super*love and accept us for what we are. After all, to love is to be loved.

Maybe, just maybe! Your guess is as good as mine.

Now, That Is Unlimited Thinking!

The body that you fly around in while you're on planet Earth, your craft for staging operations in three dimensional time/space, is a complex system of brilliance. In an airplane you have all sorts of systems—avionics and fuel lines, engines and control surfaces, empennages and canards, wires and cables, hydraulics and autopilots, glass and gauges, retractable mains and tricky tail wheels, constant-speed and fixed-pitch props, slotted fowlers and trim tabs—tons of stuff that sometimes doesn't work. Sometimes, all these little items have a mind of their own.

Your body is another story; it reacts to the attitude of the autopilot-Soul that is flying it—what you program is what you get! Are you aware what illness truly is? Let me detail for you what the mind does with the body. Your body: Have you ever taken a good look at it, a hard, close look at it? It is the most miraculous of machines. Try to duplicate even the smallest cellular division and see what you have to make to recreate that division.

The body, as it was created in the beginning, houses what are called the great glands. Some are ductless glands. The glands are called, in some parlances, the seven great seals—storehouses of the energy of superknowingness. They are also called Chakras. Your body was created to live forever. That may be a little tough for you to believe, because all you've seen is death and dying and facelifts!

Contrary to popular mortuarial opinion, when you are functioning in harmony, in perfect health, you actually live in agelessness. When the seven seals are awakened and the greatest seal of all is at work, and when the greatest organ of all time—the mind—begins to open, guess what occurs? *Harmony!* Now, we're not speaking of a musical group. Harmony—the harmony of the *hormones.* The ladies know all about hormones; the men, not so much . . . but they're quick to learn! You're in ebb and flow with hormones every moment of every day. When your body is in hormonal balance, you are in *harmony.*

One difference between your body and an airplane is, your body is prepared to regrow a limb, an organ, to recreate eyesight, to recreate any living portion of its whole self. (I'd like to see a Boeing 747 grow another engine!) Contained in every cell that helps to make up your body structure is the cell's genetic blueprint of it's own DNA and its chromosome structures. Each cell carries around its own blueprint of the whole.

Do you recall what the ancient pharaohs were striving for? Immortality. They concluded that whenever the superknowingness was such, with a scraping of their cellular mass they could *clone* a new body—*their* body. And the car and the bar could return back to them, the *car* referring to the body and the *bar* referring to the soul. That is why they kept their bodies intact.

In the arena of body preservation, they did a much better job than most of you do; for what is left of you in a little over one-hundred years is only a smear of some bones and a few pieces of costume jewelry at the bottom of the casket—an endearing scene!

Those ancient pharaohs, which many of you were, had a knowingness within them, an infinite truth, that the whole is captured in the single cell, and it is. Your scientists even this day have the ability to take a cell scrape and recreate a clone of you. Were you aware of that? You could be stamped out like car fenders if the government directed it! The body is truly wonderful, but it is a no thing unless it has the living fire, the Godfire, within it. And that is the unseen divinity that you all are.

Adjust Your Attitude

Your brain has the capacity, through the pituitary and pineal systems, to create a *life* hormone instead of a death hormone. It doesn't do that because you still live in your little fearboxes of limited thought. You're afraid of everything, including your shadow; you're scared to death to have a wrinkle on your face so you don't laugh, and by doing so you are dying more quickly than most. What allows one body to live for a very long time, and another to live for a very short time—both being genetically the same—has everything to do with your attitude. Illness is the reflection of the *emotional body* in the body.

We've discussed how powerful you are, Gods who can manifest everything. Do you know what your Kingdom truly is? It's your autopilot-Soul, which directs your entire drama as it has been programed by your attitude—this is your flight-control system. When the soul is pacified inside, then whatever you desire outside thus becomes manifest.

Every illness there ever was, was created out of a limited

attitude. Cancer is a war of the body upon you—its free radicals are out to destroy you, because you are a hypocrite within the body, happy one moment and full of hate the next moment. That cell begins to declare war upon you.

The question becomes, how to be healed, aye? If one had the grandest of attitudes, and could see his body in saving grace and in total love, he would heal his body in moments. But you can't do that with 33 percent mind-power. You can sit and visualize until you're blue in the face—blue with hot sweat breaking out on your forehead, and you feel like you'll have it any moment, and you're trying to rub your hands hotter and hotter and hotter. It's not happening—you're not equipped to heal yourself because you've backed yourself into a helpless corner of limited understanding.

If your brain were fully operational, your body would *never* grow old. The fantasy of the elves? They *existed*—ancient ones with nigh no age, riddled with wisdom. They're only a myth now, but there is a truth about that. And just now you reason in your little boxes, *What a truth—how outrageous can you be—agelessness!* I'm right and that is quite wonderful, but in your little box you expect to die. You've done everything to prepare for it—you live like there's no tomorrow, you despise yourselves, you've even purchased your own plots to be buried in, no doubt with an excellent view. And what of this paper called life insurance? Really, is that not an irony of truth? Why is it called life insurance? It should be called *death* insurance. Correct? It pays off when you kick the bucket.

Dead-Stick Landings In Progress

It's *all* attitude! You're powerful enough to have shut down your rejuvenation centers. All your props are feathered—flamed-out. How do you reverse the shut-down? Illness, anywhere in the body, is trying to tell you something. If you are nearsighted, think about what that says to you—that you only see what is in front of you, you cannot see what is beyond you. If you are farsighted and cannot see up close, what is that telling you? You don't like what you see, so your vision is somewhere out there, not in front of you. And if you're riddled with diabetes, what is that telling you? Excessive amounts of sugar in the blood, because you have learned through your attitude great selfishness. Your bodies are teaching you about your attitude by reflecting it all.

Your embodiment, your body, was created in a style that existed wholly outside of the realm of disease. Perhaps you know that every sexual disease was created by man—every one of them. Why do men die of broken hearts, which are called cardiac arrests? Because they are unfulfilled beings who are hard-pressed to make an impression in this consciousness; they know very little about emotional love and expression—their hearts give out on them, they *burst* open with an anguishing tremor, the travesty of men.

Disease just doesn't happen—you create it according to your attitude, the attitude in 33 percent social-brain that falls below survival into a state called decadence. I've been much maligned for using that word to describe the state of things. Yet, you're becoming aware that the whole of your gameboard is riddled with the diseasements of decadence—you read about them every day in your newspapers. And you contemplate—*Why?*

You don't need to be the victim of your thoughts. When the mind begins to open even 10 percent more into Supermind, there is *no* disease, there is no running out of life—there is only life!

I've heard your thoughts, you who have asked for help because you are manic depressives; you who have contemplated taking your own life. Why would you destroy your beautiful body? It won't make the illusion disappear. You want to depart because the illusion is so unhappy for you. And in that strife of unhappiness, you've totally lost what it is to create joy—your body is in degradation instead of joyration!

You can only be depressed about your looks so long before you lose them, what you have left. You can only hate your body so long before cancer takes over and does it in for you. You can only work so hard and so long to make an impression in this fickle Social Consciousness, only to die of a broken heart—ironically the failure of one to extend and express one's own self. And yet, you can change your attitude program into a joyous celebration in a flash!

And how many lovers do *you* need to lie with before you've thrown away your virtue, like pearls before swine? And sooner or later your precious, priceless body, which you don't love or hold in devout understanding of what it is and what you are, is going to die just because of *how* you are. It's most alarming that at the height of your technical age, you are experiencing the plagues. It is alarming, would you not say, and almost an embarrassment to the evolution of the human spirit, to find that the *common* cold cannot be cured? Fly off to the moon sneezing!

What could the answer be? There are medicines, the greatest of which utilizes the body's own mainline functions for a cure.

In other words, by using the same tissues that are diseased, the same system that is *diseased,* the same blood, the same immune system, the greatest cures of all will be extrapolated. And isn't it ironic that the cure came from you!

Now, that's only a physiological cure, but what about the reoccurrence potential? Guess what causes the reoccurrence? You guessed it, Mr. & Mrs. Wonderful, for no matter if you cure the cancer, if you still *hate your self,* you will *never* cure it. It will return again and again and again until it does its job. You've programmed it to.

There are many of you who declare that you are healers. To *heal,* in the verb sense, is a very mighty profession. It is also a profession that puts the healer in a very uncomfortable seat, because you can never, ever, *ever,* heal anyone of their own attitude. You may make a difference in their body but you will never heal their autopilot attitudes—it's not yours to heal. The greatest healer of all *is* the one who created the disease. Healers, if you want to punch out of the hot seat, do so—no one will see you as lesser.

Double Line Bottom Line Checkpoint

In order for you to have the privilege of observing the effect of your depression on your body, I shall gladly direct to you another runner. In other words, you're going to be fatigued, and perhaps stressed to the point where you become slightly ill—a little bit less than being well, but not so bad as being sick. Your next step is to reach for the medicine cabinet or the medicine man, correct?

This is what I desire you to do. While you're sitting there, I will playback a memory of your days' events—you will see them flash back very quickly. You will hear what you said about yourself, you will listen to the excruciating travesties for which you've judged yourself and a few others—*called yourself on,* I believe is the term. This is a rare privilege which you would ordinarily never enjoy, reviewing your days' activities. Sounds like a rather daring time-travel adventure to me! Are you with me?

In the state of awareness you'll be in, it will become very, *very* clear what the sum total of that day's attitude meant—in other words, what is called the bottom line. You're going to acquire a double-line bottom line! The moment you realize what you did in that day's events pertinent to the kingdom that is you, the *moment* you realize it, you will have healed your*self* splendidly. This only works for self, you must understand that—healers beware.

In this little display of your own miraculous wonderment, you're going to sit back, *lean* back, and you will begin to feel rather cocky. Have you ever felt *cocky?* Funny word—I suppose it's origin has something to do with a strutting rooster, wouldn't you say? When you feel that feeling, *revel* in it, baste yourself in it, *feel* the *glory* of it, because when you do that you *own* the exhilarated emotion of an accomplishment you never thought you possessed. And the more you *get into it,* as it were, the more you will own it. From there, that just opens up another part of the contemplated mind. Once you know that, you're home free.

There is more to be said about this little miracle. The joy that you will feel afterwards—reveling in it, rolling in it, and all the like—is a joy that you've been searching a dear long time for;

a joy that gives you the strokes of understanding that you *were* really something. Well, how much greater can you become? How close to self-love can you travel when you have just touched the inner God that heals the whole?

This joy accomplishes a magnificent thing—the more you're happy, the more your brain-receiver opens up; the more that opens up, the more powerful you become, the more aligned you become. Now, mind you, a blunder or two will ensue along with the strokes of understanding, for whatever you see, you must see with a judgeless sense. You cannot say, *I see good and I see bad,* because if you do you have just intensified your kingdom in a polarity that is very unsavory.

The more hours you fly in Superconsciousness, you'll discover that this flight level is not a process of good and bad. It is the process of *is*—a forward thrust that has no balance, it just is. Therefore, one does not set up the possibility of failure.

Opposites Detract

Further elaboration is required, I detect. Every time you say something is *good,* you are going to realize that something is also bad. Have you ever thought about that? That's how you think—right brain, left brain and all that; you have to have opposites. If one part of the opposite exists, the other part is not too far behind. If that's a truism, could you realize that if something is *beautiful* you will find the *ugly* of it eventually? Did you know that when you find the perfection of anything, the *imperfection* of it is not too far behind.

To time-travel into Superconsciousness, you have to master judgment. You can no longer look at a rose and say it is beautiful— you only *become* the rose in feelings . . . *Rose, it is.* You no longer look at your children and say to them, *"You're a very good child,"* because in the next moment they will be very rotten—don't you mothers know! You'll only look at them and *love* and allow them. The more you allow, the more powerful you become. This is very clever stick-work on your part, because you dictate your aerobatics through allowing the rarified atmospheres of your skyhighs, or the deep, dark dungeons of your manic lows. Roger that?

The *Is* of Superconsciousness is without the vacuum of good and evil—the opposites do not exist. If *good* exists, it creates a vacuum that sucks in the *bad*—the law of the world of opposites. The *Is* of Superconsciousness is without the vacuum of perfection, for it would suck in imperfection. Once you get on a roll into Superconsciousness—you know, rock and roll, 400-knot fly-bys, rolling reversals and all that—it is a *forward* thrust, it is the *now*, the evolution of now, it is *super*knowingness. You don't sit around and grade your activities—you just *are*.

Why is it that an FRGB can walk in absolute sovereignty, can know it and own it all? How else could you view the whole of the fickleness of humanity and still love it? You could never love humanity based on *good* and *bad,* did you know that? Think about it, because if you did, everyone outside your reality base would be rotten. Isn't that how it works? The little healing—once you get a taste of it, you can't go back. Once you begin to wake up and become sovereign, you'll never become enslaved again. It is *assured!*

I suppose you've been asking yourself, who is this character who has been writing to you between the airplane symbols? It is I, the Author-in-Command of this adventure.

When I write these words, they are the product of years of thinking activity in this lifetime, and many other light-years of hyper-thought activity in other lifetimes, no doubt. I believe it is an illusion to think that we *don't* live multiple lives— after all, where have we come from and where will we go?

Every word that is in this flightlog has issued forth through me. I've proofed the Ramtha transcripts and in some cases transcribed them myself. I have compared video tapes to audio tapes looking for flaws of presentation, trying to find the tricks of the communication, if there are any. I've observed Ramtha and Ramtha's channel, J. Z. Knight, for almost eight years. To me the manifestation of Ramtha is very real, not a fake or fraud, and it is contributing quantum-leap information to those who want the information.

I originally started playing with these *other-dimensional* communications because I had no idea what they were talking about— it just felt intriguing to my beinghoodness-self (how about that for a mouth full!). There was a need in me to delve deeper to discover what was there. I started out as a skeptic—I'm a *prove-it-to-me* person, and I hope you'll always continue to be that type of person, too.

What is this time-travel to other dimensions really all about? How does it affect you? How will it help you get rid of your stuff? Can we really break through into an age of compassion? Who really cares?

This is how I understand it. Any time you allow a thought to enter your being, you are time-traveling into the dimension of that thought. Why? How? That thought will take you to where it is. Thoughts as we know them are composed of symbols; when you think a thought you picture it, for instance *airplane*. The word *airplane* is composed of organized letters printed in ink on paper— just like all these other words—but the vibration of the word conjures up all sorts of thought-forms and word-pictures in each person who sees the word.

Everyone who sees the word sees different pictures. When a child sees *airplane* and points to a bird in flight, to that child, that's what an airplane is in that moment—who's to say the child is wrong? To a Captain of a two hundred–ton behemoth, the word *airplane* is something quite different; it means science and technology merged with perfection in man, it means responsibility for crew and passengers, it means tens of millions of dollars, it means weather prognosis, and computers, and a walk-around, and flashing lights and dials and gauges, and *V1, rotate,* and *ah* . . . as the mains touch gently after another perfectly executed mission.

See, you just took yourself on a little trip into the mind of the Captain—a little time-travel adventure. You can relate to airplanes and on-time flight, but what's this unseen-world adventure all about, you ask?

What I think is going on, is that we are beginning the communication with the unknown part of ourselves, the part that's been hidden by the ages. After all, if we *are* all things, then we *know* all things; let's talk about it! We see this blatantly through the channels as they manifest their unseen entities. Yet, what is the source of the information? Could the unseen entities simply be mirrors of ourselves, that great latent powerhouse of information that has been taught out of us by the institutions that make up this reality base?

What are the choices of the Source of information? If we label it *God*, whose God is it? I can hear the battle cry now—*"It's our God"*—*"No, it's our God"*—*"Forget that, it's my God!"* If we have to give it a name outside ourselves, humans will eventually establish ownership to it and then begin charging admission—just as I tried to do with *my* new model of the universe, and it is debatable about how *new* that model is.

And then, on the other hand, we could call this source of information *evil*, or we could call it *good*, but what good would that do? Those who aren't open to it, *do* call it evil; those who are open to it, *do* call it good. Well, *good* and *evil* are just judgment words which create word pictures of fears; not very useful in the Light Age, aye?

If the Godsource is all that there is, since we are a part of all that is, God must be in us, lowly, old us. I suppose that means that we are not the bastards of the universe, which is a pleasant thought. Let's try an equation—if we are equal to *A* and God is *B* and *A* fits inside *B,* as all things do, aren't we also *B?* Makes sense to me, but I'm sure a preacher or two will have something to say about that.

Assuming we're a part of God, since God is defined by all religions as omniscience—knowingness of all things—then, using logic, *we* must be in knowingness of all things. If we are, how do we lift the backdrops that have hidden away from us the complete grandeur of discovering the awesome extent of our reach?

I believe that the appearance of communicators from other dimensions is the beginning of the lifting of the backdrops of forever, those veils that have hidden the depths of reason from us. Now, if we are equal to *A,* and God is *B,* and *A* fits inside *B,* if we're talking to God, we're also talking to ourselves, roger that? Perhaps channelers will continue to channel wondrous, unseen entities until we learn to talk to ourselves; until God learns to talk to himself.

Manifesting Whatever Your Play

The next phase of this communiqué will be a scorcher for some— why are people ill? Because they *want* to be ill. Simple questions, simple answers. What can one say about joy? It cannot be emphasized enough. Joy, the essence of the Godfire, cannot be experienced enough in one's life, because if it takes repeating that one hundredfold every day until you feel the *joy,* it's worth it.

Have you ever known someone who was *always* unhappy, and no matter what you said to them and no matter what runners of opportunity were sent to them, they always found the *down* side of it—*always!* Disease is simply their motive.

You see a cripple and you feel sorry for him. It's not pity that you give to someone, it's *love* that you give to them—they *wanted* it that way. And you say, *"But how do you justify the brutalization of those who are innocent?* Innocence is a linear term that relates only to your three-dimensional time/space. Every moment that you think about a fantasy, every moment that you contemplate violence or watch it emotionally on your television because it's *awful,* when you're watching a drama that involves violence, did you know you're caught up in the scene? What happens when you embrace the scene emotionally? *You* become the victim. Didn't you know that? Or is this God stuff only for certain things, and does it not include other things?

Your Supermind and your autopilot-Soul are omnipresent—whatever they embrace, that becomes *law*. There is no such thing as a victim, there is only *is*. And there are many of you who play out melodramatic roles in your mind—*heroic* or *violent action* that you suppress and therefore play out in your mind. Do you know that you are manifesting your play, whatever it is?

If you end up with no limbs, or you end up crippled because you have become a real-life victim through your fantasy, you are that way because you *wanted* it—that's how it works. If you fear anything, fear it *emotionally*, it becomes a *law*. If you contemplate *anything* and embrace it *emotionally*, it sets the stage for your next drama. Everyone is the way they are because they want to be that way—they have the will to bring about such a life.

There are those who have preferred to come back totally and in complete dependence upon someone else—they have selected an incapacitated body knowing full well how the clay would mold. Why? What does it take for you to realize how grand you are? Does it take not being beautiful, does it take not being athletic, does it take being unstable in the body to realize your Supermind, at it's fullest potential?

There are many who have done that—you are bringing realization to it's zenith. It is not a terrible thing to see someone who is crippled—actually, all that is *crippled* is the word itself. It is a grand opportunity to love them for the wisdom of their truth.

Another runner is walking up on your flightline—I send to you what you would call a cripple, and when you look into those eyes you're going to see forever in those eyes. What they know in those eyes, you are groping to learn on your own two legs. That contact will teach you much about the health and the design of our natures and how we truly mold them. Switch on . . . contact . . . *go for it!*

Short Circuited

Let's discuss *want to*. When you want to heal someone, you want to take the pain away, correct? You want to make it better and easier. Oftentimes there are those who manifest their diseasements into deliriums of pain—to witness that is anguish to the soul. No one desires to see another suffer so terribly.

Do you know that you cannot take responsibility for another's illness? If you do, you've become an enslaver—you've taken it on yourself, as though *you* had created this misery for someone else, and therefore *you* must judge it and heal it. You cannot do that— they have established their own rendering. You can't even heal your own headache—how do you think you're going to heal a pro- digious problem?

Health has everything to do with one's state of mind: the body reacts according to the electrical energy the mind is delivering to the central nervous system, and everything reacts to the circuitry. That's how it works. The body is only waiting for a *moment* of restoration and a change of attitude to open up the central vortex wholly. The Supermind, through allowing, through the Godfire within, sends these signals that will heal the body. It's very simple.

You're losing your war on cancer, correct? There is a cure rising on the horizon; it will be here before the Spring of your year to come. The dynamics of that cure are very simple, and the cure is *profound*—it was under your nose all along. But the cure doesn't change one's state of mind. Disease alters and uplifts and gives a different perspective on life, certainly. But if you continue to revel in unhappidom, the *dis*ease will only return.

When is it humane to allow? Is it callous to allow someone their own truth regardless of how painful it is? Is it? This is where the wind can blow and you can falter. It *must* be allowed and it *will* be allowed in Superconsciousness, in Superunderstanding.

What is called the immutable law of the Godsource *is* the law of free will. You must understand without prejudice and bias that everyone is entitled to their life no matter how they have created it. If you can love them enough to *allow* them the opportunity to heal, to be healed, or not to be healed, without feeling the blame for it any which way, you are blasting out of your fearbox of superficial responsibility.

In the days to come, the pouring out of the diseases will become rampant—it's already happening. The plagues are here, you read about them every day. And unless the attitude of the whole of the world changes, one third of the population of the whole of your world will perish before the end of the next decade, just from famine. Famine is also a disease, a plague.

Health has everything to do with one's state of mind. If you are a miserable person, you're going to be short-circuited and short-lived. Unless you can find joy in the pleasure of what you are, you shan't ever realize a final destination in Superconsciousness.

The little miracle of healing yourself is a wonderful breakthrough. I'm certain you could write volumes on this miraculous moment, but writing won't do any good unless someone else can feel that same understanding. There are many who are feeling it. They, in the face of dreadful disease which they have created mentally, and which is acting physically on them, will be able to turn it around. They'll call the turnaround a miracle!

An adventure into *FL: SuperC* must evoke the whole of sovereignty. One cannot say, *"I am of the Godfire,"* and on the other hand be vulnerable to disease. You must *be* and have dominion over the entirety of your life.

I Wonder Why You Haven't Wondered Why

What I've advised you of is not an improbable dream, but most probably is the epic of reality lying unrealized in you. Haven't you ever wondered why you only use 33 percent of your mind? Didn't you ever wonder why you haven't kicked in your afterburner—couldn't you reason why? There are those who will cast the advice in this flightlog aside—that's all right, it's your choice, you're still loved, but at this point it has become merely unreasonable for *you*.

I desire you to look at the reasoning that lurks behind your thinking. Are you copping out because you don't want to set your-self up to fail the probability of this dream? If you are, you're hoarding life as a dream only, not seeing its reality. That's the easiest way not to fail—never to try. Don't you know yourself well enough by now, after all those millions of years; can't you see your own infinite possibilities? Or have you listened so long to someone else's song you've never heard your own? What *is* behind the backdrop? *Is* it just a dream?

And there are others who vibrate to the harmony of these words—this is your song, because nothing else works anymore. And perhaps it took this dream of the adventure of life for you to realize that—you had to become so stuck in your own Social Con-sciousness, you couldn't even *discern* reality. You couldn't even hear you own voice, you couldn't even heal your own self, because you weren't *supposed* to.

You *are* brilliant people. You've been brilliant in the ways of misunderstanding; you've played such games with yourselves, and always talked yourself out of your brilliance. You're even reason-ing that I don't even exist, because that makes it easier for you not to participate. That's all right, but what I have endeavored to in-form you of is a grand truth. And for the whole of its simple teaching, it is only a reflection of your own grandest potential. There are those who don't even want to bother to look into the mirror. That is all right, but I wonder why you haven't *wondered* why.

Just to Decorate the Planet

The hope of all the human race rests on the ability of a few to superknow, to be acutely aware of something more than their fear-box of unrealized self. These few are throttles-to-the-wall pilots of their own destinies.

If you don't think you can heal yourself, stay sick. If you *don't* feel it is worth it to put food up in your pantries, go without. If you *do* think that it is too big a bother to start loving yourself and being much more amiable toward the rest of the human race, be ugly. And if you can't live without negative and positive, go for it. Gambling is to lose, not to win. When you've lost your airspeed and your lift, if you gamble, you'd better know your spin-recovery procedures.

You declare yourselves to be *enlightened;* you don't even know what the word means. It doesn't mean to plug in some light and walk around in an austere, placid mood—it means *to be in knowledge of.* The Godfire essence isn't a myth—it is the God-source *devout* within the kingdom called man and woman. It is a heritage that only a few have been able to embrace.

And somewhere along the line, you've never thought that of yourself. Why? Why not?! How unreasonable are you? What do you think you're here for? Just to sort of decorate the planet? Dirty up the skies, the water—is that what you're here for? Are you spawns or bastards of the universe, or are you really evolved from monkeys? Monkey, monkey mind.

Yeshua ben-Joseph, and many more who existed in space-time outside of your contemporary age, endeavored and strove to embrace a concept called Superconsciousness; in order that that light could perhaps be seen through all the people who would look and see, and that the miracles might really be not miracles, but rather a way of life for a god *realized.* Why don't you think that applies to you? Are you exempt? If you are, it is by your own terms and no one else's.

In getting this Supermind-thing together, it's not a tough sector to fly in at all. I could divulge to you in one sentence what Superconsciousness can be, and manifest all the runners to you and never say another word to you. But I have to go the long way to explain and make you reason; you don't think you have learned anything unless I gab a lot! Correct?

Why am I doing this? Just to hear my own self speak? Well, I can do that other places. I'm instructing you in Superconsciousness operations because I love you. Your complex boxes of unworthiness are going to lead you astray. What is to become of you if you don't even have the knowledge to understand? What will become of you if you don't make that change that will insure the whole of your life in continuum?

Christ, as you know that idol, *is* the immaculate realization unveiled. But wake up, FRGB candidates. When you know the *ideal* which Christ reflected, you can no longer say that Superconsciousness was someone else's doing. You can no longer keep muttering that because *he* did it, he somehow pulled *you* out of your pickle. (Bah, humbug!) This is your own game, and you're coming to an hour in which you're going to have to realize that. Your prayers and your chats and your worshipings simply won't do it for you. You can continue to play blind-man's bluff. Do you remember that game?—the all-wise unknowingness leading the all-wise unknowingness. Pilots—when are you going to wake up? Perhaps when you realize you've been asleep.

Cat Launch . . . Standby!

If you embrace this communiqué emotionally while the multitudinous runners are coming forth, at the end of that sojourn within, if you have wisdomized it, then it *works*—you will be catapulted into Superconsciousness! And you didn't have to do anything but open up to *know* that it works—that's what *makes it happen*. All of this verbiage will have been worth it if *one* of you touches that brink which so many of you are afraid to break through, because it means change. Beyond, beyond into the great unknown is just around the corner of your mind, just past the milestones marked *Courage* and *Fun*.

Maybe you want to remain on deck because you don't realize that change has nothing do with unhappiness, but *everything* to do with the cat-launch adventure called joy. It *does* mean you have to think for yourselves, it *does* mean you have to answer your own questions. But really, how are you going to exist for two weeks without asking someone a question?

This is heavy furniture just to get you to *know* that you know, to bring you to a realization that doesn't have anything to do with celestial bodies or one hundred guides, that doesn't have anything to do with the uncelebrated or celebrated teachers who continue to confuse you. It has nothing to do with dogma: religious and metaphysical science is a limitation because it's just *another* law. You've heard of ghetto-blasters? I'm a dogma-blaster!

Those who can unite in a state of pure acceptance and freedom are uncovering it. Those who can look into the God-essence of Self are uncovering it. Well, if that's the case, then it means that even the cards that detail your future, even the tea leaves that form God knows what, even your cookies that divulge your fortune, they won't work. Dogma-blasting strips you of your superstitious mind, that little fearbox, and shows you a light of clarity that rings from within you and *tastes* of divine Godfire mind. If one of you wakes up and puts to use this wonderful thing that is sitting on top of your heads, I will be exceedingly happy, because then everyone can say, "Blimey, it works!"

Superconsciousness is your inherited right. You know how selfish the lot of you are? If I tell you something belongs to you, you break breakneck pace to obtain it, because it's *yours*. You don't care what it is, it's just that it's yours and *you're* going to have it. That's how you are, and it's rather smart of you to be that way. I suppose that's where that, *Go for it!* phrase emanated from. Well, what are you waiting for? A legion of angels to fly by with harps plunking to do your bidding? It only happens when you cat launch out of your box and begin to open up. *Whoosh!*

You are beloved Godfire beings who have been asleep on deck for 7.5 million years of reincarnated dreams. Well, it's time to wake up, because your turn at *ruling* the world is coming up very shortly. How do you want to rule it? The *same old thing,* or *out of the Night into the Light?*

Do you want to launch yourself up into Superconsciousness and embrace it, or do you want just to fly in circles around it, lost in the dreamfog of illusion? This communiqué is intended to offer you an explanation of what your kingdom is like, to give you an insight into something you've never seen before. Go for it!

The last time we chattered in our headsets I asked you these questions: What is this time-travel to other dimensions all about? How does it affect you? How will it help you get rid of your stuff? At the stage of life in which you are now freeze-framed, what is your input basis of reality—how do you see the world? What has influenced how you see your world? What do you think you are, and what has influenced that thought of what you are?

Let's go on a quick side-trip adventure. You've been my passenger, riding with me in this airplane which I've created, this airplane called a *book*. If you stay on board in this segment of the trip, you'll *really* peal off a few unwanted dimensions of limitation. As your Captain I'm going to shove the yoke forward, bleed back on the power, and trim us for a dive, a dive that will take us right back into the beginnings of our past, our most recent incarnation in the here and now.

As you've been reading these words, you've been traveling with me in a left to right linear progression—that is, from the present to the future, from moment to moment. And if you turn the pages back, you'll hop right back into the past where you'll read passages and words that are now familiar to you, because you have already read them, you've already lived them—they are the *past* to you.

In this dive that is about to commence, I will take you out of the linear left-to-right, past-to-future progression and drop *you* right back into your lap. Envision that you were walking across space horizontally, and then all of a sudden you stepped into a hole and *whoosh*, you instantly fell through it, leaving behind all of your conceptions of what you were and how you exist in the reality that you exist in. Okay? Are you with me? Here we go!

I'm shoving the yoke forward—the push-over—you can feel your body lift up a little as your seat drops out from under you, your seat belt snugging down on you to pull you down with the falling plane. Your first thought is, "When is he going to pull us out of this?" I'm *not*—you are, when you want to be pulled out of it. But this dive might be so amazing to you, you might want to ride it out for a while.

Now you're looking over my shoulder to find the airspeed indicator—you watch silently as it winds up faster and faster. Your body is starting to flow with the dive—the G-force of the dive has neutralized yet you *know* you are in a dive, something is definitely out of the ordinary . . . you are losing control. Your senses are unable to sense the unfamiliar environment that you have been placed in . . . you're losing control.

Why? If I blindfolded you and put us into a tailspin, even though we were spinning and spinning, you would soon tell me that the spin had stopped even if it hadn't. In fact, you would tell me that we were now spinning in the *other* direction, even though in the seen reality we weren't—that's how inaccurately we perceive reality. Because the fluid in your inner ear eventually becomes inured to the spinning sensations, the neurons signal your brain sensors that a spin has commenced in the opposite direction. Perceived reality is oftentimes an illusion.

We've reached checkpoint one in our dive. You've promised me that you will forget all aspects of indoctrination, education, fear, and guilt. You've promised me that you will just dive down with me in total awareness of essence reality, that reality which exists without preconceived notions. What do you *really* think God is? Remember, you have to answer that question without *preconceived* concepts or ideas. Slip back in time, past the time that someone sat you down and began to *tell* you what God was. Go back to the time when you *knew* what God was. I'll wait—we're on autopilot . . . *diving down, faster and faster.*

Cosmic Light Show

Progress—everyone wants to be making *spiritual progress.* Do you even know what spiritual progress is? It's not that you smile more brightly or frown more deeply—that has nothing to do with it. There is a light that exists around your body, made up of two aspects; one aspect is referred to by some as the Blue Corona Light. The other aspect—the Great Light, your aura—is awaiting acknowledgment. Both lights vibrating as one are known as your Godfire-Light. If you are stuck in limited knowingness, your Godfire-Light is very close to your body—you're in a Social Consciousness of density. In other words, you're living for Social Consciousness instead of expanded awareness.

If you are aspiring to superknowingness, every moment you comprehend something grander, you expand your Godfire-Light. Prior to putting on your flightsuit for this adventure, your Godfire-Light was smaller, closer in, because you were more in the density. After a few hours of time-traveling at our flightlevels, your God-fire-Light is now beginning to broaden somewhat. When your light broadens, that means you are hearing, and embracing what you're hearing emotionally, with your Soul . . . it becomes *super*knowledge! Knowledge expands your Godfire-Light.

When your runners all appear, prepare yourself! You'll observe some erratic light movements. That's a signal to you that you're in the process of learning something emotionally and then, in the same moment, trying to shut the door on it—I believe it's called *massive confusion.* Actually, the Godfire-Light of your entire planet is beginning to flicker into brilliance for the emotions are peeling away the illusions.

You've heard the term *aura*—do you know much about it? In every understanding that is spiritual, everyone seems to grapple to create a dogma around it—dog, dog, *dogmas;* it becomes a religion. Well, when it becomes a religion, it's yesterday's news. The Godfire essence that you possess is the Godfire-Light that is the next phase from thought. That Godfire-Light is the beginning of creation.

All of you possess your original share of light from the God-source, which is why you can't deny that you are connected to that Source. When the Godsource, the Thought, *contemplated* the thought, it created a reality. Every reality is always at a lower frequency than the created thought is, so light was born.

This *auric* light that I'm referring to is not the light that emanates from your lamps. Your auric light is an invisible, whiter-than-white light, beyond your three-dimensional senses. Yet, one who opens to the totality of Superconsciousness can see this light, because you can fly beyond three-dimensional senses.

Your auric light has always been with you regardless of what body you've selected to recycle yourself back into. For ten million years you have possessed the same thirteen-ounce autopilot-Soul which lies near your heart, which basks in this light. When you feel a flutter near your heart, that's your autopilot-Soul accepting the input of new wisdom. Your heart is a pump which doesn't *feel*, but *reacts* to the feelings signaled to it by your Soul. In every new lifetime you just slip into a new flightsuit—a different face, different skin, a different body, different genes, and different cell memories. But it's the same old you, plodding along.

Tomorrow You're a Stop Light

There has been much dogma and spiritual regulation created around one's auric light. Contrary to popular belief, you cannot tear this light. Has someone ever said to you that you had a huge tear in your auric field? You were leaking, I would presume? What could you be leaking? How could you tear a thought? Can you destroy a thought? The very word, *destroy,* is a thought, isn't it? So how could you tear the birth of a thought? Well, it just doesn't happen. If someone tells you, *aghast,* that you're walking around with holes in your aura, suggest to them that perhaps they need to have *their* spiritual vision examined.

Has someone ever walked up to you, suddenly stopped, then begun looking all around your body as if they were inspecting you, preflight checking your auric field? Then they move back a bit and with a very serious tone impart to you, *"Oh, your light is very green today, yesterday it was purple-lavender—tomorrow it will be white."* It sounds as though you were an airport beacon, flashing green and white, green and white! And tomorrow you can be a stop light—*"Your aura will be red because you'll be angry and it may change to yellow when you're sad!"*

Well, your auric light is not a chameleon. *Emotion* is the chameleon in the body, but this light is constant. And your light is beyond white, it isn't even the semblance of what one calls white. What you do see when you begin to narrow your vision and look at someone very closely is an electrical energy around their body. That is called the Blue Corona, what you are seeing; *that* is very visible. Once you attune yourself to seeing that infinite light, which is now photographed, you will be reminded that you're still alive—if you need reminding! Perhaps you would like a photograph of your Blue Corona to hang up along with your other portraits?

The Blue Corona is that eminent light that is coming down into manifested density. The Blue Corona has with it the polarization of positive and negative energy. And if you lower that energy in frequency vibration, you create mass. The mass is called gross matter.

Your scientists can define matter to the point called gross matter. The next step of that definition is a blue light. They feel they are at the end of the road, because they do not know where the matter goes. But they are beginning to suspect and realize that that blue, eerie light is the next phase, or *exalted* phase, of mass, which goes back into the Blue Corona. The Blue Corona is then fed through the variant degrees of the auric white light around you, until it becomes the optimum, the First Light. From there it is pure thought.

How could you have a tear in your Blue Corona? It isn't happening. Nor can you change colors in your Great Light, your auric field—it remains a beyond-white brilliance. What *has* changed is an emotional flush within the body. The Great Light and the Blue Corona create in harmony your Godfire-Light. Your Godfire-

Light is constant, because it represents the *is* that is constant. That is why it is called the God of Your Being.

Do you remember way back, when the Gods decided that they could *lower* their light by splitting what was called the God of Their Being? What they split was the Great Light and the Blue Corona. They lowered all of these frequencies to *become* the lower positive and negative energy. Those frequencies are now what is reflected in you! (Is the light going on?)

Without the Godfire-Light around your body, you wouldn't have a body—it is the cosmic glue that holds mass together, called love. That Godfire-Light around you holds you together and feeds you the bread of life, called knowledge. Knowledge, the bread of life? I know, *wheat or rye?* There must be an analogy here someplace? Oh well, I'll think of it.

Just Tune In!

Knowledge—how could you think a thought if your brain didn't create thought? Where does the thought emanate from? From outside you, in the Godfire-Light aspect of your being. As it comes through, the thought is changed into energy propellants, for which the brain is actually a receiver. Just like when you're enclosed and surrounded in your cockpit, you are surrounded by your Godfire-Light. Your Godfire-Light collects the thoughts from the River of Thought and delivers them to your brain-receiver.

If that's so, if genius is sitting right in front of your face, why aren't you picking it up? Because your receiver is not tuned in! You do not have the facilitator up here in your brain-slab that picks up that *genius* frequency level—that *genius thought* simply bounces off; to you, it's nonexistent.

If you had a part of your knowingness available to allow that great thought, if you were open to it, then you would receive genius and *pure super*knowingness. But your brain is just not a happening place—you're just picking up the thoughts of others in Social Consciousness, because that is the *lowest* wavelength; that leaves you with only a small part of your brain available to pick up the genius.

You've heard the phrase, *going back into the Light?* What's that all about? When you begin to open up your brain into the adventure called Superconsciousness, your Godfire-Lightfield becomes a splendid light-show happening. You are reversing back out of the density of your flesh.

Someone who is fleshy lives in a state of decadence—the whole world is wrapped around their appearance, their sexuality, and there is nothing wrong with that. It is a limitation though, because the whole world is wrapped around how they look and how they're going to blend in with others. They are the ones who are prone to the greatest disease. Their Godfire-Light is very close in, because all of their efforts to exude life slurp up their usable fuel. You fit these specs of limitation if you presume that everything there is has to do with the pleasures of the senses—you know, sight, taste, smell, touch, and hearing—if that determines your reality.

The Godfire-Light that you project around you also determines your capacity to open your thought. It also is a measurement of your emotional balance in your solar plexus area. Those who are intellectual define these flightlevels of Superconsciousness intellectually, but they hold back from embracing them emotionally. They just don't want to get involved, period! Do you know one of those? Or are those *your* specs?

Intellectual really means, *limitedness,* because everything remains conjectural once it's intellectual—it *never* is reality. Intellectuals can intellectualize every moment of every day for all the eternities that will be, and their Godfire-Light just stays close in, flickering every once in a while when they allow themselves a moment of *irrationality.* Big word, *irrationality!* Well, I suppose my scribe here could *intellectualize* every premise in this adventure, he could turn all of these fun words into *big* words—you know the kind, you run out of breath trying to pronounce one; you find them listed in the ingredients of your foodstuffs! If a thing can't be said simply, why say it at all?

How do you bring your Godfire-Light to its zenith? Simple—

by bringing forth the thought in openness and allowance, by embracing it emotionally. That emotion *becomes* and is *determined* reality. It doesn't matter if you can't package the emotion up and sell it in the marketplace. If *you* feel it, you *own* it—it has become a reality. From that emotion, your autopilot-Soul gathers important data which it will call up during the manifestation process.

Without your soul you could not accept thought—it simply wouldn't be present. Without your soul you could not be a creator, because you must possess the thought to divide it into the lower frequency realms to create anew. The thought holds itself in the soul emotionally. That's where your inspiration is born. A weeping soul is one in the birthpains of discovery.

In every segment of reality there are many who hear things but they don't feel them. Until they feel them, they can't say they *own* them. The *owning process* works like this. The moment you begin to feel—*feeling* is allowing the thought to come in—that feeling opens more of the brain to allow more thought to surge in. The feeling is like a rush over the body. In the same moment, the soul records every cell's *action* and *reaction* to that *new* thought via the feeling, which is carried through the body at high frequency energy so that *every* cell receives the feeling. Then the soul records the *collective* of the body's emotional movement. *Then* you own it—that feeling flies back out into the Godfire-Light. Your Godfire-Light begins to grow.

Conquering the "I Am Not"s

We've used the word, *Master,* in this flightlog. There's a difference between a Master and a Fully Realized Godfire Being. A Master is one who conquers himself—his life is expended in conquering the illusions of self. What does that mean? Conquering his status quo of limitation, discovering what he is not. Once he has conquered the *"I am not"s,* he discovers what he is. Simple? Simple. Once you've conquered the illusions of your limitations by *tuning in,* the Master eases himself into the left seat as the Pilot-in-Command, a Fully Realized Godfire Being.

A Master can walk into a marketplace without any adornment, nothing that says he's a Master—you know, no ash on the forehead, no rags, no long robes, no pious look, just the way you are—and *because* of your superknowingness, your Godfire-Lightfield could cover the whole of the marketplace. Just by walking by, your consciousness is so powerful, the *Godfire-Light* that radiates from your being is so powerful, that it collectively covers and embraces everyone going to and fro.

When a Master walks in the marketplace, there is a change of knowingness there, a change of feeling in the shoppers who are congregated; they even put down the *on sale* items they raced in for! Instead of feeding off greed, bickering, bargaining, jealousy, envy; instead of feeling that which you all feel at the marketplace, all of a sudden there is a tranquility. Your Godfire-Light is now feeding off a grander knowingness for a few moments—something has passed you by and you turn around and look to see what it was. It was an unseen thing that occurred emotionally.

Everyone is affected by the Godfire-Light of a Master. Have you ever entered a room and people turned around to stare at you? And it wasn't because you were wearing some outrageous fashion just to be noticed, it was just you, and people turned around and noticed. Have you ever been in a room and all of a sudden *you* noticed someone who wasn't particularly outstanding, but a feeling was emanating from them? They walk in Godfire-Light and it is a great light.

When a *Fully* Realized Godfire Being walks through the marketplace, the light envelops the *whole* city—just by walking through. The light of an FRGB (aviators are *so* into abbreviations!) can flood the perimeter of your world because they are the *absolute* Superconsciousness. The mind is completely open, the Godfire-Light is omnipresent. And when they walk, the whole of the world is lifted by their presence. What was being fed with violence, hatred, jealousy, dogma, and cursing, all of a sudden the feeding process changes and there is something kind and wonderful in the air. There is something that makes you weep and you don't know why you are weeping. There is something that causes you to pause and catch your breath. There is a wind around you and all of a sudden you shiver with a chill; you feel as if a gentle host has just wrapped his arms around you, and the exaltation is grand. Shoppers lay down their tomatoes and cucumbers and begin to look around, because they want to know where this experience is radiating from.

That is an FRGB who has mastered—*mastered*—to become, and *becomes* the light to the world. The FRGB didn't become what he is for your sake. He became what he is for his own sake—he embraced the Godsource within to become. How exalted is that moment? What does it take to lift the whole of your world from its bickering state? What does it take to change you from your dog-eat-dog society? What does it take to keep you from murdering your brothers?

What does it take to keep your mind pure, without the diversions of fantasies? What does it take to have you become amiable—to love, to allow? What does it take to love what you are, however you look, however your body is, to say, "It is *mine*, and it is a God-being that lives there"? What does it take for the men to *feel* emotion? What does it take for the women to be free of their own indoctrinating enslavement? What does it take for the borders of your world to come down and the whole of the humanoid experience and drama to become as one? It takes a Fully Realized Godfire Being!

Did you know that in the face of love there is no war? In the face of love there is no competition. In the face of love there is no fear. In the *soul* of love there are no troubled waters, and that is a great truth. If that is true, why is your world living and breathing in unrest instead of peace? If in the face of love there is no fear, what does that say about the current flight status of your Earth-gameplane?

It blatantly says this—that no matter who *says* they are fully realized, they haven't achieved anything yet because the consciousness of the whole has not *felt* the Godfire-Light experience of a true FRGB—not even in your neighborhood!

So you continue to act and react, you continue to live in a Social Consciousness of good and evil, positive and negative, beautiful and ugly. That is your little flightbox that you live in— you're just flying around in it, bouncing off the walls. How could you ever venture outside your box and do away with all of those *things,* those *identities* that you are?

The FRGB-rated pilot is the resurrection of the divine entity inside—resurrected from the inside to light up the outside. And everyone possesses the *inside* Godfire-Light—the whole of the world, seen and unseen, possesses it. Who is going to power it up to light up the outside?

Center Focal Point Center

In Stage-I flight, a Master masters the stages of limitation—the polarities of good and evil, negative and positive, perfect and imperfect, accepted and rejected—all of that is Social Consciousness. The Master masters everything until it emerges into the center focal point of balance which is the factor called *is*—now you're flying in a flightlevel *beyond* judgment.

You master every *thing* until you secure that center focal point center, the *is* factor. This means you are certificated in the *Mastery of Allowing,* the *Mastery of Loving,* the *Mastery of Seeing the Now,* and the *Mastery of Being in Knowingness.* You're only cleared to land at center focal point *center* by depending upon and trusting inevitably the Godsource within, your great knowingness. Anyone who acquires his Superconsciousness certification will also be FRGB-rated—they are one and the same.

Today you are Masters; tomorrow you may be FRGBs. In Stage-II flight as an FRGB, when you touch down at the *is,* you wake up to Superconsciousness, because then you have conquered it all, you *own* it all. Then there *are* no laws. The *is* factor is unconditional love—how could it be confined by laws? The *is* is lawless. That's why the SARRs (Spiritual and Religious Regulations) are such a limitation. That's why good and evil is a limitation, because you only end up worshiping the evil! You worship what you are frightened of; you respect what you are frightened of. Strange, but that's the way it is on your planet Earth in the flightlevels of limitations.

The *is* and the Godsource within are lawless. Nature also, through the balance of life, is lawless. It is *evolving*—evolution fits no law. Your evolutionary patterns have changed grandly—it is in the flow of the universe to move forward. The forward thrust is called forever—the FRGB is within that thrust. Your name is *forever.* And it is not that you have to do anything, it is that you *allow* everything.

Try to Sidestep Precarious Positions

Those who make a dogma from your Godfire-Light, who lay a trip on you and say that you have a tear in your light—they certainly aren't allowing *you,* are they? Those who call you *sinner* certainly aren't allowing you, are they? In order to understand someone else's Godfire-Light, you have to know beyond the knowingness of *your* situation—you have to know their whole situation, and that is a rather precarious position to put yourself in.

In some, the Godfire-Light has extended so far around the body, and the density is so powerful, that every emotion manifests as a disease in the body. Like flying by wire, your body is *reacting* very quickly to any move that you make. That's why it is said that *every* thought manifests, *every* word manifests—they manifest visually in your body as disease. If you are diseased, change your thoughts.

Prove it to you? When you are *stressed out* and your blood pressure goes up, what do you think is happening within your body? Reason it—isn't your attitude affecting your body? When you become tranquil and peaceful, what happens to your heart rate? And when you have to make so many decisions because you think you have to, what happens to your heart rate? You have to measure it on an altimeter, it climbs so high!

And when you have to live up to everyone's expectations of you, when you are *fighting* to hold on to being the center of attention, and you end up visiting the medicine man and he shakes his head, saying "You have heart disease," guess who created that? The more *stressed out* you are, the greater your risk of illness.

Why can a Christ or a Buddha or a Mohammed ascend and you can't? Because you don't have the mind to understand that there is no such thing as death. Because death is in *your* dogmatic belief—it happens every day, that's the *real* world. Your brain hasn't opened up to the functional part that sees beyond death and dying and flies into light.

Flightlevel: SuperC

This is the flight plan: The Master is flying toward center focal point center. Every moment he is mastering himself, his Godfire-Light is growing. When he winds it out to full brain capacity, the whole of the brain is opened up; the mind is in bloom, the pituitary looks like a grand flower, and everything is on *full power*—he has attained FRGB status. Also, in this power setting the body has changed—the body has stayed forever young, the body no longer contemplates dying because you are the one who contemplates it. Those cells would live forever if you allowed them—they were created to.

Your Flightlevel: *Superconsciousness.* The Godfire-Light is growing, the Master is becoming, the body is changing and takes on a light appearance. And in a moment you ascend, cleared into the great beyond, into the end of time. Why? Because when the mind is totally open to Superconsciousness, the FRGB that you are has resurrected itself *totally*—you and the Godsource are *one* and the *same,* your kingdom is at hand, and in an instant you lock on to the next flightlevels of consciousness.

How do you catapult yourself into ascension? Your desire flows outward and upward at a 45-degree angle, and everything that the *Is factor* is rides with it. Your desire to vault into the forever thrust is simply *law,* and your body begins to vibrate at a faster rate of speed than three-dimensional understanding. If your mind is wholly open as an FRGB, then your kingdom is at hand. Your mind has dominion over all things—you are the Master of all universes, all dimensions, all levels, all consciousness.

In the moment that you desire to time-travel to forever, the bodily frequency changes from the three-dimensional–understanding vibration to the Blue Corona vibration—the FRGB takes on a hue of blue light and becomes almost transparent.

The FRBG then pulls the Blue Corona vibration up into light energy. Then you become a blaze of light. And as you are blasting off from this three-dimensional adventure into the thought called Forever, your Godfire-Light begins to fade into a *brilliance* that you can no longer see—in a moment the brilliance disappears.

. . . we're still diving, are you with me? Checkpoint two. Now that you've created some word-thoughts around the ideas of *god,* I'm going to disengage the autopilot and increase the speed of this dive a bit—shove the stick forward a little more, add some power, see if the wings stay on.

And *here we go,* blasting straight down through time—back, *way back,* we're going to dive right back into your mother's womb, into this microscopic being that is growing in there, which will someday become a frightened, guilt-ridden human being struggling for survival. You!

Look at it—see yourself as you immerse yourself into the body, with all the expectations of the adventure of life. And then, in the now-moment, feel what you are, what you've become. From the great hope of the adventure of life to the bastards of the universe in only a few, brief years. It's sad, isn't it? Do you think God would have bothered to create life so it could be miserable within itself? Why create it at all, if not for the *joy* of life?

Let's click in the autopilot again. Let's take a little trip inside the womb, surrounded as you were in the cushioned waters as a baby-god making ready to enter back into the Earth-plane, the Plane of Demonstration. What did *you* want to achieve? What did *you* want to accomplish? Why did you decide to incarnate in an earthling's body? What was your play, scriptwriter? What did you want to demonstrate?

Did you return to be subservient to a vengeful God who *says* he loves you, yet will cast you into a *hell* if you don't walk his line? Did you return to be subservient to little pieces of paper that have numbers printed on them, which are called *dollars*? Did you return to be subservient to a substance, a liquid or a powder or a weed that puts you into an *altered* state of consciousness while it destroys your brain cells?

Did you return to do battle, to wage war? Or did you return to love in peace, to live in harmony with all things? Did you return to play the game that was being played, to live the lessons that you wanted to live, just to live them; not because of some karmic retrospection or because some God was waiting in some unknown dimension ready to clobber you with a frying pan if you didn't?

Are you squirming in your seat? Let's increase the dive angle a bit—hold on! Do you feel the speed increasing, do you hear the roar outside as you think yourself back in time, back to where you were before you decided to sojourn on Planet Earth. Where was it? What were you up to? Was it in another dimension, in another universe, another galaxy? Are the scenes you've seen on Planet Earth familiar to you, or are you a stranger to this land?

Go find a picture of yourself when you were a youngster. Stare into it through the lens of a camera, close up—immerse yourself into that scene and pull the moment down from your memory banks. Do you remember the youngster as you? Or was that you when you existed in another dimension? Can you tell me all about it—what happened that day and when, who you were with, what it was all about? Can you remember the names of the others in the photograph? Who's that over in the corner . . . old what's-his-name?

117

You gents reading this, go put on a whiff of Cologne that you've had stashed away—smell the memories conjured up. You ladies, pick up a glass doll dressed in lace—inhale the innocent pleasures. Where did all of that go? Even a whiff of hot popcorn will carry you back in time. Or play a game of Monopoly, win or lose.

Boyhood, girlhood, womanhood, manhood—what happened? How did you end up lost in this dive into infinity, this dive from which there is no escape, this dive that continues until you pull us out of it. Do you want to pull out of it? Or are you on autopilot, so lost in it you don't even know you're in a dive?

I'll see you on the other side of truth, you who can envision what God is, but who won't claim the vision. I'll see you on the other side of truth, innocent one.

Destination 8

ON FINAL APPROACH

Gentle But Firm

A voice alerts your consciousness . . . *"Flight* nine-seven-two, Clearance Delivery. When I can I'll turn you into Blue Ridge, it'll be about the zero-ten radial.

"Roger, Clearance, nine-seven-two."

You order your first officer, "Put the girls down." A chime sounds as the passenger compartment fills with a pleasant voice . . .

"Ladies and gentleman, the captain has turned on the *No smoking* and *Fasten seatbelts* signs for our final approach into Los Angeles."

You order your first officer, "Flaps, four."

"Flaps set, four degrees."

"That will help you descend to ten-thousand. You can use the spoilers also."

You key your mike, "Clearance Delivery, nine-seven-two. Are you gonna turn us on the Blue Ridge arrival pretty quick? Thunderheads are billowing."

"Nine-seven-two, you can proceed direct Blue Ridge now, cross Baton at and maintain niner-thousand."

"Rog', direct Blue Ridge, Blue Ridge arrival cross Baton at nine-thousand, thank you sir."

To your first officer, "Set altimeter at niner-one."

"Roger, altimeter, niner-one."

"Shoulder harness, landing lights."

"Check."

"Disconnect autopilot."

"Check."

You key your mike to tell the rest of the world . . . "Regional approach, Flight nine-seven-two, heavy. Descending through nine, have romeo."

The world was listening . . . "Nine-seven-two, fly heading two-thirty-five. Descend to seven thousand."

"Nine-seven-two, heading two-thirty-five, out of nine for seven."

And the world directs . . . "Nine-seven-two, heavy, turn ten degrees left, reduce speed to one-eight-zero."

"Nine-seven-two, wilco."

To your first officer, "Ten degrees flaps, please."

"Ten degrees flaps, rog'."

You start the approach checklist . . . "Continuous Ignition—*on.* Seatbelts—*on.* Radio nav' switches—*radios.* Altimeter flight and nav' instruments—*set and cross-checked.* Airspeed bug—one-three-nine, *set and cross-checked.* Flight attendants notified—*down to no smoking."*

"Nine-seven-two, heavy. Turn right heading three-four-zero. Contact approach control, one-one-nine-four."

"Three-four-zero, nineteen point four. So long."

"Approach, nine-seven-two, with you at five thousand."

"Nine-seven-two, expect runway one-eight, right. Fly heading of three-five-zero."

"Roger, three-hundred-and-fifty degrees."

"Nine-seven-two, turn left to two-four-zero, descend and maintain three thousand."

"Nine-seven-two, two-four-zero, out of five for three."

A stark warning alerts you . . . "Nine-seven-two, heavy. Traffic, ten o'clock, a mile northbound, twenty-four hundred, unverified."

"Thank you, we're looking." As you strain for a glimpse. You report, "It's a blue jet—or is it? . . . No conflict."

Another turn is directed . . . "Nine-seven-two, heavy. You're six miles from the marker. Turn left heading one-eight-zero, join the localizer at or above two thousand three hundred. You're cleared for ILS approach, runway one-eight, right."

"Roger, all that, appreciate it."

They want you to slow down . . . "Nine-seven-two, reduce your speed to one-six-zero please—traffic is bunching up. Contact tower, one-two-six point five-five."

122

"*Reducing speed to* one-six-zero, tower frequency one-two-six point five-five."

"*Nine-seven-two,* heavy, regional tower. You're cleared to land, runway one-eight, right. Wind, zero-nine-zero at five, gusts to one-five."

"*Thank you,* sir."

You bark to your first officer, "Before-landing check. Landing gear—*down, three green.* Flaps, slats—*thirty-three, thirty-three, green light.*"

"*One-thousand feet.* In the dark of that rain cloud, on glideslope. I'll call 'em out for you."

"*Seven hundred,* six hundred, five hundred, *watch your speed.* . . . You're gonna lose it all of a sudden. The wind shear—there it is, push up the power, ride it, . . . push it up . . . way up . . . way up, up. . . .

All right! Well, done. Settle her in back on glideslope. Right on . . . three-hundred feet, *have runway in sight;* two-hundred feet . . . one hundred; crossing threshold . . . *squeeze* that yoke, flare . . . nice and gentle. Hold that nose up while she glides out of the air; hold her firm but gentle . . . fifty feet, hold her so they won't even feel this touch, thirty . . . twenty . . . ten . . . *mains touch, so gently.* Hold the nose wheel off . . . reverse thrusters, hold the nose off, watch the center line; nose gear ten feet, five . . . balance, hold it off. *Touchdown,* three down and *oh,* so gentle." Just like a dream.

"*Blue Leader,* you're cleared to land, runaway one-eight, right; follow the heavy."

"*Blue Leader,* roger tower."

You watch from the ground as a speck on the horizon becomes six sparkling jets sweeping toward you in a delta formation. You first see the lead jet, then his two wingmen, then their two wingmen and, hiding from your vision, the slot-man. You wonder, are they going to *land* in this formation?

"*Blue Leader* has the ball, follow me down." Your five wingmen respond, "Roger, leader."

They sweep out of the horizon, their shadows growing on the land as they approach the runway, 500 feet away, in tight formation, each pilot's attention focused on Blue Leader. Now 300 feet away. . . . Now 200 hundred feet, still 36 inches apart, not a waiver from anyone. You watch from below, wanting to be a part of above. A child next to you screams in glee as he sees them for the first time.

"Everything's down and locked, landing checks complete, on glideslope."

"Roger, Blue Leader."

Blue Leader is 100 feet . . . then 50 feet off the deck. While still in delta formation, Blue jets Four and Five touch down simultaneously. Four seconds later, Blues Two and Three touch down simultaneously. Four seconds later, "Blue Leader's on deck," as they slow, rolling together, still in delta.

"Tower, we're all on deck . . . except for Blue seven. . . ."

Left Behind in the JetWash

Those of you who watch from below, wanting to be a part of above, how powerful are you, innocent ones? Could you land a heavy? *Could* you focus so intently that you make happen what you *want* to happen?

As a Fully Realized Godfire Being, through attaining *Flight-level: SuperC* and *Supermind,* you *can* fly past all levels of dimensions. You *can* time-travel back through thought and *reverse* the pattern of thought into gross matter, then reverse it from gross matter back into thought *simply* by the desire—that's how powerful you are.

There have been a few FRGB candidates who have ascended, who have kicked in their thrust-reversers and blasted back out of mass into thought. My guess is that you think ascension is a fable? It's a truth. Yeshua ben-Joseph died specifically on a great tree loving all his enemies to prove that life exists beyond death, and he *proved* it, blatantly, even to the most doubting of his followers.

124

Buddha ascended on an island before over *five* thousand commoners, ascended into the heavens with the whole lot watching, to prove where the FRGB rockets off to. Left behind in the jetwash was a legacy of truth, of joy—an ideal which unfortunately became an *idol.* Yeshua ben-Joseph, your "Christ," has become an idol rather than an ideal. I, Ramtha, ascended in front of 2.5 million of my army on a wonderful day on the northeastern side of the Indus River, because I desired to become the wind—that was my ideal.

To understand the potential of Superconsciousness flight, identify it with the absolute consciousness of the FRGB, that light that floods the perimeter of your world. But *FL: SuperC* isn't just a word—a word only becomes intellectual. It is a profound emotion that must be experienced, enveloped, embraced—the feeling has to be there or you'll never get off the ground!

What I have told you about your brain is a very scientific truth. My communiqué was not shrouded in occult truth, it was not shrouded in dogmatic truth to become a myth, it is a *truth* that is real. The kicker is that no one here knows how to express it! That's the reason I'm here. If you activate this flightplan, you *will* soar into *Flightlevel: SuperC.*

My Flightlevel Is Omniscience

I have briefed you on your roles as the forgotten Gods. Do you remember? It is a weighty truth. What flightlevels do you live in? You live in a world that is filled with terror; you're afraid to take moonlight walks with your lover, you lock your doors while watching horrific *entertainment.* (You *can* turn it off, you know!) You live in a fantasy world that begins to manifest, and you wonder why it all happens to *you.*

You worship, worship, worship. You are seekers, seekers, seekers; always seeking, never finding. My purpose in appearing in this demonstration of outrageousness, this feminine form, is to leave you with nothing to follow except *you.* That's what you've needed to know for so long, that the truth of everything is, indeed, *within* you.

All the secrets of the ages are locked up in there, just waiting for you to *switch on, contact,* let them out. The dormant and latent Superknowingness has *always* been there—for ten million years! It *is* your divine right. But the tragedy of it all, and why so many will never evolve to *Flightlevel: SuperC,* is because you have hang-ups in your soul memories, in your conscious, everyday, boring, mundane lives which you allow to jail your minds. You've grounded yourselves!

Wouldn't it just be hunky-dory to jet around in *Flightlevel: SuperC!* You would love to be able to do that; wouldn't it be wonderful to be that powerful? Wouldn't it be the grandest of things to be a light to the whole world—be the first on your block to be a light to the world, sound good? And, of course, everyone and all of your peoples could feel the love that you feel. And, naturally, the world, for the first time since Adam could count, would be unified in a spirit called brotherhood, aye? And instead of destroying life, it would be perpetuated. Just hunky-dorus.

Do you know why you can't? The G-force, *guilt.* You're so locked in by your personal guilt, you cannot travel beyond it— you've pickled yourself, shot yourself down. Listen up! I know all about your abortions, I know about your molestations, I know all about your fantasies, I know what you were contemplating when you were contemplating because I was there—my flightlevel is omniscience. I know about your infidelities, and it doesn't make any difference if you actually *did it* or not; when you've contemplated it *emotionally,* you've done it, because *that* is the reality. The bodily activities are only the aftereffects.

I know about your lack of love for the Godsource, because you don't know what it is, because you can't *possibly* love yourselves. I know and I listen to you who contemplate the idea of how you have abused your children—how you have left them for your own, personal gains. I've listened to you who have hurt people and abused them to exalt your own selves—I have listened to it.

I've listened to the man who contemplated spilling his seed

last night, because he was having an erection, and he thought about whether he should do it or not, and in the throes of pleasure he finally gave up to contemplate something that was *maddening,* because the only way he could ejaculate is through violence—I saw it.

And I listen to the sweet souls who weep and weep and weep, because what it meant when they read this flightlog was that they were turning their backs on their creed and their faith, which meant they were turning their backs on their *families,* which meant ostracism.

I have seen the ones who contemplate their reliance on the stars, on the astrology that they have depended on for so long for answers, trying to figure out why it doesn't work when seemingly it once worked, faced with the question, *What am I going to do now?* How are you going to change that feeling, which so many have come to know you by? How do you walk out of that enslavement and still not offend your customers?

And how do you tell your Board of Directors that your products are contributing to the pollution of the planet, that your corporation is furthering its destruction and you want change? What would the stockholders say? And how do you tell the lobbyist that you aren't interested in pursuing his proposal because it contributes nothing to the nurturing of the planet? How do you tell him, he who helped you win your election? How do you tell your conclave that you can no longer cry *sinners* to your congregation, because you know another truth, that all things are love? There are no easy answers here, only truth.

I have seen those who hate people of different races, who don't want to touch them, who think they are better than they, and yet sincerely try to have a loving consciousness, but are hypocrites because they are riddled with the guilt of their despite—they can't feel beyond it, they smell inside.

There are those who *still* despise people from different religions. I mean, how long do people have to suffer because someone said you're supposed to despise them, because your parents said, *They're all the same.* Why, *why?* The question is, do you go against the grain and become an individual, risking the abuse of others because you *are* the way you are? Or do you just sit in the puddle you've made for yourself? I see your guilt and fear and I feel it.

Being contemplative is facing yourself. You can never become *fully realized,* until you have fully realized who and what you are. The purpose for all of the runners? They are mirrors, the reflections of what you are; they will accentuate your different personalities so that you can look and *embrace* what you are. And if that means you cry a thousand years, *cry* a thousand tears, because if the release is there, let it flow—the fear is not worth dying for, is it? If it means you burn this book a thousand times, do it—let the tears flow.

Flightlevel: Freedom

All your anguish can be plotted from your emotion system named *guilt,* the G-force which is backed up by your *fear-of-rejection* systems. Once your *guilt* and *fear-of-rejection* systems are secured within you, you can radio-call *Flightlevel: Freedom* with no restrictions.

Guilt is the modus operandi of Social Consciousness. Guilt is the key that locks you in and *you* are the jailer. Guilt—its primary objective is to enslave and hold back. The dogmas in religion have laid the heaviest trips on people, including the debasement of women by labeling them soulless for eons—they are still suffering under that slander.

What does the G-force sound like as it reverberates in your Soul? It explains so eloquently that God, the Father, the love that is, no longer lives within you; that you are *not* sons and daughters of a living God, that you are something that He simply created and you are to serve Him, serve Him, *serve* Him, serve Him!

When you hear this tirade, you curse the Godsource within because you really know you're not that rotten. But you *God-damn this* and you *God-damn that,* and I hear it and hear it and hear it, and I wonder why you are doing that to yourself, because every *damn* is a damn of self. You are *damning* your own divinity—no wonder you are so close-minded and limited.

God was taken out of you according to religious law. They made it *blasphemy* for one to hold himself equal to God's light. So in their litanies they kept removing you from what you were— according to them, the light never existed in such a lowly creature as *you*. Their purpose? The greatest enslavement there ever was, save the fall of women, was when someone realized that if you remove the *divinity* of the human drama from humankind, you can control everyone who will listen by speaking in the name of the Lord. It worked! It *still* works.

Let's reason it through to see if we can put the light back in you. God made everything, correct? What did He make it out of? Well, if God made everything and He *was* everything in the first place, what did He make everything else out of? *Himself!* Now, wouldn't that mean that every cellular mass emanating from the thought is God-inspired, *divine* purpose, and all that?

So how could anyone reason that the Father is out of you? Where did He go? He was there all along, but to the masses of common people who were ignorant and superstitious—you know, superstition: garlic, white candles, making the evil eye, amulets— the fear of abandonment by the Father still lingered within their soul memory.

So you began to hate God, and then you began to feel guilty because you couldn't understand why God would condemn you to eternal hell for thinking an evil thought, when the thought was just there. Why would God do that to you? Why? Why weren't *you* loved by God since you really, deep down, loved Him? Why were you going to hell? Why would the Father do that to *His* children— you could never imagine that fate for your *own* children. But who could you talk to about it? Where could you go for therapy? Everyone you talked to was just part of the illusion.

And if you would question, they would say, *Never question the law, never!* That is an enslavement of the greatest proportion— *never to question.* When you are silenced by your own desire for knowledge, you suffer at your own hand—you're a controllable bunch. And all they had to do was say they were speaking *in the name of God,* and automatically you are either accepted or condemned. For eons in your history I have watched this.

If you refused to fit into *their* illusion, you were excommunicated from their church—doomed to eternal damnation, because you really thought you were part and parcel of God! Your history books reek with the tears and blood of those who have been hard-pressed because someone *speaking for God* didn't like them—they were burned, tortured, their limbs were hacked off while confessions were solicited, their children were massacred before their eyes in the most heinous manner, all in the name of God. Those pages smell!

Now, you sit here reading, filled with a plenitude of feelings, and perhaps you are a little horrified; perhaps you are feeling uneasy because this sounds like blasphemy to you. Think about it— why would you fear that? If you were *never to question,* it meant your mind was suppressed. If your mind was suppressed, your life only consisted of survival and appeasment activities. And that meant that you were at the mercy of *every* neurotic orator who was a prophet—whoever spoke *in the name of God,* you were at the mercy of that neurosis.

The Platform of Self-Failure

Everyone incarnate on this planet has lived through this castigation in all those lifetimes. Within your autopilot-Soul there is a tremendous guilt factor that keeps you from linking up with the divinity of the Godsource within you—you *still* feel *un*worthy.

That unworthiness is the platform of self-failure for everything in your life. That is the foundation of your insecurity and your un-love for self that radiates out to others and then out to the planet at large. How could you expect anyone to love you when God doesn't? Reason this communiqué backwards; reason it to its most infinite understanding, which is where it all came from. Give me your readback, please!

This is how it is: You *all* are the sons and daughters of the living God, the Godfire of all that is. The greatest adventure of this Godfire intelligence was for the Godsource to become man and woman. The enlightenment and the engagement thereof would be called forever the *resurrection* of the Fully Realized Godfire Being. The resurrection occurred when the Godsource could walk in your body, which He made, to experience the adventure that the Is had created—the whole sandbox of the universe—to transcend to the furthest parts of its understanding, into the most dense gross matter, and then to return to itself in a blaze of white brilliance. You will witness this resurrection in your lifetime.

For you to know, there is nothing more dense than gross matter. Therefore, the greatest apex of the Godsource's understanding would be for Superknowingness to be immersed in the adventure of gross matter. In other words, no one ever became a Fully Realized Godfire Being in totality without becoming man or woman. Through flesh and blood, the window to the whole of forever is revealed. The *is factor* is understood when it is *realized* in density, because density is the realm of God unrealized. All of you *still* don't realize it because you believe your collective mind *is* realization. There are some surprises in your logbooks for you!

Some flight students don't like surprises, and because you still don't realize you're divine, some of you just want to exit out of this body, out of this situation—it's just too *damn* hard! You know, *punch out,* pull the ejection handle, eject out of life; so some take their own lives. That, of course, is their will to do so, and they go to another flightlevel of realization.

But they still have within them the same emotion that caused all their miseries; it's the same old them. They've achieved nothing by punching out, only postponing the inevitable. So, we will *tune in* to them a few eons from now and watch as they *work it through* in another flightlevel. As the universe turns, aye?

For those who stay on, hang around, endure, strap themselves in, through simple mind they begin to reason the God factor—*God is all that I am.* And through that understanding they begin to realize the amazing and *complete* suppression of their altered-ego mind—remember, *never question?* Through all the eons of religion on your Earth-*game*plane, you are still taught never to question, never to contemplate, never to go beyond the written word!

The written word is history, that's yesterday's news and it's old and yellowed. Ever seen a week-old newspaper? Yellowed! Today's word is in your autopilot-Soul, it's what you *feel* in there that lifts the persecution of the ages from your aching back, so you can stand up straight and fly right into *Flightlevel: Freedom.* As long as you live never asking a question, you're a controllable bunch of followers. *Today* you are still controllable.

How easy is it to control someone? Lay a heavy on 'em; you know, you do it all the time. Make 'em feel bad, *guilty*—you know what that's like. Lay those little innuendos on their emotions and let them rest there, as though suspended for all eternity. Watch them slink on home, hurt and upset, crying out. And you think that's *very* good for them—they will walk home and start sobbing and *really* thinking about this situation. That means *you won!*

I see those games. You're reenacting that drama over and over and over. When you have your target locked on, you blast them, with guns and missiles; you do it every time! Why? Because every missile launch against your enemy adds substance to yourself—makes you feel a little taller, a little stronger, a little more worthy. There it is again—your guilt—so you try to rationalize the lack of the Godforce in you. And then you wonder whether you fit in with the universe.

You feel like an outcast and it makes you miserable. How do you think a thought of your own without it being a sin? How do you live without living in sin? They say to you to *love God with all your might,* but you hate anyone who doesn't believe the same as you do! Even the most distinguished of hypocrisies always reveals itself eventually. How are your hypocrisies known? Because every war that ever was, was a holy war—slaughter in the *name* of God. Both sides would pray to be victorious and solicit the power of God to enslave the other. Isn't that an irony? That drama is still being played.

Fogged In

Let me ask you, would it be easier to convince someone of something if they were solid, or fragile? In other words, is it easier to convince a strongman that he needs help, or would it be easier to convince a weakman that he *needs* help? If you have your answer, would it be easier to convince a strongman, a person who is whole within himself, that he needs help; or would it be easier to convince a weakman, a person who is riddled with misery, insecurities, and guilt, that he *needs* help?

The onslaught of redundant Guilt which has assaulted your autopilot-Soul, which makes you feel you are not divine, has permeated your FRGB status completely—your autopilot has you flying around in a fog of guilt. If someone gave you a radio call in your fogged-out flight conditions, it would be welcomed, aye? Ever been lost in the fog? And if the call is, *Jesus died for your sins,* you're grateful, because you are so indoctrinated that you are guilt personified; you *desperately* want to break out of the fog.

Naturally, no one considers that the *saving* radio call could have emanated from the same source that fogged you in! And, of course, Jesus is the *only* one that broke out of the fog—everyone else, for *all* time has just been *fogged in!* Have you ever—I don't even need to ask this—could you ever wonder or ask the question, "What happened to all those poor folks before Jesus's time? Are they just doomed? What happens to them?" Civilization has been attempting to *civilize* for 10.5 million years. What happened to all the poor suckers that lived more than two thousand years ago? Good question, but you've been told not to question. Can you see that's only a ploy?

Yeshua ben-Joseph, *Jesus,* was a great FRGB—still is. It is *The Law,* the dogma of religion and the rituals of spiritualism, that have twisted and created an idol which has separated you from your Supernature. An idol, by the way, that you could *never* live up to.

Tender ones, you can't live to please something unseen. Tender souls, you only have to live so that the consciousness within you, your true Superconsciousness, is *always* at peace. No law will ever do that for you—that is the sighting of the individual vision as you emerge from your dreamfog. The guilt that you've carried for eons has made you *in*secure, the weakman, because if you're not loved by God, *who* is going to love you? What is to happen to you on the *Judgment Day?* Doesn't that send a *fear* wave through your body, just to hear the words *Judgment Day?* That is how insidious the indoctrination has been.

How many hours must you hear about how rotten you are, read about *all* your sins in all those analogies in *The Book,* feel the insecurity, the un-love, before that emotion of utter hopelessness becomes a *solidified* truth within the precious, Godfire being that you are?

And once the hopelessness is etched on your Soul, it keeps you within the perimeter called good and evil, it keeps you in the framework of limitation. It keeps you in the flightplans that say you are *not* divine—*Don't bother even to try to fly.* And who defines the good and the evil? Your enslavers. Who defines your framework of limitation? Your enslavers. Who says you are not divine? Can you venture a guess?

Haven't you ever wondered why two thousand years ago somebody *got it together,* and why not today? I know, you just needed to keep your calendar perpetuated. After all, every time somebody *got it together,* you would have to start counting your years all over again—that would be very confusing!

The reason no FRGB has arisen since Yeshua ben-Joseph, is because ascension went out of style; you know, like last week's best-seller, it went out of vogue—out of sight, out of mind. No one has allowed himself the worthiness of the self-love of the God-source to arise. That is yet to be seen, and when it is, it certainly would make for some *news,* wouldn't it!

Yeshua ben-Joseph said to his people a simple truth. He never preached about hellfire, but about the goodness of the Father within. And he said to all people, *Let it be known that what I am, so are you.* He said, *The Father and I are one, just as it is in you!* And he said, *The Kingdom of Heaven is in here, my kingdom is not of this earth, it is within me.* All great truths. Why didn't you listen? Well, where could you read *those* words? And the words that you could read, told you it was *blasphemy* to compare yourself to Jesus of Nazareth.

Sinners from the Word Go

How does it feel to be sinners from the word *go?* Well, I suppose you are aware of that—you are, you know, *sinners!* You've heard the word? Everything you do is wrong! And you can only be forgiven by them. That's too bad—I thought you were quite jolly good beings myself! But some of you just *insist* upon being guilty.

Let me tell you about the vibrational frequencies of the G-force. When you feel guilty about everything you do, there is no joy in life. How could there be? After all, you aren't divine, you are bastards of the universe—orphans and all that. Well, you must be orphans—Jesus was the *only* son of God, remember? Since you are so *lost,* your vibrational frequency is one that vibrates in utter fear.

You're a generation that fears the bomb. You're a generation that is at *holy* war with everyone—your neighbor, your family; the beliefs are all different, so ostracism is running rampant. You're desperately afraid—you drug yourselves into oblivion, you shoot up and shoot down, you take a toke to get high because *you* don't have the power to create a natural high yourself, because you just aren't *there.* You're copping out on understanding—you've just backed up a hundred million years.

You drink your wine, not because it is the ascended grape, but because you want to feel enamored and loose. The men froth at the mouth when an esteemed lady walks by. And, of course, they are the *epitome* of Social Consciousness—give them a few glasses of wine and they become leaky barbarians, because it is a catalyst to express a joy that they don't own. If you did own it, it would show in your Godfire-Light, and it doesn't. That joy that is the all-consuming fire, which is *just* there, isn't there, because you're still fogged in, guilty about everything you do.

So you pick up this book about a destination called *Freedom,* catchy title! You read a little bit about *Flightlevel: SuperC.* What you're gaining is something that is really without words—a grand emotion. But here's where it gets tricky for you, a sticky wicket, how is it said? You're up against *The Wall!* You're coming up against the big G-force—*Guilt,* and you don't know how to handle it.

Here's the *guilt-force,* blatant for you to see: How do you get beyond your drugs and your hard drink? How do you get beyond your terrible fantasies and your horrific entertainment? How do you get beyond your religious persecution? You're in the guilt-force full blown! Because you've sinned and lost the love of God, you give the hatred that you feel back to everyone you touch—you give it all back, tenfold! You're just compounding the hatred against you; it will manifest in your reality base. You're just flying from one fogbank into the next.

Why can't you fly out of the guilt-force? Because you've been so indoctrinated with the concepts of what's good and what's bad. And once *you* know what's good and bad, you go out and judge everyone else on what's good and what's bad in their lives. Here's how that thrust reverses back on you. What you've judged bad for them, *you've* been doing, and you feel the guilt-force head on! Remember, if you *do it* in your thoughts, you've done it. Your guilt compounds and compounds itself and goes around and around until you're just spinning out, constantly. No wonder you drink, and shoot up and down and sideways!

"Why can't I give it up," you cry! *Why don't you want to give it up*—I sigh. It's a very difficult jetroute for you to see, because I'm asking you to reason your own iniquities. You really don't want to know that you suffer from this terrible disease.

The guilt-force emotion leads to *dis*-ease, got it! You don't want to cough it up because the guilt-force is familiar, it is reliable, it is the *real* world, and because you do not love that which you are. Because you are not loved by God, why go on? And isn't that the lot of everyone else also? Who *does* feel good about their self? Who *is* happy in a world of grief and fear? Who *knows* they are loved by the Godsource for ever and always? You see, it's status quo to live in the guilt-force.

Breaking Through the Guilt Barrier

How do you break through? Well, take a look at you. You have done innumerable things—sit and think about a few right now. Find a few memories? Were you quite the charmer or did you make a fool of yourself? Did you hit a home run or did you strike out? Did you graduate with honors or were you on the bottom rung of the ladder? Is Dad proud or Mom mad at you? Most who contemplate focus on the *bad,* the *failures* of their life. And one *failure* is enough to cancel out a thousand successes—strange, but true.

So when you contemplate all that you've done, it *hurts*—you're reminded what a silly lump of clay you really are. Because it hurts, you don't want to touch anything that is messy. You know, we don't want to ripple the pond; we don't want to confront anything that is uncomfortable because that means we've done something *wrong.* And you're an *adult* now, so get off my case, *right!* Underneath your layers of self-guilt hides your Godfire-Light. Let's turn up the juice, fire it up, shine it out!

When you master self-guilt through your own understanding, you release yourself to fly into *FL: Freedom.* Why do we say, *through your own understanding?* In the lawless universe, only you know the laws for your self. Your laws are not contained in any rule book or preached from any pulpit, written in any law book or government release; they are discovered and earned through living life.

If you expect to receive a certificate to fly into *FL: Freedom,* we can't present you with one. But you can earn one and present it to yourself by owning this simple understanding; that what the Godsource created, He created of Himself; and that *all* that is the wonderfulness of life is from that great divine Is. The endowment of the Soul in the first light is God manifest in the intelligence of humankind. Since you possess a Soul, you are endowed in the first light. If you can *allow* yourself to climb out of the guilt-force to reason this, then you will begin your ascent into *FL: Freedom,* that wonderful space called *I am God;* and because *I am,* I am loved.

Who cares if the whole world despises you? If you are loved by the Godsource, you own it all. And who is the whole of the world but that unfortunate lot who have forgotten their divinity, who live in fearboxes? They all despise you for *you* anyhow! If you are loved by the Godsource, that is enough; that will give you the courage and the understanding to go for it all—*Superlove, Su-per*mind, Superknowingness, *FL: SuperC, FL: Freedom.*

When you time-travel in these rarefied atmospheres, you really get down to basics. What have you done that you feel so guilty for? Who is it that you feel guilty about? Will they die for you—think about it! Why are you living for them if they won't? What are you suppressing for? You had an abortion? Is that act worth dying for? Millions of men spill their seed every night—the sperm *is* alive, squirming in a stage of life. They don't feel any guilt for their act, why should you for yours? Take the guilt-force and convert it into knowledge; then it becomes wisdom.

You've abused your children? Is it so late you cannot love them? Go ahead, loan them the car! Are you living in quiet solitude so you won't ruffle the family tradition? Are you reading this flight-log in the closet by candlelight? Will any of them die for you when your moment comes, because you have lived for them? What have you proved living in the closet? Have you even been *born* into this lifetime? What mirror of divinity have you reflected, what intensity of the Godfire-Light were you? Just a dim, dim, shadow of a light to other dim shadows of lights.

I Had a Lot to Come to Terms With

In my life I was a great conqueror, a great strategist. The seeds of my people flourished on the Persian Gulf, and along the Indus River and in Tibet and Cathay. Even the Ionians who were of ancient Greece, they were my people. And I was the biggest bastard of them all for I was the great conqueror, the *Ram*—that meant, *The God.*

I slaughtered and I hacked because I was a barbarian who was filled with anger, hatred, and ignorance. I was conquering myself, the *whole* of myself! And any excuse to abolish tyranny, no matter how minute, I marched. Mine was the most terrible army there ever was because it was considered the *immortal fleet.* I had no fear, that is why I never perished—*none.* I was fearless because I wanted to do battle with the unknown God due to its *blatant* unfairness to my people and my mother and my life.

It wasn't until I saw my own blood that I woke up. There's nothing quite as touching as seeing your own blood—your immortality takes a dim view of fearlessness. I saw it flow like a scarlet river on a snowy floor; the floor seemed perfect, except my blood found a crack and created a pool. I convalesced on a rock for seven years healing my savage wound, sitting and being humiliated by the irony of the situation—being taken care of by women, the *great God's* dung and urine being carried away.

Well, I was humbled, aye! *Humble!* And I sat there and watched the coming and going of seasons. And I began to watch the splendor of a sunrise, and the waxing and waning of the enchantress moon, thinking all along the stars were her children. I saw generations of the nightbird in his nest nearby come and go.

And I watched the wildfowl in their seasons, and I felt the bitterness of cold and the anger of the sun at midday. I watched the wind whip through the rocks and blow my cloak askew around me; then it dashed off into the riverbed and through the olive orchards, and I saw an unseen power turn olive leaves from emerald to silver; and I watched it blow up the dresses of the women revealing alabaster knees, and saw the frolic of children giggling in its wake.

I had a lot to come to terms with, because the more I began to realize the subtleties of life, the more I found the unknown God. And the more I realized, I knew that it was all an illusion. In that I healed myself from my guilt, because I began to see that not until I realized it, could I own it and be free of it. For me to *own it,* it took ignorance and barbarianism and tyranny until I realized the illusion. And then I forgave myself for all of my moments. I had no regrets, because everything that I did made me what I was.

Where does wisdom come from, after all? Look at you—how can you ever become wise? Do you think abstaining from life creates wisdom? That only creates ignorance. Everything you've done, which has been hanging and suspended in your emotional soul for 7.5 million years, you did for the *adventure* of it; then you were caught in the emotion of it and it is still sitting there in the fog. You may be twentieth-century entities, but you're 7.5 million years old and backward, because you haven't resolved the emotion and *owned* it. You haven't allowed your mind to think; you would rather bask in superstition.

The reason you did what you did, is that you *wanted* to. That *want* has nothing to do with the guilt-force. When you don't *realize* that you did it because you wanted to, that's when you live in the guilt—you're afraid, you're unworthy. When you own everything you did—*everything,* from selecting your family to accumulating your wealth—when you know you did it all *for* the adventure, to *know,* to own that wisdom, then you are on your way home.

Just how loving is the unknown God? The Godsource has allowed everything—allowed, allowed, *allowed;* from your most barbarian thought, to your most hideous fantasy, it is allowed. Why are you, then, suspended in life? Why do you keep recycling back? Why are you allowed to be here in your corrupt, *wretched* ways? The only answer could be that you are *waiting for the moment of realization to occur.* Only at this flightlevel do you *realize,* for only here can you blatantly witness the dreamfog of the illusion.

The Devil Made Me Do It

To live in noble virtue is not to abstain from life, it is to *embrace* life. What does a man know who lives in a cave as a holy man? What does he know about women? What does he know about commerce? Is he afraid to look into the eyes of a woman, lest he become a fallen man? What has he mastered? He has mastered a cave, he has mastered an austere and simple life. In the next life, he'll come back raping and pillaging everything in sight. It is a truth! Many of you were holy men.

In contrast, how would an FRGB allow a woman to be a woman? How would he know about the tenderest of emotions, and about the fragrance of the nape of her neck? How could an FRGB have dinner with an enemy? How could he know the frustrations and the hopes he feels for *his* people? How could an FRGB forgive his enemies? Because he wouldn't have any, he had been it all!

NOTAM, listen up! In order to own all the illusions that the human experience presents to you, you have to have *been* it all. Otherwise, the curtain would never lift on the drama of your God-fire essence realizing. In other words, if you never *were* anything, what could you realize? How can you be *everything?* By loving everything, embracing it all, knowing the emotions of it all, and becoming the *wisdom* of it all. You do that by looking at what hurts *you.* You won't wake up from this dream until you look at what hurts you in your consciousness, then love it as the Godsource loves you.

You have a bad conscience? What hurts you, why do you feel bad? When you are alone in the night and the bed is empty beside you, then you begin to think about it, because it all comes home to you. Perhaps that's why you're always frantically looking for someone to lie with—so you don't have to be alone with you. And you can turn on your music and blast your brains from here to kingdom come, trying to *get hip,* but you know you are just hurting more and more—you're just side-slipping around where it's really at.

When you're alone with you, you only have to be there for a

moment to feel everything come home. When you look at all your *atrocities* and allow the feelings to come up from the depths of your soul—all the things that you've done—they will be resolved, they will be owned. If you don't, they will continue to eat at you— hurt, hurt, *hurt*. No matter how many coats of new paint you put over them they still smell.

You're afraid to be alone because you know what haunts you. Only when you allow it to come up, to meet it emotionally, do you return to your kingdom. Only when you *reason* it—*I did it because I needed to know and now I know and understand*—can you then return to your kingdom.

Do you know why Yeshua went into the wilderness? To con- front his devils—that's where the *devil* thing started. The *devils* were his limitations—*limitations*, not *temptations!* He had to face them and he did. That allowed him to return for the baptism of the dove. He owned it all, save death. That aloneness in the wilderness afforded him all his nightmares, his desires, his longings, his com- pletions, his incompletions, and he met them *all*. He went out and *lived*—devil spelled backwards is *lived*.

Welcome to Destination: Freedom!

What is it you don't understand? *Who* is it you don't understand? Do you understand the man who is unhappy emotionally and works himself to death to try to prove a point? Do you understand and love him? You can't criticize him any longer because you have *been* him. Do you understand the woman who is insecure and un- loved because she knows she will be wrinkled one day? Do you understand and love her? You can't criticize her any longer because you have *been* her, you have *felt* her frustrations and anguish.

NOTAM: You can criticize and judge anyone you want— *everyone*—but that means, in order to realize your *self,* you will have to recycle and return to *be* them, so you can understand and love them. Are you up for that? Just so you can love *you?*

Here's the science of it. When you condemn someone, all

you're doing is reflecting the hurt that you feel inside yourself onto them. You're just lashing out because you feel *forty lashes* inside! One who hates humankind is one who is unresolved with guilt within himself—he hates what he is, so he projects that on human-kind. Anyone who reflects back to him what he is, he attempts to destroy—thus holy wars. Really, he is destroying himself, that's where the irony lies.

You're cleared into *FL: Freedom* when you own it and it doesn't hurt you any longer to look at the emotion. It doesn't hurt you any longer to look at a baby someone else cuddles and think that you destroyed yours. It doesn't hurt you because you are at peace with it, because life prevails; life goes on and on and it was *your* choice. Now you can hold the babe and love it; now you can live the rest of your life in peace, and you understand those who *choose* those things; you don't need to condemn them. If you love them you own peace, if you judge them you own war, and those days are coming to a close in this time.

When you own everything you've done and you look at it, then you can look at everyone; and instead of hating them for the mirror they are, because it reflects your hate, you can love them and allow them and understand them, because they reflect your love and allowing and understanding. *That* is the FRGB conscious-ness—welcome to *Destination Freedom*. You no longer need to judge people because you understand them.

And it only took a little bit of wisdom to achieve that, and now you are loaded with it—you *smell* of it. Your Soul is like the ocean bed of sand—unresolved pearls, irritants. Like an oyster, the more you own them, the more the irritants turn into the pearls of wisdom. Then you fly home from your dreamfog and awaken loaded with goodies. If there is *one* item you remember from this flight instruction, let it be this: *Hatred of humankind emanates from one who is unresolved with guilt.* All the other flightlevels are within easy reach when you own this one.

Punching Through

Facing your fallacies? This is where it gets touchy for you. Because many don't own up to their own decisions, the residue of their lives becomes everyone else's fault. Hesitating to punch through this feeling of guilt backed up by fear is the *one* thing that blocks you from time-traveling into Supermind.

Let's see if we can further the *punching-through* process. Your next runners—are you prepared, *thumbs up,* and all that? Do you know where the wilderness is? Well, if you will remember, it is a few miles out of town—go that way, or is it this way? Well, go find it, wherever it is! It will be an excursion into self-love to go there and meet the Godsource within. And I assure you, it will visit you.

Go—don't take your blaring music, that kills the cells. Take foodstuffs—leave behind your drugs, leave behind your strong drink. Drink water only, and eat meagerly, but eat. Leave behind your books, which are romantic novels, which are slaying novels. Leave them behind, leave it *all* behind. Take off your jewelry, it carries vibrations in it—leave it behind and head away to a wonderful place. Take the paint off your face and let your hair be wild and free—for the first moment just go and be.

I think it would be jolly good for you to find a tree and put your arms around it and ask yourself, *What does that tree know that I don't?* Why is it still going to live, while you are going to be dead and gone? It will be flowering over your grave someday. What does it know you don't know? And when you call the wind, because you need something to help the emotion come, I will come to you. Speak to the Godsource within you and allow the emotions to surge forth.

When you venture into the wilderness, you'll learn what it is and why it exists. The wilderness, nature, is a noncondemning consciousness. Have you ever heard a tree talk about you behind your back? Were the birds chattering about your new hat? Hardly. Nature *allows* you because you are the Godfire essence—it simply allows you. It also *knows that* you don't know what you are, and it allows that *un*knowingness, so you touch that which you are.

Do this for you at least seven days—at least. And I am the wind in your hair when you go. And in those hours and in that quiet, much cosmic business will present itself to you—remember Jesus's trek into the wilderness. You venture cautiously out to the wilderness as a confused nincompoop and return as a master of the illusion. (You have the funniest words on this Earth-gameplane of yours; I wonder who invented nincompoop?)

Your trek to the silent monuments is the beginning of going home. It is the beginning of loving you and nurturing that divine aspect that you thought would be found through religion. But this is *real,* not superstition. During your sojourn, I will send the memories of yesterday to you. And they will be of the smallest nature, the most delicate of traumas, the most subtle of desires—the conflict between father and son, the jealousy of the mother toward her daughter, the competitiveness of friends, all of it *simple.*

And the memories will march on you like a legion, and in their presence the memories will cast you into some magnificent daydream, and one by one you will make your peace with them. And after the march, if you think about it and it *still* hurts, you still need to own it. For when you return from the peaceful monuments, you will be on the threshold of breaking over this great thunderstorm in your path that is called *insecure guilt of limited mind.*

What is it to look at your father's picture and not blame him for the lack of love that you felt—how about your lack of love for him? You will own it, and from that you will love your father because you have loved your*self.* And through that, that feeling carries on for an eternity. And what about your mother? Like you, she has the Godfire essence within her—yes, *even* your mother! You'll learn to understand that she is locked in her own trauma, just as you have been. How could you expect a supernatural mother, when they are all dealing with *their stuff,* just like you?

The Picking Process

The wisdom of allowing will begin to emerge when you begin to own *you*. Then you can love your mother, because you love you and understand you. Then, when she picks on you, you can allow it, because you know she is just picking on herself. And while you're in the picking process, you start picking up the pieces of blame. Are you familiar with this one—blaming everyone for your failures, blaming everyone for your neurosis? Does that sound like you?

When you return from the wilds, you meander down your blame list with a smile of freedom on your face. You realize you created your neurosis because you wanted to. And then you start picking up all the guilt trips you've laid at everyone else's feet— you start 'fessing up to them because you're not the helpless sheep anymore, you're an all-knowing, Godfire Being with unlimited understanding. Since your understanding is unlimited, you understand *you* made it all happen—it was your inability to perform life. To know that is a bounty.

With that ownership emerges a mystical gleam. It *is* difficult to own all your past blame of everyone else; you've spread it all over the world, as far as your thought could carry it! As difficult as it is to own it and no longer blame anyone for who and what you are, there is a glee that uncrumples when you start to reclaim it.

It means that you're taking back your power—you're coming home. Your brain begins to ignite and light up; you are passing the thunderstorm of guilt and insecurity; unresolved joy begins to brim to the surface because it means you *are* the Godfire, after all. You have emerged into that subtle, infinite knowingness that allows you to peak out the joy.

How happy could you be continuing to blame everyone else for your mistakes? How happy have you been blaming everyone for your traumas? Not happy at all. When you're *happy,* you are in full dominion of your life—you're free! If everyone owns a piece of you, what is that called? That's being in jail, imprisonment—

how could you be happy behind the bars of the thoughts of others? And that's where you are—locked up—if you live for their thoughts of you.

Powered Up Again!

See how simple it really is to understand it? Once you understand it, you can own it. And when you own it *all,* you have secured all your power back, you're *powered up* again. You can sleep at night like a baby, going into delta, to the exaggerated consciousness, and from there you glean from the soul its cobwebs to wake up in joy!

Joy and that mystical gleam are signs that you're coming home. They are signs that you have accomplished something that therapy never could. They are signs of a will that is awakened and a truth that is not autistic in it's manifestations, a truth that is not fanatic. A fanatic is someone who doesn't own it all. One who owns it all knows it—it's just there.

The ownership is a peace, a profound peace—*unresolved joy.* Then you've transcended beyond the thunderstorm blocking your path, then you *know* you're the Godfire, then you *know* you're divine. You understand everything you've done in this dreamfog, this slumbering dream of 7.5 million years—lifetime after lifetime after lifetime. Then your built-in alarm clock rings and you wake up.

FL: SuperC lies just beyond that thunderstorm that blocks your jetroute home—it's as close as the nose on your face, which you've learned to love! The wilderness jaunt will do grand things. And if you're strong enough, you'll 'fess up and own everything thereafter. And before you speak you will learn to speak like a God instead of a nincompoop.

Speaking about your language, are you aware that your language totally lacks divinity? Are you aware that your common speech is *illuminated* with curses? More than fifty percent of your

147

speech is augmented with a swear word, astounding! I suppose you don't know that what you speak manifests.

When you return from the pristine wilderness, you will relearn to speak, because whatever you say *is*. Then you will contemplate your common word and realize that it is *law*. And what sings from your mouth will be like a heavenly symphony. When you return, you will be time-traveling on a different route from everyone else around you.

Don't pack up your sleeping bag and your tent and slip into your four-wheel whatever to be different; do it because you love *you*. Whatever else happens after that is all right. This is the bargain: I will bring up your past. If you allow, allow, and *allow,* and then own and own and *own,* you will pick up the pieces of your life that you've left at everybody else's doorstep. Once you've reclaimed the blame for your *un*successful life, you will be breaking out into the clear at *FL: SuperC.*

Now, contrary to some thinking, a trip to the *wilds* is not an excursion to New York! Although it is fairly wild there, I do suggest a more peaceful setting—you know, trees, greenery, peace, mountains, *not* ski lodges, the desert, *not* Las Vegas, lakes, not Lake Tahoe. What you want to look for is unspoiled, untouched, quiet, tender, virgin, off the beaten path—places that don't take credit cards, addresses that read, "General Delivery." If you ride in on horseback, all the better. Try it, you'll like it!

When Is Beauty Seen?

When you open up the brilliance of your mind into *FL: SuperC,* when you open up the flower so that it blooms and bears fruit, who's mind will be opening? Yours. Therefore, you don't give away your power any longer, do you? In other words you don't ask questions like these any more—*How do I look today? How am I doing? How is my light?* You keep traveling forward into supermind by being super-*you*, by living a life that is centered around the nucleus of the Godfire essence within you.

Who should you be listening to? The Godfire essence within your autopilot-Soul. Who should you be seeking succor from for wisdom? Your great Godfire-Light radiating from your autopilot-Soul, and your knowingness reflecting from your Supermind in the all. How do you know when you *super*know? You will know when you know; there just isn't a question any longer of what you're doing because it just *is*.

And how will you know that you're going to be beautiful? When the word, *beauty,* doesn't exist any longer in your vocabulary. Beauty is the unseen essence—it is the spirit behind the mask. When the word doesn't exist in your vocabulary any more, you have become it. For in order for you to see beauty, you would have to be outside it looking in on it. When you *are* it—moving along in the flow of it—you don't see it.

Here is an analogy to help you understand. When you ask a little child, *Are you happy?* he doesn't react to you—he doesn't know what *happy* means because he *lives* in happiness, he doesn't know anything outside it to compare it to. As he grows, he learns to be outside happiness, to be in *un*happiness. Now he can perceive happiness, because now he can look at from where he is, in *un*happiness.

Well then, how will you know that you're going to be successful? When it is no longer important to you, when you *become* success, when it isn't outside you, when you no longer look back on it and say, "Ah, there it is, *Success.* It's not where I'm at so I'd better get to it." *Success* owns you then, instead of you owning it. And, of course, the next law that follows is, *if anything owns you, you are enslaved to that thing.*

What does it mean to be owned? Let's bring out some examples—to be owned by your job, to be owned by your auto machine, to be owned by the mortgage on your house, to be *owned* because someone else owes you money and you want it. To be enslaved by anything outside you is the war of Armageddon—it is called the Valley of Zion, and the battle of the Christ and the anti-Christ. The *anti*-Christ is not a seven-horned devil that rises from the sea. The anti-Christ is your altered ego. What else *could* keep

149

you from becoming what Christ was? Only your altered ego, because you ask yourself, *what would others think, how would it look socially?*

Why, if you had your own truth, everyone would be mad at you and you couldn't live like that—you couldn't bear to have anyone think ill of you. That's a devil of the Christ—altered ego, the limitation, the battleground. The FRGB has dominion over everything. When you arrive at *FL: SuperC* and hold that altitude, nothing will own you. You will own all things and have the power to control all things in your life—*all* things.

Well, since I've been reading along with you, I've decided to try some of these adventures. My vacation was coming up, so I decided to escape into the wilderness. At the last minute a friend offered his ranch in Montana, "at the end of the road" as he said. The place sat on a hilltop at six thousand feet. I planned to stay for three weeks, secluded, away from everything and everyone, except the cries of the morning birds and the rustle of the evening mice.

I had never spent time in the wilderness, except at Disneyland on the Jungle ride. I used to tap water and city lights and alarm clocks and suits and such, heading off to the wilderness in search of stars and silent nights.

I drove for two days, saw Yellowstone and more of the "land of the free and the home of the brave"—remember? I saw a funny bumper sticker along the way—"In gold we trust." On a moonlit night, I arrived at the gate and made my way to the main house. Stars, I saw *stars,* and from the *ground!*

I found the loft-type bedroom and collapsed into a contented, restful sleep, not knowing the beauty that would awaken me. The next morning, as blue sky and greenery filled the room, I found myself on top of the world—well, almost—looking out the window down a fertile valley off into the great beyond. Two mountains surrounded me, topping nine thousand feet. It was hard to believe the front yard turned into fourteen feet of snow in a winter's blizzard, temperature dropping to forty below—today it was 80°F. above.

I spent my first day figuring out the systems of the house—hot water, hot tub, the air-tight, the well, the pump. I cleaned, arranged, unpacked—I had packed in food because the nearest town was sixty miles away—an all-day trek on these roads. On the second day, I settled in—my mind kept telling me what I *should* be doing, but there was no phone to answer and no flightline to rush off to, no restaurant to savor, no TV to watch, so I just started listening to the wind. I realized that my checklist for breaking out of *my* illusion was quite simple and clear cut—I wanted to own anger and prejudice within my being forever; I wanted to see my altered Godself absolutely; I wanted to see my Godself absolutely.

Remember that quotation, "Power corrupts," and that other one, "Absolute power corrupts absolutely"? Here's another one for you. "Absolute fear corrupts absolutely!" I wonder if *fear* is the emotion that prompts the reaction of power? Maybe. Here's another one I heard—"Absolute God loves absolutely," and "Absolute love uncorrupts absolutely."

It's really quite simple to be like God—just love as God loves. I suppose the tough part is figuring out *how* God loves! That's where all the rules and religions come from—trying to figure out what should be loved and what shouldn't be loved. It's easy to figure out that a fawn is to be loved, but what about a baby tarantula? We know we should love baby-birthers, but what about murderers? Maybe absolute God is absolute love, and when you contain that within self, you've owned anger and prejudice; you don't emotionalize your reaction to fear any more into anger and prejudice, you *own* it. And when you do that, maybe you can forgive and allow all of self to love all things.

Why love all things? What you *know* of all things is what you *think* of them. And for you to know a thought you must have been that thought—felt it, *known* it in your being, *been* it. Therefore the thoughts of nonlove for others are really thoughts of nonlove for yourself, as you have felt it and known it.

Why love all things? Because you're not your thougths—you *are* thought. If you *are* thought, you are all things. If you love all things you love yourself. Simple! To feel the love of others it seemed that I must feel the love of self first. What stops that *feeling of self* process? The emotion of fear, *un*owned, stops that feeling of self. The emotion of fear has a way of masquerading as the knowingness of love, but there is a difference. Talk to you in a bit; I'm going to take a nap. . . .

When Does Success Become the Smell?

The pursuit of sovereignty is quickened by the desire called want, but how does *want* fit in with personal success? Humankind has itself between a rock and a hard place—you've reasoned yourselves into a vice. You hesitate to change, to evolve, because you feel that is *un*spiritual. You hesitate to think for yourself because that is blasphemy. You hesitate to be a genius because you ask, *what would the neighbors think?* What does a true, Godfire being look like? Where are the examples? How do they act, especially in the area of personal success?

Evolution in *FL: SuperC* is accented by reaching to grab and embrace that portion of creation called genius. Genius is just around the hard place in the road. I have never expressed that it is ungodlike to be a success at who you are—never. That is a God *being*. On the contrary, when one lifts oneself out of the dogma of good and bad, of poverty consciousness, of richness consciousness, then he is at the apex of understanding—he has dominion over all things.

Many are in a continual quandary about losing their wealth. Some are in a quandary about losing their poverty. Essentially, it is the same puzzlement—they feel that movement in that area, *change,* will create a crisis point in them in some way. That is a very real fear in a lot of people, and I sympathize with it. That's why I say, if it makes you happy, keep it!

Of course, when I say that, usually they are placed into an even grander puzzlement, because they have no idea what happiness *is.* If you live your life in wealth, having wealth is being happy—worrying about it, wondering who's stealing from you, trying not to pay taxes, looking for *the best* rate of depreciation and investments, wondering who your real friends are. Well, I suppose that's happiness for some people. After all, what's the choice?

And if you live your life in poverty, being poor is to be happy—not knowing where you will slumber tonight, wondering if you'll eat tomorrow, trying to remember the place that gave you a hot meal, hoping it won't be too cold tonight. I suppose that's happiness for some people. After all, what is the choice?

If the flightlevels you're flying in *make you happy,* if they bring forth unresolved joy, embrace them. And then again, if your life makes you unhappy, keeps you in a box, change it! That goes for everything in one's life. And don't give me that *I-can't-change-it,* song and dance. I *know* you can change it; millions of people every day all over the globe change it. That's a cop-out and unacceptable in *FL: SuperC.*

Success is not necessarily how much gold one acquires, or how much poverty one endures. *Success* is one's achievement of any endeavor because one *wanted* to achieve it and it made them happy. That's the apex of success. In contrast, a lot of people live in a fearbox, convinced that their discernment of success has to live up to someone *else's* ideal of what success is. Of course, that ideal is to have endless lieutenants at your beck and call, to be powerful, to be a ruler, to possess hordes of gold; or to be riddled with stench and hunger, in poverty.

There are many ways to look at success; it means none of those things. Gold and poverty are the same thing, they are made out of the same Source—*Is.* When one begins to fly in Superconsciousness, one goes forward into the idealism of expanded mind.

That expanded mind continuously enraptures one in the scent of achievement. That sense of achievement is a security that is the same as unresolved joy.

When does the success begin to smell? When it doesn't make you happy anymore; then it is an entrapment. And unhappiness sneaks up on you very mischievously. The bloom that you needed in order to reach that success is very soon off the rose—you find yourself *jailed* by the grind necessary to perpetuate that success. Remember this simple truth—the jetroutes to *FL: SuperC* do not belong to an organization, they do not belong to a book, they do not belong to a country, nor a dogma—they belong to *you.* And there is only one route—that's *yours.*

How will you know if you're on the *correct path?* You possess a built-in inertial navigation system that feeds you data constantly. Reason this—the correct path brings joy! That's the jetroute of the flight student who is mastering the eloquence of an FRGB-rated pilot.

And if your route jets you a little too close to a thunderstorm or two and the feeling of joy is lost, punch in *unresolved joy* again to correct your heading around the thunderstorms and head straight for joy. Unresolved joy is the exacting, electrifying emotion of the Godfire coming forth in you. In a state of joy there is no hate—when you're happy, the world shines along. When you're in joy, you are unjudgmental—that's why it's such an *exalted* emotion. And when joy is *unresolved,* it is forever.

Now, I hear you reasoning the pros and cons of throwing everything away so you can set your heading for unresolved joy. You're thinking, "I am pretty miserable, but not so miserable that I want to throw everything away." And then one morning you wake up and riot and throw it all away; and the next minute you want it all back wondering, *Why did I throw that away?* And then you blame it all on someone else: it was *their* fault, you really didn't want to do it, you thought you were going somewhere. You went somewhere all right, around in a circle in your fearbox; you were bouncing from one wall to the next. Because you're still in your box, your reasoning capacity is limited by a limited mind.

Who said to throw everything away? *Changing it* doesn't mean to throw the dishes out with the dishwater. Let's be sensible about this. If all of the world's corporations decided to work toward the uplifting of the planet, they would create an *economy* around it. In other words, *Hey guys, there's money to be made in the uplifting of the planet!* And that's probably the only way it will happen, aye? Instead of creating the budgets to destroy, let's create the budgets to perpetuate. It does make sense; how can you continue to profit if there's nothing left?

What Does Make You Happy?

Assess where you're living. If you're living on zippers and that makes you happy—stay. If you're living where the earth is shifting and that makes you happy—*stay;* but do reason why it makes you happy. If you're living in the cities and that makes you happy—stay.

On the other hand, look at your life—all of it. Have you succeeded with your perceptions, or are they just fleeting moments of glory? Are you suffering the slings and arrows of your own achievement because you're spinning your wheels? Boredom is a sign from your autopilot-Soul that you've learned everything there is to learn from that adventure, whether it is relationships, business success, unsuccess, ownership, poverty, whatever.

If you're climbing to the top of the mountain you have made and that makes you happy, continue your ascent to the summit. Do be aware that to stay *at the top* requires the momentum possessed by an FRGB; arduous, indeed, in the business world. But fairness to all will be an honorable achievement in the future sunrise.

And how honorable is it to be able to walk away rather than engage in a battle of ownership? It is grander to walk away than to stay and fight for some miserable cause that has only canceled out your joyride. And it is odd isn't it, that when you walk away, they almost follow you out the door wondering why you won't do battle with them? These are the flight systems that you must become proficient with to ascend and maintain *FL: SuperC.* No one else can do it for you—no one. Change is the optional law in your life.

Think about your life for a moment—contemplate it. What couldn't you change if you wanted to? Isn't it rather exciting to know that *you* created it all! You see, you really are a grand manifestor, but you haven't given yourself credit. And if you've manifested in the *negative* as you call it now, you *know* you can manifest in the positive—the difference is just a tweak of your mind.

Whatever you have created has nothing to do with the mass that sits in front of you; it has everything to do with the genius inside you—the real treasure lies inside, not outside. And every pickle you've pickled yourself into, *you* made it and *you* can change it—you've created it all! It takes a dignified and noble flight student to humble himself enough to look evenly at his life. The keyword in your flightplan is the emotion called joy; unresolved joy keeps your heading from deteriorating.

Give Me a Break

There is a natural abhorrence in your country toward those who are successful. They are worshipped yet despised—it is jealousy that sees through green eyes. It says a lot about someone when they create their own idea and take it to its zenith.

And it says even more when they can turn and walk away, when they call for clearance into the next flightlevel because it is finished at *this* flightlevel. If you can't sell what ails you, have you ever thought about giving it away? Am I being impractical? I am being the Godfire essence. If it has you behind bars—enslaved—if it is holding off your blast-off into *FL: SuperC,* why not give it away? I can see it now—the New Age shows up tomorrow morning and no one can attend because they can't sell their old-age hangups! Such is life. Apparently, holding onto your hang-ups mean something.

Do you see how the dreamfog keeps you lost? Those who are trying to break away and ascend into the next flightlevel are still stuck in the fog of the old one, because they refuse to break out of it. Breaking out is just a tweak of your mind. Maybe somebody someday will say, "Do you love this? Do you want it? It's yours. Goodbye." Well, some would say that is a very true test. But what is the purpose of your flightplan? To link up with Superconscious-ness—to be one who has complete sovereignty over his life? When it's very clear inside your knowingness to change, *make* the change. The change will not be at a cost, but will be of value, allowing the next opportunity to land.

Practical—have you heard the word? Many often rely upon practical sense rather than *common* sense. And because of that, in order to look the part, they do many things that don't make them happy in the process. However you adorn yourself, however much gold it takes, stones it takes, however many *designer this-and-thats* it takes—whatever—if it takes a loin cloth and a shaved head and ash smeared across your forehead, if it makes you happy, *go for it!* If that is your next step in achieving understanding, let it ring.

But give me a break—know *why* you are doing everything you are doing. Why are you still married? Because of the children, of course! That is really laying a trip on the next generation. You're creating the guilt-force for the next generation who must follow in your footsteps—*Mom and Dad stayed together for me; we have to stay together for little Herbie!*

Are you staying together because of social security? There are many that do, you know. Open up and climb to SuperC—all that is in the Godsource will flow through you, to you. There's a par-amount difference between one who dreams grand dreams and one who makes them happen. The next step during your climb-out is being a doer—*do;* accept the aggressiveness of bringing forth the dream into manifestation.

And there are those who feel utterly helpless and hopeless,

who depend upon others for everything. That is the dreamfog you are lost in; it is being worked out. When you tire of that adventure, wake up. Use the facilities of brilliance to move forward, because that is what will happen in the New Age—sovereignty of self.

Whatever it is, if it doesn't make you happy, walk away, give it away to someone else who wants it. Let it be *their* next dream; let it flee from you. You're emptying out your limitations when you do that. Then you have *room* to grow, to allow magnificent things to fill the vacuum of those seemingly empty places. When you hold onto yesterday, when you hold onto dead and dying adventures, you have no room in your box for greatness.

The Cast System

Some of you are having difficulty with this. Well, redundancy of flight instruction and flight systems saves lives every day in the airlines industry. You won't mind if we utilize a little redundancy to try to break through your barriers?

Making the decision to change doesn't mean that the cast system is now operable—well, you cast everything away and then regret you did it. The pass key here is to look at why you hold onto it. Why *do* you hold onto it? Because someone expects you to, because the stocks are up, because the money is good, because you wonder what your husband or wife would say, what your Board of Directors would say, what the *bull* would say?

In order to poke through the guilt barrier, you have to understand why you are still caught in the web. In other words, what are your habits and excuses that still ensnarl you? Once you detect that those barriers are operative in your flight-system, you can look evenly and squarely at them. And whatever you walk away from comes back to you on the wings of a dove one thousandfold in greatness. That is why the rewards of noble virtue are so spectacular—they fold back on you in big ways.

When you're on top of the mountain, what brought you there?

Honor, allowing, courage, virtue, strength, fortitude, noble character, eminence; excellent qualities—*nobleness,* not very many know what that word means, those ancient qualities that have long since been forgotten by your social system. Those qualities belong to an FRGB who is Pilot-in-Command; without them he is not a master of his own destiny, nor can he love the whole world, nor can he *release* the whole world and love it no matter how it looks to him.

In *FL: SuperC* there are no extremes. If someone is in need of a dollar and that's all it takes for him to survive, and then there is another in need of fifty *billion* dollars, they're in the same difficulty, aren't they? It doesn't make any difference, it is *still* where they're feeling. Amounts determine nothing; it is the *emotion* that determines everything.

You can flit around and say, "Oh, I have a bag of worries that is unbelievable." You wear your worries like badges; you know, you've heard people talk about their illnesses—they're always trying to outdo one another with their gallbladders. It's a competition! Well, worries are the same thing. But let me tell you a secret, listen. When you were expanding upon your worries to them, and you thought that they were listening to you, guess what? They were thinking about all of theirs in competition with all of yours—they never even heard a word of what you said! So where are you at? Speaking to yourself as usual!

Can you see, are we breaking through the fogbank? It's *all* attitude, and attitude is *all* emotion. And emotion is very clear— either it *is,* or it *is* in the not that it is. In other words, you must *feel* the unresolved joy, you must *feel* the forward thrust that stretches your mind to an inconceivable place, to new flightlevels, because that unresolved joy is the feeling outside your fearbox. You've always been the victim—now victims don't exist, there is only Godfire.

The FRGB is one who owns it all right where they are, for they have broken through the dreamfogs of necessity, they have burst through the dreamfogs of security, they have smashed through the illusion of the lack of love of self, and they have blasted out the other end of the time-travel tunnel to meet the Godsource face to face. And when you do that you are all there is to be.

A Heightened Space of Nauseousness

Listen carefully. Your shooting up and shooting down and toking your weed is killing you. It *is*—you heard it here. You try to justify it by saying that it brought you into a heightened space of consciousness—that's a laugh! What you're experiencing is a slow death in all of its hallucinogenic glory. Your brain cells are dying by the millions; you're experiencing death, not life.

Well, where do the hallucinations materialize from? Why did you have the visions? Because you have diminished your brain power to such an extent that the drug, acting as a catalyst, brings the vision to the surface. *You* think you are seeing a heightened consciousness; you are seeing your own nightmares and fantasies.

You can justify your habit patterns all you want to; it's your truth, it's your life. But please comprehend totally that the life that flows through you is excellent quality. It *is* a high and it *is* the vision, it *is* the absolute knowingness and it *is* the joy. And to experience that, you need nothing in your hands or in your body to act as a catalyst to make it happen—it is all within your soul.

I know how you justify things to fit your comfort zone. It's quite all right for you to do that, but can you fathom that you are still bouncing off the walls of your box? You're *not* time-traveling forward and your brain isn't opening up to anything—it's closing down and dying. When you've slain the cells that do not reproduce, you've cut yourself off from your own Godfire-Light, your own glory, what your Godfire essence is.

Then all you are is a living machine that's enslaved to its next moment of accelerated illusionary joy. How would you like to fly with a drugged up Pilot-in-Command? No way, right? If you can find the answer to your habit in these words, you'll own it. Then it doesn't own you any more as you soar off into the wild blue yonder.

Let It Be

At *FL: SuperC* you'll find that all your priorities are changing. When you've lived and dressed and done everything for everyone else, you're going to find that you're losing interest in that masquerade. And I wouldn't doubt that one day you will sit back aghast and wonder, *Am I losing it?* No, you're gaining it.

What you are losing touch with is the fogbank of illusion—you're *gaining* the clarity of reality. The reality is the *unknown—that* is the mind of Superconsciousness. And if you sit there and you don't have anything to do, and you're not motivated to do anything—*sit there*. I sat for seven years on a bloody rock! Could you sit on a rock for seven years? Hardly, your Timex would lose control! You're in too big a hurry to die; you couldn't sit on a rock for seven minutes.

This is a process of letting it be. There are some very divine words you should familiarize yourself with—*allow* and *be*. When you punch them into your thinking processes, they will allow the mind to quicken and bloom; they allow the emotions and the troubled waters to gurgle up so you can see them and then own them. Then you are in control. While all of this is occurring to you in your little world and in your consciousness, it is noticed. It is a brave and daring thing to break out of the fogbank that everyone else is lost in. That will cast you into the limelight as being an individual. You've drawn attention to yourself.

There are many who do *anything* for attention. They just don't have the love lock in their power/love center, nor the security lock in their autopilot-Soul center. Have you seen the colorful hairdos lately? That is not a judgement, just a comment. Once you're on the jetroute of thinking that opens your mind, you *do* step out of the mundane and outside the ordinary into the *extra*ordinary. I wouldn't think you would need to place a signal beacon on your head, though!

It *does* take courage to be alone. Blooming into an FRGB is an alone process, for who do you relate to? *Who* knows what you're going through and how you need to handle it? If they knew, they would know for themselves. Who do you talk with? The wind, the Godsource within.

While you're jetting around in *FL: SuperC,* you're also moving toward the original consciousness called thought. Thought is the *is,* and from it all things issue forth in profusion. The sunspot is emanating from the *is.* The solar wind is a result of the spot of the *is* on the sun. The new weather patterns are a result of the shift in the solar wind from the spot of *is* on the sun.

Here's something intriguing for you to process: The thought that Superconsciousness is moving into, is to be in link-up with the knowingness of the *is.* When you travel in *FL: SuperC,* you'll eventually link up with the *is! That* knowingness is going somewhere—it is the *is* that forever is unfolding; and with that you begin to be in link-up, connected with it. Instead of being well connected about town, you can be *well connected* in the forever.

The Curtain Is Coming Down

Your drama is coming to a close. The Aquarian Age is upon you— the *is* age. This is the return of the fully realized Godfire being. It is the awakening, it is the Superconsciousness, it is the new time. The metamorphosis is occurring on all levels. The sun is going through a metamorphosis, your earth is, your galaxies are; you will discover a new planet in your solar system that is metamorphosing. Everything is moving; it is unearthly, literally. And as soon as your brain opens through Superlove and *allowing,* through holding onto what you are, you will link up in the flow of that knowingness. In that knowingness you will be in the full flow of life. Then you are called forever and ever and ever and ever—then your knowingness is absolute. Then you realize that life, the *is,* the thought, is *on-going.*

Can you guess why transcendental meditation doesn't work? Within you is reflected the Supermind—the mind of the God-source—and you try so hard to still that reflection within. How can you still the mind of the Godsource? How can you still forever?

You would have to vibrate at its pace in order to *think* it was standing still, correct? Then, you would be *in* Supermind; then there is no time when you are at equal pace, there is no distance, there is no measure, there is only *is.* Your time-travel adventure would just stop! You would have arrived. You would be in the forever heaven—the forever, ever heaven that is eternal. You would be in the *Is* that is the great beyond.

The Magician's Magic

Want is the key that unlocks the door to *FL: Freedom.* It has nothing to do with chanting until you're blue in the face, living in a cave, wearing a nasty loincloth, walking around dirty because the dirtier you are the holier you are—you're just dirty, that's all. Oh, how I love to bully around in those china shops. Just dirty!

Want is a divine and *powerful* word. It is the *all-powerful* word that you own because want is like the magician's magic—I *want* this! To *say* the word *want* in your intellectual consciousness is a very far cry from the absolute *desire* of the word want. You say you want a lot of things, but you really don't want them— you're just uttering words that are meaningless, boring sounds. Want is something you *feel*—it's a feeling, a *need,* a desire. Knowing your flight status as an FRGB flying at *FL: SuperC* is all you need—everything else just begins to happen. When Supermind kicks in its afterburner, everything else just falls into place.

And if the ride gets too hot for your britches, at any moment you can shut it down. Whenever you don't want to go forward, you'll know it because you don't *want* to go forward—it's too hard. You're still loved—I *love* you.

If you want to see this adventure through and you're uncertain what lies beyond the dreamfog, remember this—you're leaving everything dreadful behind. Beyond the dreamfog lies the reality. And in the ughknown there is no serpent, there is no mugger, there is no condemner, there is no fiery pit. In the great beyond is the adventure of paradise, and you only get from here by awakening out of the dream.

Whenever you go forward you leave behind the fears. When you go forward it is called the virgin movement. In the past, when you've *thought* you've arrived, you made a clutter at your landing site—you carried all your junk with you! Naturally, the kingdom you created there was a fearsome kingdom—it contained all your excess baggage that you've been trying to dump behind for so long.

Going forward and *really* changing, leaving the clutter behind, is a natural action of a Pilot-in-Command who knows his heading. And any time the turbulence gets too tough, do a 180-degree turn and fly back into the fogbank. Anytime you want to sit there and be depressed, *be* depressed—it's all right. Any moment you want to cry and feel sorry for yourself, go for it—really wallow in it, you deserve it because you *want* to. It is all up to you. *FL: SuperC* is totally optional.

There are some of you that are too comfortable in your comfort-zone miseries to change. Your life will end on this Earth-gameplane, and wherever you go and whatever you do after that is another adventure; but remember, your flightbag is still loaded down with all of your prejudices, your limited opinions, your hate, your bitterness, your self-pity—you're carrying it all with you. How could you ever see the light at the end of the time-travel tunnel when you're too busy looking backward, saddled down with all your excess baggage?

It's a Fragrance You Can't Buy

FL: SuperC is the will of the Godsource arisen within humankind. How does this play in the drama of your real world? For the first time *ever* it gives you control *over* the drama—it's an illusion, you can rescript it! Soon, you'll be able to see the drama for the illusion that it is. How will your new vision affect your social life? What will it do for your state of mind? Well, you'll have a lot of headaches, because blowing past limited mind sometimes is painful. The pain is not a physiological pain, but an emotional pain that manifests the physiological pain.

How you are in this peeling process depends wholly upon you. When you stop needing proof about everything, you begin to wake up and just allow, allow, allow, *allow.* Then you don't need to have all these side adventures that you go off on, trying to prove you're right. You know? Sliding up to someone and saying the classical, *I know you from another lifetime. I bet you have a problem with blah, blah, blah, blah, blah.* And they say, "How did you know?" And you answer very stoicly, *Because in my knowingness I know that now, I can see.*

Guess what? I never knew a Pilot-in-Command who made a big deal out of being an expert pilot—it was always the ones who couldn't get off the ground who bragged! Anytime you have to be braggadocios, that's a sure tip-off that you're not sure what you're up to; so some of you *must* go and drag a poor, innocent person, who is so vulnerable, into your sandbox and muddy him all up, kick him out, and leave him as confused as ever! When you have to start laying, as the term has it, your trips on others, it just means you don't own them.

In the wilderness it's a very simple life—a little food, a little water, mixed with lots of love. The love is free, the food is harvested from your garden. Pure water is plentiful in the wilderness—mountain streams, deep, dark wells; cold, pure, fresh, clean, there for the adventurer to find.

Life *is* survival, survival *is* life—why all the panic? We're all survivors, why not live to watch the movement of the wind in the trees, to watch the clouds as they are blown across a pristine, sapphire sky leaving shadows of joy dancing across the land? Why rush off hither and yon to do this and that? Why not go back to the land?

Go find a spot, your own special place. Homestead it, bring the kids and dogs and cats. Sleep outside under the stars; feel the wind as it caresses your weary, precious body. Why strive to achieve? To achieve what? You already are what you are—grand, glorious, divine, a fragrant perfume in the whole scheme of things. It's your social conditioning that tells you you're *not,* that haunts you, forces you to strive, to be *upwardly mobile.* Why strive? For what? There will always be someone else who has more.

When our constitution was signed our economy was agrarian—we lived on the land, we ate from the land, our children danced in the dirt barefoot. When our constitution was signed the three largest cities were Boston, Philadelphia, and New York. Jefferson said they were the sores that plagued the body politic, because it was there that the infestations began.

When the Declaration of Independence was signed—you remember: "That all men are created equal . . . endowed by their Creator with certain unalienable Rights; that among these are Life, Liberty, and the pursuit of Happiness. That to secure these rights, Governments are instituted among Men, deriving their just powers from the consent of the governed." Remember?

In Jefferson's day, the population of the largest city of the Union did not exceed thirty thousand people! What would Jefferson grumble about today, I wonder? If he were running for office would we even elect him? In those days of valor and pride, there was a *human family* consciousness that pervaded every soul—there were no slums, those who had more assisted those who had less, personally. If your neighbor needed a barn, you raised one; if your neighbor needed food, you shared yours.

Why return to the land? It's from whence you came and where you go—it breathes, it's *alive*. The land is plentiful as you move away from the major population bases of the millions and millions. There are millions and millions of acres untouched, off the paved main roads, awaiting the touch of your fingers in their soil. It's cheap to buy or you can trade something for it—your house, your fancy car, your savings for a rainy day. It's cheap—a few hundred dollars per acre instead of thousands.

Get back to the wilderness, to what it is and what you are. It will move you and smile back at you and ask, "Where have you been?" You don't buy these words? Spend two weeks in the wilderness—alone. Borrow them, beg them, buy them, those two weeks.

Slow your pace, slip your watch in a drawer. Sit—do nothing and listen. Watch the movement of life, feel the earth breathe, as it ebbs and flows with you, a part of it returned to breathe with it. Look out across vast panoramas, watching the peace, listening to the silence, feeling the isness—all that is holy and divine found as far as the eye can see, not contained in musty caves or ornate cathedrals but all over, open, free, available to all, no admission charge.

Go where it is to see it, be a part of it, feel it; know what you see outside is the peace within you, as in all things in equality. Inhale the clean air, smell its freshness as it was just made for you over the next hill, over there by some trees, whose purpose it is to be. Live in the joy of what it is—leave your cares behind, know you are right on time. Feel the light of the sun as it feeds your being with love, caressing you with warmth from the womb of celestial wonder.

In the wilderness you can know what you are, get back to basics—simple, easy, pure—atonement, at-one-ment. Get back to what you are—be you, know you, love you. It is simple. It is.

Simple . . . Is

Who do you suppose are the meek who will inherit? They are the salt of the earth. They are the *un*glamorous, they are the unspoiled, they are the simplicity of life. They ride around in old, rusted automobiles. And in their furrows, and in their hovels they wear a smile; and behind perhaps weathered skin and fading eyes there is still a light that shines, and there is a joy on their face that you wished you owned.

And you ask them, "Look at you, you're working in this field, you . . . you, you don't have any nice clothes to wear, and you're sitting here with simple mead and simple bread, and wouldn't you like a few bucks?" "No," they answer, "I don't need it. What do you have that I don't have? I don't have all your worries, and I don't have all your unhappiness—I just *am.*" The meek who inherit this new age are not the braggarts, they are not the mongrels who seek succor from famous people—what will that do for you? The meek who inherit are the common people—they are FRGBs inside, and they don't lay their trips on anyone, they just *are.*

You can see it in them—they're wonderful; they have a glow that you don't own no matter how many facials you've had. It's a fragrance you can't buy, a look that you can't imitate, a feeling that you can't duplicate until you own it. They know that their truth is *their* truth, *their* reality, and they are quite contented to proceed in that reality. Any moment they step out of their reality to lay it on someone else, they have lost the reality they owned. It is that within that is simple, *simple,* simple.

For You and You Alone

There are many who, the minute they hear a voice coming forth within, feel prone to channel it to the whole world. As if the world wasn't confused enough! Apparently it's not good enough for the voice to be there just for you, it's not good enough just to have the Godsource within you awakening. You have to go out and lay your trip on the whole world. You'll never make them happy, because you can't be answerable for their life. When you have all the answers for them, you own their life—that puts you in a precarious position, being the dictator, the enslaver.

Listen to the voice that is important for *you*—your Godsource, *you!* The voice never says, *Go out and gather a multitude and let's hang this on them!* That's not how it is at *FL: SuperC.* That voice is for you and you alone. You're the adventurer in your dreamfog; *you've* collected the memorabilia of experience—*your* experiences. What good does it do anyone else to hear about your excess baggage? Good question?

In the autopilot-Soul of everyone is the memory that there is safety in numbers. It has long been in the religious memory that when two or three or more are gathered together, they automatically form a religion—in other words, they lose individual truth and begin to blend a law of consciousness.

The memory that you keep pulling up is to *belong* to something—that is the compensating energy force of the fear of abandonment. These are *very* strong emotions. Your being is riddled with these memory-fears. They are *so* powerful, if there is anyone outside your group, it becomes almost a *holy* thing to destroy them if they don't surrender. This has been proven throughout history. What these fears have exhibited blatantly for you to see, is the *lack* of the love of God, which would allow another God the love of God. It is insecure, bitter dogma that enslaves both the enslaved and the *enslaver!*

Why can't you be alone in your realization process; why *can't* you fly at *Flightlevel: SuperC* without a fanfare from your constituency and a sermon from your preacher? Is it so impossible for you to be *you?* At those flightlevels, sovereignty is what will open the mind to embrace the soul and engage the kingdom. You won't be able to party with three of your friends over tea and crumpets saying, *All right, let's become. Let's share experiences—I'll lay mine on you, you lay yours on me; have another cup of tea.*

Well, I suppose you could, if all you wanted to do was chatter. But destination *Freedom* is about resolve and conviction, it's about changing what doesn't work into what *does!* These flightlevels that you can soar into will break the bonds of the past and propel you to where you've never flown before, breaking away into the glory of forever. I'm not really sure you want to break away.

The Promise of Forever Fulfilled

There is an hour coming when higher and lower selves, one million forty-one guides, all the dietary elements for enlightenment, the quotations, the philosophy, the passages, the abstinence, they will not amount to a hill of inedible beans. Look around at your world— everything you see here will be unfamiliar in the new age, outdated. And those of you who are so big and so bold, won't even be cleared to *FL: SuperC* because you're locked up in metaphysical journeys that go nowhere. Isn't that the truth?

What has all your chanting done for you lately? What has all the burned incense accomplished, besides making your house smell good and create a lot of ash that you have to clean up? And all the candles that you've burned? What have all your prayers accomplished? And all your alms? Can't you see it isn't happening? Wake up! It's only entertainment, just another fantasy. What's *super-* knowingness, pure and simple? If you know how to know you will be sustained—if the whole of the universe threw up, you'd know how to go with the flow. Basic truth—we shoot basic truths at you!

It's really quite simple. Instead of praying for peace, *be* the peace that you are praying for. Instead of praying for love, *be* the love you're praying for. Instead of praying for health, *be* the health you're praying for. In other words, be a light to the world; *be* the example so that they can see that it works for you. Then they'll try it. See how it works?

Destination Freedom wasn't concocted to force a truth down your gullet. It was designed to engage you to look and see and own for yourself. One who wishes followers tells stories of cosmic mumbo jumbo. And yet, not one of their words can manifest a runner, can manifest a glory that is undeniable. So, you end up on the receiving end of mumbo jumbo, and it makes for good daiquiri conversations.

Yet, I'm criticized because I challenge you; I'm at the top of everyone's list because I engage you in life. Well, if you think *this* is cosmic mumbo jumbo, just wait 'til the runners arrive. There are a grand few of you who are going to wake up out of the dream-fog and own it all. And the promise of forever shall be fulfilled.

To the Rest of the Common People

Superconsciousness is a super reality. It transcends the dreamfog of intellectual science, and it goes beyond the obscurity of science, of religion and dogma. It is the *is factor* of the great unknown—the unexplored, the forever universe of understanding. *FL: SuperC* is your link-up to the heritage of what is called *is*—the Godfire alive in you forever.

To fulfill the prophecy of the return of Christ is not to look into the heavens or to the East, but to the within—to justify your illusions and to own them; to go beyond into an understanding that is illogical and irrational, into what is called Superlove, which no one owns. When you see it from outside your fearbox, it is simple; escaping from your box is difficult.

Waiting for you is *FL: SuperC,* your birthright. The Crown of Thorns of Christ is your birthright. The salvaging of your king-dom is your right to live. Your divine right as a God is the im-mutable law that *allows* you to be whatever you want to be. But the allowing is fixing to take a great and gigantic change, which is wonderful, and those who possess Supermind recognize it and know it.

The time has come to press toward you and send the runners. I challenge your minds and gaze into your faded faces to see if you're *getting it,* because I realize there is coming an hour when you will try frantically to remember what was said here. And because you will be trying to remember *frantically,* you'll never remember; your memory experiences about the future sunrise just recall frantic, frenzied hysteria about something that is not even fearful—it is divine.

What is your contribution to the future sunrise? Perhaps your daring Soul, perhaps your doubting mind, perhaps all of the hardships that show much of your character; that quality will sustain itself forever. And, after all, what is peace? It isn't peace marches and *love-ins* and frantic demonstrations—it's consciousness. And when you feel it, *everyone* feels it. It's like the memory of the Master walking in the marketplace, and it is the unforgettable experience of touching the Godfire-Light of a Fully Realized Godfire Being. You are adding to the quality and the beauty of the whole everywhere by being you.

Your flight instruction doesn't just stop the moment you close these pages. I will facilitate your adventures on and on and on by the runners who will challenge your little world and press you into Superknowingness, if you want them to. No, it doesn't end here; the adventure will continue to jet you around in all sorts of flightlevels, altitudes you haven't begun to conceive.

And if you tune yourself acutely into the infiniteness of Superconsciousness, you will know it. The flight plan of your life will be marked up with a variety of changes—as your mind opens, as nature is on the move, you will be in synchronized harmony with every *thing,* all in all.

That is your next adventure—the next flightlevel, *Superconsciousness.* It's all up to you. You're on your own to know, and you're on your own to answer your own questions. You're on your own to be in tune with nature, for there you'll find peace. Peace is a consciousness, it is an attitude—in *FL: SuperC,* you resound with that attitude. This moment that you feel, let it stand for generations to come, and it *will,* for what has been your flight instruction will induce a new age and a new peace and an unforgettable love that hasn't been on this Earth-plane for eons—all because of you.

You are loved, not because of your face, your fame, your money, your no money—those do not matter. You are loved because you are the *common* people, and through that commonness there is the *whole* that is represented. You are loved because your life is touching the world in synchronized harmony. You are important, more than you have ever dreamed.

So what is this adventure called *Destination Freedom* all about? It's about everything that you *feel.* But it is more, because it gives hope to all the rest of the common people.

Destination 9
IN-FLIGHT BRIEFING

2100Z
For Your Eyes Only

Your flight instructor commands, "Try to raise Whidbey."

You punch in Whidbey's frequency, "Whidbey NAS, Blue Seven, do you have us?" Your answer is static.

You punch in an alternate frequency, "Whidbey, Blue Seven, can you fix our location?" You squelch your receiver—*craack, cracklcreees, hisssss.* "No response . . . what happened?"

"I'm not sure," your instructor wonders, "I just smelled something and blacked out for a second, I'm . . . I'm a little dizzy. Or was it a second? I have 2002 Zulu."

You check your watch for Universal Time. "I have 2032 Zulu."

"Wait . . . I think I'm picking something up!" you shout.

". . . craacklehiss . . . squack . . . there . . . craahiss . . . once was a planet, beautiful it was, emerald green in its color, and the other planets smiled upon it. Its hills were filled with green, and its brooks and streams and lakes and dreams were filled with the laughter of lovers and the bright eyes of mysterious things swimming and multiplying and laughing and living."

"What the hell did you pick up—a kid's show?" your instructor questions.

"I don't know. I'll . . . I'll try another frequency."

". . . And then one day a most unusual appearance appeared, a two-legged creature that stood erect . . ."

"Same guy; I'll punch in another frequency," and you bang up your radios hunting for a clear channel.

". . . and looked to the heavens wondering what it was doing here on this most beautiful planet. It walked and wondered, and slept in the grass and ate the mysterious things that were swimming around, and sucked and passed gas to its heart's content."

You tell your instructor, "He's got all the frequencies blocked. Any ideas?"

"Yeah, he sounds like a comedian. I've checked all the systems—they're all green. Let's listen in—what other choice do we have?" You settle into your seat as the voice continues.

177

All the creatures and the rocks and the minerals that were living on this emerald planet before the two-legged creatures appeared just watched them and smiled. And then they moved on, because the place was big and the two-legged creature was small and couldn't move too fast, but had a mouth to form sounds and a brain to think of sounds to form.

As time passed, along with a lot of sucking and passing of gas, another two-legged creature appeared, one with soft and curvaceous body features as compared to his rough and hairy hide. Who would know which appeared first? Since they were each alone, would it matter?

On a blustery, warm afternoon, amid the sounds of the forest crackling in the wind, they saw each other for the first time. They were startled, and the hairy one, thinking it was just another *thing* to eat, took a bite. Well, imagine his surprise! The soft one clobbered him in *his* soft place and she ran off while he limped off in unfamiliar agony.

As the shadows moved across the landscape, they continued to eye each other, peeking out from behind trees and rocks. One day, the soft one, from behind a tree, held out something for the hard one to eat. It was an offering of friendship. The hard one moved forward from behind his rock, and reached for it. It was then that they looked one another in the eye and saw what they were. In fear, the hard one grabbed the fruit and rushed back behind his rock; the soft one giggled. The hard one bit into the fruit. *It is tasty,* he thought. And night fell and the hard one thought about the soft one amid the stars.

Amid their evening with the stars, the hard one decided not to try to eat the soft one; the fruit she offered was tastier anyway. And the soft one, in turn, decided not to clobber the hard one, for as she looked into his eyes she saw herself. To their surprise, the hard one and the soft one found rest and thrill and joy in the comfort of the other. And possibly more significant, they decided to break fast together the next morning! They met at their favorite rock. It had a particularly spectacular view.

Soon, as time and more gas passed, there came along another

one, this time emerging from the contours of the soft one. All three of them were surprised! And the two-legged creatures began to multiply or add on to each other, and they also divided. Soon there were a variety of soft and hard ones, all different sizes, shapes, colors, and purposes. Memories were quickly faded in this place, so they didn't remember that they had emerged from the same source, *were* the same purpose, *are* the same thing. All they saw were differences, and the hard ones began beating on the soft ones, again and again.

The soft ones, like the mysterious things in the streams, simply moved away to other parts because there was still room for everyone, although you could see that if the hard ones kept multiplying there wouldn't be enough room for everyone in some time understanding.

Well, soon that *some time* arrived. It was quite a surprise to everyone, because it seemed that the pretty green pasturelands were now in short supply—there just wouldn't be enough for everyone. Of course, the outside observer could see that the hardest of the hard would *never* have enough, and eventually the soft ones would be crushed against the rocks that they hid behind. The Emerald Planet was starting to look brown.

And then one day, a bold and outrageous two-legged creature appeared. He was a visitor from another time dimension. He had a window into the future and could see things that the other two-legged creatures couldn't see or didn't want to see. He was called *outrageous* because he traveled around from village to rock cluster, talking to the soft ones and *infuriating* the hard ones. I will translate his simple message for you to ponder, and then you can decide if you are a soft one or a hard one. The message begins. . . .

This message you hear today is like a window. All the coverlets have been drawn back so you may see the distant horizon. This message is for one who is mature in spirit. Do you understand that term? The message that you will hear is certainly not for one who hides behind spiritual cloaks, not having the courage to live in real understanding on the Emerald Planet. Rather, such a one lives in the realm of airy-fairy.

The message will impart to you an understanding that is applicable to your *bare* existence. It is certainly not one for children's games, for those hours are over with: 2100 Zulu is just a few ticks of time away.

I am very pleased to see that you have the courage to listen. The *courage to listen* is the desire to gain the knowledge that will provide you the opportunity, through choice, to make the proper decisions that are important to your *life*. Whatever is working with you in your future and even in your Now, is affected by *your* choice.

You won't remember everything you'll hear in this message— you had a tendency to fog out, to fog what you did not want to hear. That is the altered you filtering what is conducive to its inward being. So you will have memory lapses and then, in moments of pure light, you will hear it *all* and will understand it all. This message will impart to you a clear vision of what is coming, not only to what is termed this Emerald Place but inevitably to your own small intimate world.

Everything has already happened, so the question, *What happened?* is really irrelevant, except to curious folks like you. And we are *folks,* all related in the family sense to all that is. *Everything has already happened?* you ask. Yes, everything *is* the future tense, meaning that everything that you see is seen in the light that emanates from what you call the future. The *now* is the light of thought that has manifested into light vibrations and then into mass vibrations, for you to see, touch, feel, smell, and all that, just as this radio message is a message that was created long ago in *my* past, depicting an event that happened in *your* future.

You two *fly-boys* have intercepted the message; you will have a few light-years to play around with it before it reaches the ears of the others on the Emerald World. If you don't understand past, present, and future, just think of them this way: The now is a thought from the light of the future; the past is a thought from the light of the now. Therefore, the future is the thought and the past is the thought; consequently, the *Now* is the *expression* of the thought of the future and the past radiating in light. Therefore, there only is *Now—what you think.* Simple? Simple . . . you'll get it, as your eloquent flight instructor keeps telling you, and you will.

I can hear you musing, "Who is this voice that is speaking to me. I'm already confused over all the other voices in the universe. Now there's a new one who is instructing the flight instructor!" Let us leave it at this—this new, *unfamiliar* voice is *you.* Simple enough? Universe—Uni-verse; one verse. Simple.

Let's get into it, as your flight instructor would say. In order to destroy anything, the *thing* must first be created, wouldn't you say? And if everything is Thought and you can't destroy a thought, what could be destroyed? Nothing . . . good, you're thinking right along with me. Let's look at you for a second. Here you are listening to this radio message. Since you're listening to it, you must be alive in some form or another. And since the future has already happened and since you're still alive, you must have survived whatever—correct! That should relieve your fears—always remember that; you always survive the drama.

Well, what is it you will be living through? If I said, *whatever you want,* you would say I am an extraterrestrial airy-fairy, as the term would have it. Since this is you talking to *you,* I would beware of your judgments on self, because that will create your now moment. If nothing can be destroyed, what can be created? I suppose that is an intriguing question, because if everything *is,* what *isn't,* that it must be created? Nonsense, you say. *Gibberish,* you say. Well, how is it that you can create a building, a temple, a machine that flies in the sky, when before it wasn't there? A good question, I say. What was it that was created? And how is it possible to create it without bricks and mortar; how can you just create it by thinking it into being?

If you can look at things in the vast scope that is properly theirs, you will discover that everything is within you, has always been, and that you will never be without. You can understand this by seeing yourself in the now moment, which is a reflection of the future light. Are your molecules still held together? I assume so. Is your blood still coursing through your veins? Apparently so. Are you inhaling and exhaling, sucking in and passing gas? Traditionally so. Well then, what is there to be worried about? Oh, I see; you want a window out onto the future. You want to know what went on out there that brought you here to the ludicrous state that you are in . . . remember, this is you talking to you.

Are you now prepared to stuff yourself into a pair of speed jeans and grunt yourself into a new cosmic realm where you create what you think? Or are you planning to ease yourself into it, with the grace of a vintage two-winger, as it flutters into a grassy, green pasture on a sunny, summer's day? Shall we look out the window into the future? . . .

The newscasters would say: Words as they were known only imparted realities that were known. Emotions that were not known were crippled by words desperately. But the words that were given in the message had a living fire all their own. They were so intertwined with destiny, they had a revelation. Those words came into being because they simply evoked the inward vision—the Emerald World's people could see what heretofore they had not seen.

And I would say, from the vantage point of my uni-verse: There was much more occurring here than can be put into verbiage, before the end came. There were many levels involved in this demonstrative level called *life* on the emerald green sphere. And many of those levels were beyond words, they could not be uttered. And if they could, you could not understand them, you who are listening to this message. In this message, therefore, you will hear words that really don't matter anymore, because their destiny was chosen. You are just living in the light of that moment, which to you was a future and to them is their past. But to everything that is, it is the now.

So for you to hear these words, they might allow you to change your tomorrow. But most likely they won't, because words most often fall on deaf ears, just as these vibratory radio signals are floating around in the void of space-thought, landing on deaf ears. If you could listen, the words you will hear will allow you to understand what happened then, and perchance keep it from happening to you. Nothing that can be uttered will be held back from you. And that which you will hear, you will react upon it by choice.

Choice—it is very important that you understand my meaning here. Choice is the inalienable right that *every* living and breathing creature in the universe, seen and unseen, possesses. It is the endowment by its creator of free will. *Free will* is the ability to choose, and from that choice instigate cocreation with what is termed the eternal *Is,* the Mother/Father Principle, God Almighty, the All that is the *All,* The Source, the God/Goddess Principle, and Pancakes on Sunday morning.

Free will. It is what sets you apart from the angels, for you embody the mystery of all other life-forms. Free will, choice, and a soul has been breathed into what you are, to evolve through the processes called life. A *choice*—everything that you choose to do, you do. That instrument is called *choice* within the Soul; your *right* to choose, one of the greatest gifts you have. As those who have lost freedom and liberty will weep to you, they have *lost* the right to choose. Up to this point in your time, as it is so termed, your choice can be activated. For those who had smiled with blank faces on the Emerald Planet, their choice was gone.

One choice that always remains is the choice to be in fear. Once *fear* is the choice, all other choices are irrelevant, for fear is that which keeps your guardian at your door, holding you in a holding pattern in life. You can choose to fear or to learn; you can choose to advance according to this knowledge or be weakened by it; you can choose to utilize this message in your life or discard it. It is up to you what you do with what you hear here, for what is given is knowledge as it is seen. This living word would manifest for those on the Emerald Planet, for the living word was already in the throes of manifestation. Many of these things you will hear were already in the processes of happening, and many are yet to unfold from that happening.

Now listeners, the two-legged creatures of the Emerald Planet were very fickle, slippery creatures. They lived by rules of what was called karma, eternal sin, and all those things of limited teaching that belong to *limited* understanding. It would take me a multiple of lifetimes to define what karma and eternal sin are, just as the creatures themselves have been trying to define those terms for thousands and thousands and *thousands* of years. Yet, even though they could never define them, they insisted upon believing in them.

And then there were those who decided, with choice at any one moment, to change their minds, which changed their destinies—as simple as one, two, three. How? Destiny is the *moment,* the *now* as it is seen *now.* And if you can wake up in the bright or misty morn and change the whole attitude of that which you are, when you are no longer a sniveling scaredy-cat and you wake up as brave as a bear with a new innate knowingness, your now, your *destiny,* will change.

All lives, as were theirs, were very flexible, all based on choice. Choice—isn't it grander to *love* than to hate? Isn't it grander to *forgive* than to war? It was all their choice. To talk about the future of those two-legged creatures was simple, because whatever their attitude was collectively, it produced the manifested destiny in each and *everyone's* life.

If you look out your window right now, you will see an ever-changing universe blooming into view, moving eternally forward. For the most part the only things in this ever-changing universe that had not changed were the two-legged creatures. Nature is what is termed the splendor of God evolving, ever changing, ever moving forward, never achieving perfection, for that is what is called a limitation. And yet, in this ever-evolving universe, there is one species that refuses to evolve—the two-legged creatures—because of fear.

In this message, I will address the predictability and the manifested destiny of the two-legged creatures as a whole. This will intimately affect who you are, because the manifested destiny that is predictable will radically change your lifestyle—it is supposed to.

Survival, yes, was a very important subject to the two-legged creatures. In the days that came upon them, it was imperative that those who were on *their* own path, moving forward in alignment with nature, would survive the many things of grim that were to come. All those *adventures* you will learn about in the days to come. This message will allow you the opportunity to survive everything. This message will also give you enlightenment, lifting you out of superstitious fear and dogma that have kept you in ignorance, causing much solicited pain to the two-legged creatures. Those who would survive all things that were coming, were those who were enhanced with knowledge. So let us begin, and shall you listen.

The principal and *only* reason that the two-legged creatures were stuck in their repetitious pattern was that they had altered themselves from what they were. They had created an anti-you, an altered self. It was termed by them the anti-God—something in opposition to what they really were. Since they thought they could never be the *God* image, they functioned in the *anti*-God image, which they constantly repented for and were supposedly forgiven for, but nothing changed on the Emerald Planet.

The anti-God was referred to as the *wickedness* of man, a familiar pattern that *all* two-legged creatures had lived through, birthed since the first of their times began on the Emerald Planet. This unseen, altered form had become the image and identity which was projected and *seen.* Since it was all that was imaged and identified, singularly it alone must be fed—*always,* all ways. It was like a hungry beast that required constant attention, yet there were other beasts that hunted the two-legged creatures.

When the Hard One and the Soft One lived through their altered personalities, they divided their divinity. They took part of their divinity, their anti-you part, and used it to keep their *power up,* the power of saving *face, doing* all the right things, *saying* all the right things, living *all* the rights ways. And yet, the divinity that was suppressed within them was the great You, the God/Source within. *That* would be called the stagnation of the Soul, which never evolved for thousands of seasons. The divinity that was had all gone to keep up the image.

Image. When one lives according to an image, there are certain things one must do to keep the image alive and well. For the two-legged creatures, *certain things* would become the very threat to their own lives! It wasn't so much the soft ones—they owned a certain contentment in just being what they were. It was the hard ones, the strong ones, the ones brutal in manner and speech, who brought barrenness to the Emerald Planet. Have you ever seen two bulls head to head in a pastureland? They may be alone in that pastureland, and the pasture may extend as far as the eye can see. Yet, they square off with each other, head to head, neither giving an inch to the other. Who's pastureland is it? They will fight to the death and then claim it as theirs only.

It was the hard ones who wrought the thrust of change responsible for what occurred in that Emerald World; the famine that occurred, the economic collapse that occurred, the war that ensued. I am going to speak about the hard ones. In your world you would term them man—*men.*

In creating the division from the soft ones—women—it was necessary, eons ago, for a man not to have an association with a woman. Why? God was seen in a masculine image—God *was* a man, his *Son* was a man, and the *Holy* Ghost was also a man, or so it was said. The casual outside observer would consider this quite absurd, for after all, without women, how would the place have been populated? Without the women, none of the men would have been there to make the rules against the women!

From the man's perspective, the *man* was ultimately divine and woman merely there to *serve.* She could only obtain divinity through the *pleading* of her husbandman to higher sources, so they said. In other words, the women were the trash of the street, only respectable if their mates *gave* them the respect through the virtue of *allowing* them to clean out the cave and knit. The women, being soft, really had no choice in the matter, for they were simply slaughtered and flung on dung heaps if they didn't want to clean the cave or knit. So, rather than being food for the night animals, they accepted their distinct characterization of being soulless. Not much *choice,* would you say?

Man, for fear of showing his *woman* side, his feminine side, had to take on certain emotional powers that would allow him an exalting and yet separateness from his women. Consequently, all of the gentler emotions are suppressed in his body. A man could not weep, nor show compassion or tenderness, for if he did he would be considered weak and therefore be considered a woman, who was *certainly* not divine. The man had to be an *achiever,* he *had* to be a winner, could not be a failure. *Failure* was indicative of a woman.

The two-legged creature, man, soon began to realize that it was *his* duty not only to impregnate the women of the Emerald World, but to see to its other affairs, its business of government, laws, and politics. An image began to be created in man—a lust for achievement of self that would drive him to the *ultimate* powerplay.

On this Emerald Planet, *every* generation of the seed, every lifetime that each two-legged creature experienced, further cemented the division of men and women. A casual observer would wonder what happened to love, the freely moving essence that brought these creatures forth in the first moment. Where had love gone? Lost in a song, for man's ultimate achievement was not to love. His ultimate achievement was to have power. Power *empowered* the image he had of himself, giving him credibility, an essence he desperately lacked. That *power* had, in many ways, separated men from their women, even during their mating seasons. And perhaps that separation created even more hatred.

The battle between man and woman became prodigious. They would not share the joy of procreation; mating became a battleground. They could not share equally the earning of a livelihood; men would earn more in the same marketplace as their women. They could not share equally in the governing of their society, for men were the lawmakers and the enforcers of the law. Where woman's ultimate achievement would be to have her perfect man love her, the *perfect* man's ultimate achievement would be business and power, not the love of the woman. You can understand why men took lightly the affairs of their mating seasons, as we shall term them. Fornicating, rolling in the hay, meant *nothing* to them, only a sexual gratification and release—*power,* frustrated power.

As their centuries began to wind on, this spurious image of man became more and more powerful. It was man who was the king and it was *man* who was the warrior. It was man who was the conqueror, who would always create wars with his brothers, often using the excuse that it was the *Will of God.* Why conquer? To appease this unseen, altered *you,* this great image of self that he *had* to live up to. Every lifetime the goal of the male soul would be to achieve power; it wasn't love—love does not belong in the altered self.

What is power? The ability to control, to own others. If you became a conqueror and conquered another conqueror, you had acquired power—or so they thought. But the power was so fleeting, because the populace was so fickle. Soon they forgot that you did anything at the circuses, so the men had to go out and conquer some more. And they had to keep it up to glorify themselves. And that glorification suppressed the natural glory that is within them all, which they never understood.

They were not aware that their altered self stood as a guardian to their soul, their subconscious, not allowing anything in that did not fit *its* image. In other words, for a man to say to himself that he was loved, your altered self would say to that thought, *"Remove yourself,"* and the thought would never reach the soul. In every lifetime, the altered you only lets into the soul that which fits its image. That's why the two-legged creatures had been stumbling in a rut for so long.

These men continued to battle, to form governments and kingdoms, often formed in the name of god—*their* god, whichever god it was. Thus began what was termed the *terror* of country conquering country. Yes, can you imagine, before the end came, a human misery began that went on and on for thirty-five thousand years, and most recently six *thousand* years in their time!

What was most important to the conqueror was that he ransacked his victim's treasury. The conquerors would borrow treasures from all over the Emerald World. From the ancient caches of a race, from the common people who worked hard for their riches, the conquerors would simply loot the prize for display in their own territory. Ancient artifacts of immense *personal* value to citizens of the conquered kingdoms would find themselves sitting in mausoleums, as decorative centerpieces in driveways, in foreign museums of art.

And with such pride the conquerors would tell their children about the long, lost civilizations that they destroyed. And they would look upon their war spoils with great immodesty—"Yes, yes, yes, this was the most important painting of the Mesormoreckians," or whatever citizens of the kingdom had been called. And their patrons would gush, "Oh, isn't that wonderful! It is brilliant! It is a work of art!" Yet no one ever asked, "How was it acquired?"

Stolen treasuries were *revered* as an accomplishment—the looting of an owned, *conquered* kingdom. And the looters were very self-righteous. They went to war, they conquered, they *owned* as if they had a right to what they took. It was nothing to assail a dead king's tomb and take his treasures for the sake of the story, *history,* as it was termed. That was simply the way that it was, as they said, for the sake of all people, to understand their ancestors. Yet, all it really was to the casual observer was the act of robbering, legitimized.

This robbering and looting activity went on for quite a while, as the shadows moved across the land. Those who were called kings were very wealthy. They possessed all the gold they needed to take on any march, to take any stand for any purpose. Those who were less wealthy and, in consequence, less powerful, were in peasantry to the king, compelled to do his bidding, to till his fields, to wage his wars. For their servitude they were exchanged mead and bread, which sustained them. They knew no other way, so they were contented with this meager sustenance.

As the conquered lands grew, the conquered hoards grew. Power was being redefined by the extent of the lands your kingdom controlled. And then power was redefined by the extent of the wealth of the people your kingdom controlled. Your wealth would eventually be defined by product, what your people produced.

The kings took the peasants from their lands, where they were sustaining themselves rather nicely, and brought them into villages and townships. The pirated lands were raped; forests were torn down, and in the place of majestic, great-grandfather trees, grains were planted. The product was sent to the conquering country to feed its hoards and its mobs in the marketplace. Politicians had to keep the mobs happy, *had* to keep their bellies filled, had to keep entertainments in front of them, because it was important to have votes, when elections came into style.

What was the fate of the exotic lands of some of these conquered countries? History would rather not remember. Lands once covered in lush, ancient forests, once fertile with treasures mined carefully so as not to disturb the balance of the soil, were *ravaged* by the conquerors, the so-called Kings, over time. In the days before the end, all you would see were vast wastelands, deserts that were once bountiful, *thriving* forests.

All this raping and pillaging of lands and people went on for quite a while, until there appeared a wondrous man, who would be known as the Little Corporal. Prior to the appearance of this little person there was a group of kings who controlled the Emerald World in the time of the Circuses. In those days it wasn't really necessary to go out and acquire financing for a march—they just simply marched and took what they wanted! But now came along this great little conqueror with dreams of glory and a rhetoric of *Liberté, Égalité, Fraternité,* of succulent vision that would resurrect his country again to its preeminence in the Emerald World.

Yet his little country was bankrupt, because the people, the mobs if you will, overthrew the aristocracy—you may have heard the chop, *chop, chops.* As a result, the commoners rid their country of all noble blood at that time. The mobs had blamed the noblemen for their intense poverty, and they were quite correct.

So the Little Corporal appears, galloping in on his white horse, to lift his beloved country of fragrant vineyards out of the gutter, to set it again in its ancient place of preeminence. And along comes what is termed a dally of an individual, who sees that he can make a tidy return. The little conqueror is financed by this *financier*—he's given a *substantial* loan to go out and conquer, with the understanding that whatever loot he brings back to the Empire will pay back the debt. Now remember, women stayed home and *men* were doing the marching. Well, a few of the *weaklings* stayed behind and took care of the women.

This little Emperor's first conquest gave birth to what will be forever known in all universes, seen and unseen, as *Grayball.* The Gray person who threw the opening pitch of Grayball, from whom the little Emperor secured the gold, started a wonderful system of supplying and financing conquests. It provided his family with a very nice return—it turned out to be a *very* lucrative business: war-making, *Grayball.*

One curve-ball idea that occurred to this early financier was that in order to finance war, he must not swear allegiance to any country, so he didn't—maybe it should be called a screwball instead of a curve. Soon his business began to spread. Grayball playing fields began to sprout up everywhere; others wanted to play. He realized that to be the entrepreneur and to set up financing for anyone else who wanted to make war, not having an allegiance to any country allowed him simply to be there to fulfill the need. The power behind this pitch was that he would collect *much* more from the victor than he could lose from the loser. Screwball.

This first particular Grayman had no woman whom he cared for and loved. His wife did not age handsomely, as the term would have it. But she gave him sons and they quickly learned the skills of Grayball, enhancing it beyond the inventor's wealthiest schemes. This treasure of sons, his divine heritage, this *first team,* would go on, and it did. We could call them the Brothers Grim; you will appreciate my meaning soon.

This man now saw an achievement in his altered self of *ultimate* wealth. *Ultimate,* meaning *all* of it. Now, listen: No one wants money for itself, but rather for what it can do. And to this first Grayman, obtaining wealth was the key that unlocked the door to what is termed power. It wasn't money he passioned for. It was the *power* to fulfill his need, to maintain this image that he held of himself in his altered self. He had never felt the love of a beautiful woman, he never knew the giggles of a precious child, he never understood the simple happiness of the peasants tending their fields. All he knew was the sensuality of *ultimate* power.

This wonderful Grayman soon realized, when one of his investments yielded a massive return, that he could work both sides against the middle, and he did. Soon this man and his sons, the Grayteam, were collecting a nice return from everyone involved in a conflict. They found it to their benefit to *generate* conflicts. The more they could generate conflicts while feeding the altered selves of lusty kings, of lusty conquerors, the more they profited and the more powerful they became. They financed both sides; they ensured that they themselves would always be the winners. Some would say this was smart. Others would say it smelled, of the stench from the battlefield.

One of the sidekicks to all this power was to have the ability to put their sons—the seed of their seed—and the people they owned into very influential offices. In other words, if a rambunctious king were to say, "No thank you, Mr. Grayperson, I'm giving that esteemed position to my third cousin, once removed," then this nice, tidy, little Grayperson would say to the king, "Well, how unfortunate that is, because I really felt that the person I recommended would do a splendid job. And since that can't come to pass, I'm going to have to ask you to pay me everything you owe me, as soon as possible."

And, of course, the king would return to his castle and quickly realize that his kingdom was in foreclosure. He would call his court jesters aside, drink and wench the night away, bite his nails, chew on them, curse, gnash his teeth, and return the next morning to the tidy little Grayperson, bowing profusely and chanting, "Oh, I would *love* to have your person fill this office. What an appropriate appointment that would be. I appreciate your suggestion immensely—how droll of me not to see the brilliance of it right off." The Brothers Grim.

Why was it important to them to place their sons in ultimate positions of control on the playing field? They knew all about the law of returning to embodiment through their offspring— *reincarnation,* I do believe is the term. They *knew* they could return to the Emerald World at any time through the seed of their seed, to reap the rewards of an endeavor started, say, two or three generations before. They knew all about the immutable law of reincarnation, but they weren't telling anyone else about it.

Since the Little Corporal's time, the influx of the Graymen grew and grew, and yet they kept the power within themselves, within their families. They began to set up banks, they began to influence governments, they began to influence the kings of those governments, the so-called leaders of those governments. And those wayward countries who wouldn't play Grayball found their gold cut off; they found themselves alone in the world marketplace, without foreign relations. The casual observer might ask, how could the power be so centralized so efficiently? Everything was starting to move through the power of gold. *Whosoever holdeth and controlleth the gold, was his Nibs!* An old adage.

A great man who was of the lineage of these beginning Grayteam activities inherited this wonderful business plan after the turn into this lost civilization's eighteenth century. (As a side note: They counted time from the appearance of what some of them called their "Lord and Savior," whatever that was.) He continued the plan within his own hands and his family's, and those who were chosen to work with him as his teammates, began to control the continent that they lived on. Every war since the Little Corporal's first was manipulated, set up, and financed by the Grayteam and their families. And if the inkling of war didn't exist, they created it, at any cost. These brothers *are* grim.

Remember, these families had no allegiance to any country. They had no allegiance to any country's laws. And they had no allegiance to any religious belief. They were on their own, which allowed them to pursue their morbid business plans quite nicely. They created dictators out of common people, feeding them through their altered self. They created assassinations. They created what is termed blame, outbreaks of violence, and dissension, all for power—*money,* yes, but the money bought them the power, because every man had his price and every kingdom certainly had its price.

What was the man's name who perpetuated and embellished the plan in their 1800s? He will know it when he listens to this message, for he *will* hear it. Is it important for you to know? Should I shield you from this understanding, or would the knowledge help to protect the Emerald Planet from red cinders of grief? Or perhaps I have already told you the name, and one day you will recognize it. If you recognize it, remember it, because recently it is this *same* family which began the crumbling of the equality of human beings all over the Emerald World.

In the year of *their Lord,* eighteen hundred and fifty-seven, this familial dynasty had placed its members in important positions throughout the continent, in what was known as the New World, and in other places around the *Old* World. These individuals were beholden to or in an alliance with this family. The Grayteam was in full swing. These colleagues were in the positions of governmental and economic decision making worldwide.

In eighteen hundred and fifty-seven, there was a meeting in a place where a big clock chimed in the town, just around the bend. At this place all the wars that would occur on the continent and in the New World were plotted, down to the last war plotted, which was the number two war in their system of counting world conflicts. Yes, as far in advance as one hundred years they were able to plan their activities, for the perpetuation of The Family.

Members of these families are also the same individuals who created a revolution in the New World, a battleground between Northern and Southern brothers and sisters. The Brothers Grim were in a coalition with munitions makers, who *also* had no allegiance to any one country. They *created* this outbreak of war that occurred in the New World. It was manipulated—the North wanted the wealth of the South. The battle cry was not hurled because of the enslavement of the human being. The enslavement was merely an excuse for it. Those who were called *slaves* were already in the process of receiving their freedom, long before this outbreak occurred. The war, which wasn't very civil, was created to control Southern wealth. *Slaves*—what a hideous word!

There lived at this time a tall, thin man who split rails. He was the leader of the New World and he did not relish the split between North and South, nor between slaves and freemen. He was a great King, I wish you to know, and there has not been another like him since that time. He had endeavored since his election to stop buying money from the Old World. He realized that the Old World was in control of the New World through the powerplays of money. He knew also what was being created to set brother against brother, and how they would be duped.

He desperately endeavored to secure for his country and for its people the right to mint their *own* money. And when he had made the decision that his country should print its own money, for the sovereignty of the people, *without* interest, he was done away with posthaste. He posed a threat to what was already a deeply rooted system on the continent; a system that at present was controlling the economies of the Emerald World, and certainly that of this new and raw nation. It was reported that a madman pulled the trigger. It wasn't a madman who destroyed this wonderful man—it was a hired assassin. The money continued to flow to the New World, to be supported by outside interests.

Now, as this message is starting to heat up the airwaves, I desire to bring you to a place in time that they termed the first war. They called it the *Great War*. Perhaps you have heard of that term, the Great War? I do believe they also called it *The War to End All Wars*—it didn't and it wasn't. In any event, this war was created and financed not only by the bankers in the raw New World, but by the bankers who owned buildings near the big clock around the bend, and who also lived in a place where they made cuckoo clocks in the winter because it was very cold.

A *scuffle* was created that would bring forth the proposed taxes that the Grayteam wanted, for they would reap the rewards of that taxation. The deaths were created to *force* a *tax* on the people of the New World. The war was created to get them *involved,* to incite them. It was also *created* to bring the Continent under submission and to extend further the Grayteam's control of money in the New World. And so it went about as planned. *Tax*—another hideous word—to break the back of the mule, to tax its strength and sap its ambition.

I desire you to remember, the banks in this New World, and those near the Big Clock, and indeed those in other countries on the Continent, *supported* this war. How else could it have been waged—who would have financed it? The people of the New World at this time were just discovering freedom, and opportunity, and land. And yes, there were hard times, but they had one grand unseen treasure that caused them to sail away from the Continent in the first place—*freedom!* They could worship according to what they believed, they could live as they *chose* to live, and they were not suppressed by tyrants from their homeland.

The New World was not made up of people with one specific creed; it was the melting pot of the Emerald World. They called it the Land of Milk and Sugar. And there was *freedom*—and everyone was enjoying that freedom immensely. They had just quit a horrible war with an *insidious* enemy who lived on a small island to the south of the Land of Milk and Sugar. The hero of the Sugarland people was a cowboy called Rough Riding Ted. A *cowboy* was a man who rode horses to chase cows. Let me tell you about these Island *mercenaries* he conquered. They were once a great island of grand people; they were not revolutionists, they were meek *farmers*. They had no revolutionary designs and yet, the Sugarland-ers, through their propaganda, were taught about the *enemy* below them and the threat to world peace posed by this small country of *farmers*. *Propaganda*—another hideous word!

Well, it was a wonderful ploy; the munitions people had a hand in that. They were the ones who created it and imported the disputers and the revolutionists—it was staged, like a stage play, though not quite Shakespearean. And so the Land of Milk and Sugar went to war to wipe out the cigar-growing insurgents. Do you know who they slaughtered? Those farmers who didn't know what the big deal was, who had *never* thought about a war, but only their harvest, their children, their love of God, the belief in their Church. They had harmed no one, but they were the insurgents and had to be done away with. That war was created by the Brothers Grim.

Let me tell you about this first *great* war. It took a lot of convincing to entice the Sugarlanders into it, because no one wanted their hands muddied. The Grayteam, owning most of the media, owning what was termed papers to read, told their writers what to write and their editors what to print and what *not* to print. The Grayteam owned the tools of communications, because it was desperately important to have control of what the people read and heard. Only then could the Grayteam control what the people thought. Well, the Grayteam went on and on and *on,* on a Graymedia campaign about the patriotism of the Land of Milk and Sugar. And on and on about those who did *not* see that the banner of liberty should always fly freely; they were to be considered traitors.

There was a very hot political campaign that went on in Sugarland to ensure the people's involvement in the war. There was a little incident that finally broke the camel's back—or was it the mule's? It was a sinking ship that captured the imagination of the Sugarlanders, inciting them to fight for what they thought they were losing, their freedom. They never knew that the passenger ships leaving their shores were already carrying contraband to the Continent. And they never knew who really sunk that ship.

So the Sugarlanders entered into it, dug in and involved themselves in the scuffle. And how brave of all of your sons and, yes, some of your daughters to perish in that war. You sent your children off to war, patting them on their heads and clutching their photographs to your hearts; you sent them to die painfully alone in cold, blood-soaked, and muddy trenches while the economy rose everywhere. The standard of living was raised in Sugarland and everyone was happy, except those who were dying in the trenches, cold and alone.

The battle cry said, *It was a war for liberty, to free the Continent from the menace and scourge the enemy!* What a lark! It wasn't that at all. The *enemy,* in this case, was a people who brewed dark beer on the Continent and danced away their cares all night while banging steins together. The enemy lurks in the shadows.

When it was all over with, not to count the misery of the war dead, the Land of Milk and Sugar had borrowed *enormously* to support its war debt. Therefore, it was subtly suggested that the way to repay the loan would be *again* to tax the people. So the tax was raised *a little bit more.* The Sugarlanders began paying taxes to pay off the loans from the Grayteam for a war that was instigated by the Grayteam. But the Brothers Grim wanted the taxes to go on and on, and on and *on,* because they wanted the people to be indebted to them, as they already were on the Continent. *Ultimate* power—another insidious word.

A lot was in the wind during this time in Sugarland history. Not only was their media owned by the Grayteam, the Sugarlanders were being taxed for a war, never really understanding *why* they had to fight it. They never really understood why their children had to die; they never *really* heard the story, you see. And then along came another king, one who was . . . who had an accident. He didn't want to play ball because *he* did not want to install in Sugarland a national clearinghouse for the money supply. So he had a small accident and soon the Sugarlanders ended up with another leader.

Now, all along, the Graymen really did tell the Sugarlanders who was the best man for the office, the office of leading *their* country. The Grayteam really required the person in office to play ball for them. During the naming of their kings, there were a lot of them who fell by the wayside. And as you would have guessed, a lot of them had been forced out of office by scandal. There was not *one* king forced out of office by scandal, who was not unjustly accused. And all of their kings that have died in office did not die by a madman, but rather because they were supposed to go—they weren't playing Grayball. Their conscience moved in the way, their *patriotism,* their defense of *we the people.* In other words, the

Godfire within them was waking up and saying, "This is not right. In all due conscience, through the mercy of God, I cannot do this."

The Grayteam had offices in various places where they mapped out Grayball strategy. The little matter of a wayward teammate would be brought up at the meeting; the umpire would simply say, "Bench him!" The next ballplayer would be waiting in the dugout for his chance to play and, of course, that person would put on his uniform and play *Grayball.* Everything would continue on, the status quo.

The families of the Graymen, by what was termed nineteen hundred and twenty, had grown to twelve families. They were the individuals that owned the international banks and, literally, the land of the cuckoo-clocks itself. The rules of Grayball they were playing said that gold could no longer be convenient for carrying around. The Grayteam created paper money, rather worthless pieces of paper with colorful ink all over them that all the Sugarlanders began carrying around. To treasure this worthless paper, the Grayteam created a bank in the city where the big clock chimed—they owned that Bank. They created a major so-called *National* Clearinghouse in every major country, in which *they* would print money according to their desire and *their* plans for power.

Does this all sound like a game to you? Well, it was—little pieces of paper could buy the Emerald World! And what was most amazing, all the Sugarlanders bought into it. Finally, in the Land of Milk and Sugar, after a few unfortunate incidents, the National Clearinghouse Act was instigated, drafted, lobbied for, and passed by the Gray Playmates. And what that meant was that the National Clearinghouse could now print money in this country, *paper* money, which was no longer necessarily backed by stockpiled gold reserves. In other words, the paper is worthless!

The Gray Playmates had created a *world* economy based on a *worthless* piece of paper through their manipulative control and their ingenious plan. Not too many years ago, it was against the law for the Sugarlanders to own gold. It all had to be turned back in because gold, you must understand, had always been their bartering power, their *trading* power, for nearly three thousand years. What was the powerplay behind all this? The more that you could strip away the value from any one human being, the more controllable they became. Are you with me, whoever is listening to this?

Soon, for surreptitious purposes, the National Clearinghouse was incorporated and legalized. It printed, *In God We Trust,* all over its paper, just in case anyone asked. It was run by what was termed an appointed director, who was *appointed* by an executive committee, whatever that was, which was appointed by the President, whoever he was, and the President was often *appointed* by the shadows, whoever they were.

Now you have a banking system on the continent that loans the Land of Milk and Sugar money, and yet it does not loan the Sugarlanders *enough* money to pay back the interest on the loan. So, if your overseas goods aren't selling as well as they should, you would never, *ever* be able to pay off the loans, because they are incurring *interest. Interest*—another hideous word!

Because they couldn't pay back their loans, because the interest was eating them up, so to speak, the Sugarlanders started doing strange and wonderful things, such as mortgaging everything, selling things, pieces of their country, possessions and the like, in order to facilitate what was called a National Debt. The National Debt was really a national *disgrace*—imagine bringing a nation of Sugarlanders to their knees with some *worthless* pieces of paper. To show you how ludicrous it was, they were in debt to themselves and the Graymen earned all the interest!

To ensure this debt would be paid off, the income tax was raised *just a little bit more.* And then on a day they called Black Tuesday, everyone lost everything they had in the fall of the Stock Papermarket. The value of their paperstocks plunged frantically, and people plunged out of windows, wiped out . . . *splat.* The plunge was quite wonderful for the Grayteam. The controlling families who had people in important places were given the legal right to buy up powerful, immense wealth at bargain-basement prices— a *fire* sale, I do believe it was called. The fall of the Stock Paper-markets? It was planned as well. Now you're *really* tuned in with me.

As the shadow passed across the land, the Sugarlanders found themselves paying a burdensome, unmerciful tax. They also began to notice that they didn't have much money left over at the end of the week to do with as they pleased. One economic theory would say that they were paying with a dollar whose value they didn't control, and they would never again enjoy a discretionary income.

Their National Clearinghouse was not owned by any of them, it wasn't even owned by their government—it was owned of itself. Sugarland was falling rapidly into debt, and it would soon be running out of sugar. An economic depression was on the land. *Nature had messed everyone up*—so the accusation went—and people were trying to find a way to blast out of a sluggish economy and out of poverty. The Sugarlanders didn't feel so free any more.

So the Grayteam, ever willing to provide ongoing entertainment, created a rather *large* battlefield to play a new inning of Grayball. They would call it *The Day of the Beast*. Actually it wasn't a day of the beast at all. It was simply the further implementation of the Grayteam's plans for the *ultimate* powerplay. The real *great* Beast would make itself known later.

The beast that everyone blamed for the war that ended with a big bang? He would not have been anyone had he not been *financed*. Those who financed the country of the Dark Beer did so playing on the megalomania of the so-called Beast and the megalomania of a country that thought it was the cat's meow—funny term, but you'll understand my meaning. The Grayteam simply *played* on their lust for absolute power, exemplified by their leader who quite frankly, walked very funny, looked a little bit like a goose, and enjoyed wine rather than beer. This megalomania caused the *death,* as they termed it, of fifty *million* Freepeople. The slaughter and stench were unimaginable—what a game Grayball was!

Let me tell you, that limited two-legged creature who they called The Beast, had such a craving for ultimate power that he envisioned himself as *world* emperor. He envisioned himself to be *the* number one person of the entire Emerald World. He was given the strokes by the Grayfolks who supported him. The *Beast* definitely had allegiance to his country, but he also needed a way to continue to confiscate other's wealth. He did so by destroying many very precious Freepeople while ravaging the beauty of their countryside; all in the name of legitimate robbery, you will remember.

I want you to know something. A bank in the city of Tall Buildings in Sugarland helped finance this beast. The banks of the Big Clock financed this beast, though they were at war *with* this beast—funny game, Grayball. The reserves of Sugarland, their nickel, their coal, all things that the Dark Beer country did not possess as natural resources, were *shipped* to them. Any honest historian would have to ask, "Who *did* they import their steel and metal from? Their fuels and technology? How could they create their war machines?" With financing from all the countries that were literally *owned* by the Grayblokes.

All the unsavvy Sugarlanders said in one chorus, after being prompted by the Graymedia, "It is a terrible atrocity that is occurring in this Land of the Dark Beer. I suppose we should get into it," for a beautiful and loving people were being slaughtered because of their religious beliefs, just to stir the fire, heat it up a bit.

And the politicians were wailing, "We cannot let the greatness of Sugarland wane when her very allies are under attack by this monstrous beast!" And, "If we don't do something, we won't be able to suppress the invasion of their way of thinking. We *have* to dive into it to preserve our liberty!" And the bands would play, and the young girls with batons spinning would strut past the grandmothers, and tears would flow, and men would look for their rifles, and young boys would learn how to be men.

Listen, it was a *game*—Grayball, unfortunately *created*. But blessed were the common Sugarlanders who *again* sent their children off to war, to die in blood and pain while the economy rose, and the Freepeople *worldwide* were making more money, and the standard of living was being raised everywhere and everyone was happy. The same old story; how many lives does this cat have?

What plopped the Sugarlanders into *this* battleground? Another sinking ship, and frantic radio rhetoric, and lurid headlines. Black Sunday. And the war was financed, of course, from the west side of the water. And more money was taken from the Sugarlanders to put the war machinery into operation. Taxes were raised, and the National Debt was rising incessantly, as water boils when you heat it, but without limit. And so they battled and fought and maimed and invented more tools of destruction, until someone came up with the big *bang*. The next inning of Grayball was about to begin. Have you ever wondered why the so-called Beast didn't invent the Big Bang? After all, he had all the technology and wizardry and money to do it. And they *were* working on it. Because the game would have been over! The cat's meow, really now.

So the Big Bang bangs, and the Sugarlanders were told *they* won the war. They really didn't win the war. The elite Brothers Grim who instigated the war *still* lived in their wealth and were still running this world. The true conquerors behind the horsemen, the shadows, didn't receive a scratch. And not one of their sons went to war—daughters yes, sons no. Their wealth had increased *enormously* from that action. For you who are listening to know, there would never be a long march again, not in this dark age of the tyrants.

In these dark days the Graybankers had become international. They had loaned to poor, struggling countries, trying to lift them up, to put them in the swing of things—*up* economically, or so it was said. And, of course, the desire of the Poorpeople was to have a Freeocracy. They wanted to live just as the Sugarlanders do! They had a real desire for that; it looked good on the box and in the papers, so they were ripe for revolution. The insurgents, waiting in the dugout, now rush out onto the playing field. Next you bring in a military government from the bullpen. You now have the polarity that you need to keep people at odds with each other— you've heard it; the *right* and the *wrong,* the *way* and the *truth.* Another inning of Grayball is in full swing—fun!

In actuality, the military government would only be on the playing field temporarily. It was only there to feed even further the

Poorpeople's desire for freedom and liberty. From this inning of Grayball, the munitions dealers make chemical factories full of money, the defense departments make aircraft carriers full of money, those that represent the *right* and the *way* make holy temples full of money, for they are the guiding lights, don't you know. Munitions are shipped from all over the Emerald World, even from the Sugarlanders, *of course* in the name of business, to the people who are fighting for their Freeocracy. What a laugh!

Once the scent of *liberty* is on the wind, this poor farmer who once lived in tranquility on his land, who didn't have to pay taxes, who could feed his family, who loved his God and could have his Church, now finds himself working in a fervor, marching in strange streets of strange cities, shouting for *Freeocracy!* He's been duped. He has no idea why he's doing this, because he's been subjected to a social conditioning that has been intentionally created to serve the Grayteam. And, of course, we all know, Freeocracy wins out in the end. And the big, bad military *insurgents* who were infiltrating to enslave the hordes, are whipped to the side, so liberty flies free in the wind again—of course, liberty being symbolized by a woman with a bare bosom. And the Brothers Grim grin again.

What does this Poorworld country need now? You guessed it! It needs substantial *loans* to develop its economy, to make it like the Sugarlanders'. So, the international bankers are *very* happy to give them *billions*—do you know that term? More than a few rolls of it—*billions* of that paper stuff—you know, it would make a nice fire. Why do they lend, knowing full well that those wonderful leaders in power in this new government don't know their hind end from first base? Because they *want* them to squander the money, they *know* they're going to squander it. The Grayteam *knows* they will never, *ever* be able to pay their loans back.

Next inning. Not long after the embassies are built, the banks are *forced* to call their loans. The leader of the Poorpeople who are now quite a bit poorer says, "Well, Mr. Banker, we just don't have any money to make this loan payment," and the international banker smiles, "Sir, that's quite all right, eh, we can work something out here. We will trade off your debt for the rights to all the natural mineral deposits in your country, and all the oil that may be found off your shores or in your country. We know that it isn't worth much, but since we exemplify the word, *nice,* we will be *nice guys* and take that mere pittance in exchange." The leader is elated—"What a deal!" he mumbles, as the Graymate pours him a glass of champagne in a plastic cup that looks like leaded crystal.

That was how Grayball was played, before the end came. Those little, poor, struggling countries weren't countries anymore. They were trying to become a Freeocracy, like Sugarland, but they weren't really countries anymore. They had become part of a borderless system of ownership that was occurring more and more in the Emerald World at that time—a playing field without fences.

How many Poorworld countries had their loans called in before the Voice sounded? Quite a few. You'd be amazed at how quickly the Grayteam gets down to playing Grayball, and how subtle and mechanized the land will become after that. Industry moves in; *things* outside the control of the people take over because *they* have moved in; the proud natives of the land will be swept off their land and herded into the cities. It doesn't matter if the farmers don't farm any longer. It doesn't matter if the rain forest is torn into splinters. It just doesn't matter—developers are moving in, pulverizing the forests, financed by the international bankers, all in the service of an elusively defined illusion called progress.

And the Poorworld people were wondering why they are hungry in the cities. And where is their food marquis, who appears to help sustain them? Riding in on a white horse, I presume.

Soon on the Emerald Planet there were only three countries in the *world* that were not absolutely owned by the Brothers Grim— *absolutely* owned. And even in their case, the Grayteam had control of their currency. Two of those countries were at war. Yet, no one in Sugarland knew or cared about it because they weren't told about it by their media, so it wasn't of much interest. The other country had sort of been forgotten, in a sense; it was very poor and impotent, so nobody wanted it. Everyone else, including the great enemy of Sugarland, the Land of Vodka, was controlled by the Grayteam.

You will find this interesting. In the Land of Vodka, a leader appeared from out of nowhere, spreading the gospel of an idealistic society. He was able, through a revolution, to overthrow their last royal leader, unmercifully murdering all of his family and ridding Vodkaland of every aristocrat, in order to incarnate his idealistic theory of society. The takeover was financed by the same international bankers. Why? To create the stigma of Idealistic Socialism that could be used to brand anyone as an enemy anytime the Grayteam needed an enemy.

Vodkaland possessed the largest gold supply in the Emerald World. It was also ripe for a new form of government, and received it. The *new,* New World Order of the Grayteam would be taken from the writings of a man who was an elitist, who borrowed his ideas from a Philosopher called Socrates. And God knows where Socrates stole his idea from, but the elitist society was refined with every new leader—we'll call it Elitism. A New World Order? What's this all about? Stay tuned in.

Were you to create a new World Order, how would you structure it? Would you create an idealistic governing team to control the world super-efficiently? And I would suppose that the upper echelon of leadership would be composed only of an elite few? And naturally, only those leaders who were *responsible,* wealthy, and powerful enough would control the Emerald World, and the mediocracies, and the animalistic attitudes of the rabble in the streets, as the elitists would identify them. Who then would lead the new World Order?

There is a hint for us to consider, passed down from Vodkaland. Their elitist-revolutionists said that the common people had no intelligence. They also said that the greatest danger to Elitism was a mediocracy, a middle class. Therefore, the Freepeople *had* to be suppressed and controlled. Their schooling and education *had* to be governed. They had to be told what to do and when to do it. Everything would be governed under law—that was the idealistic society: totally controlled, totally efficient.

And oddly enough, all the Grayteam had to do was to keep telling the people of the Emerald World that they *were* free, and they would keep playing their game. You could keep taking away more and more of their freedoms, taxing more and more of their property and income, as long as they had wine, and mead, and pocket change to jangle at the end of the week. They thought they were free, *even* if they had to work their fingers to the bone.

You think this is a comedy? I think it is a tragedy, for that New Order society had been instigated, created, and financed for many levels of purposes, the ultimate being the creation of a new design for this society in just a few years—the New World Order. What was the New World Order? There will be many messages sent to you describing the New World Order. It would be novelized, put into motion picture form, into dramatic plays, songs, and dance, all for the Freepeople to see it, for them to choose.

Do you see why Elitism *had* to be created; do you see why Vodkaland had to exist? Just as, in the smaller countries, revolutions appeared out of nowhere to shake the very foundations of the Peaceful Governments, in order to instill a new World Order, there had to be a polarity that would allow the people to *beg* for leadership, for a change from the fear of the insurgents. If there hadn't been a Land of Vodka, what would the munitions dealers have made those last few years before the Voice came?

If it was not for Vodkaland, who would have been the enemy of Sugarland? That little island of farmers south of its shoreline? Listen, because the Sugarlanders have always felt that their liberty was threatened, they've placed their nose in everyone else's business—they were told to. After all, Elitism from Vodkaland was a threat to Miss Liberty and her bosom—an attempt to get her drunk in order to seduce her, we suppose! All along it had been a manipulation, what was termed a sinister game—Grayball.

Do you think the Freepeople of Vodkaland are ruthless and hard? Do you think they are without souls? Do you think that within them lies no wonderment regarding what created all this? Do you think that when they worked with the simple earth, they didn't wonder at the seasons and at the growth of a single seed into food upon their plates? They were just like the Sugarlanders, for they were children, *gods* of the living force. Why had *they* been afraid of the Sugarlanders? Because *their* media was owned by the Grayteam, and *their* people were told precisely what you elitist pigs are really like! Pigs in a poke.

If it had been up to the Freepeople of Vodkaland, they would have opened their borders to the Sugarlanders long ago. It would have been an exchange of brotherhood and life rather than an unnatural one. Imagine the control, imagine the *control* of one Grayman who could overpower an entire nation of human beings. *Great* altered self!

And I know you will find this hard to believe, but a wall was constructed out of iron to keep a whole *nation* of people contained within it. Would you not say that was the most hideous slap in the face to humanity you have ever heard of, in any dimension or spacetime? I was there just the other day in their present day as they term it. I looked upon it. Imagine—a wall could keep *out* a whole nation of people. Amazing!

How could a wall of wire enmesh and entrap millions of people, you wonder? They were ensnarled in an attitude of subservience that was allowed to flourish in this Emerald World, an attitude that accepted things as they *had* to be. Those people who were wrapped up in the barbed wire lost their freedom. And soon, the Sugarlanders would lose theirs, because the ideals that gave birth to their nation didn't exist anymore—*the land of the free and the home of the brave* did not exist anymore. The fabric of their laws of rights and freedom—*liberty, bared breasts*—was rotted through by the manipulation of the Grayteam, by laws and bylaws and interpretations and rulings and programming and propaganda that simply commandeered the original intent, to lead the country lightyears away from its original purpose and design.

And most important of all, the Sugarlanders had grown fat and lazy on their cans and sweet tooth. How and why? The bodies that they occupied and were continually reborn in, were genetically derived from their forefathers and their foremothers who seeded this great land with the emotional fervor of freedom. These pioneers were not warlords—they wanted to live away from conflict, in what was called peace, to be left alone. Genetically, the

Sugarlanders had a natural inclination not to make war, except on their neighbors, which wasn't really called war but a *domestic dispute*. It was just as brutal.

In any event, the Sugarlanders wanted *freedom*—not an insidious word. But what happened in the Emerald World was that the *definition* of freedom took on a rather obscure meaning. To them freedom was to toil in their fields, to *labor* in their cities, to drink their brew, collect their wages fairly earned, go out and party hearty, and have lunch. Lunch? Why don't they just say, "Let's go eat!" you wonder. *Lunch* was fashionable.

And they had to have entertainment. They sat back and stared into a box that sent them pictures of their whole world. Their whole world *was* this box—it entertained them, it hypnotized them, it controlled their emotions; their whole world was *lived* by this drama. And guess who controlled the box? Grayball was alive and well, being played actively on the box. Since the Sugarlanders were hypnotized and entertained, what did they care who ran their country, as long as they had their wages, their brew, their entertainment, and their days off—paid.

In that peaceful lethargy is secreted the remarkable attitude that was the reason why this country was ruled, why the Emerald World was *run* by tyrants. The people didn't want to be bothered, they didn't want to hear bad news, they didn't want to have to get out and vote—what a nasty thing, it was raining; *the system didn't work anyway!* They didn't want to be bothered by the decision-making process in their country. They would rather play games on shows on the box than *make* the news—you know, smile at the camera and impress your neighbors.

Is it painful to listen to this? It should be—there is a mechanism in everything, seen and unseen, that is triggered by the loss of freedom. That mechanism flutters and patters, and grinds and grates, and hustles and bustles until freedom is returned to it, *real* freedom. In this day and time, the bare-breasted libertarians have, for the most part, been creatures of the past; bare-breastness being deregulated, to allow magazines and moving pictures that teased the population with scandalous entertainments. What do I mean by scandalous entertainments? You weren't *in* if you didn't do it, and you were *out* if you were caught doing it.

This was, indeed, an interesting world to look in on, for every person who stood up off his fat behind and spoke out, endeavoring to enlighten the pacified masses, to help them gain an awareness of the Freepower of the sleeping, dreaming middle class, was ridiculed into nonexistence. And you would think that the Graymedia ridiculed the Freespeakers into nonexistence. They didn't have to. The masses were so pacified by the propaganda, they did it *for* the Grayteam—what a *laugh!*

The sleeping people of Sugarland were doing the work *for* the Graymen; they were fulfilling the plan of the Grayteam's World Order. All the Graymedia had to do was to tell the hypnotized masses via the box or the papers that someone was out of his mind, or that he had committed some *indiscretion* in his gossamer past, and that's all the mesmerized masses needed to laugh the Freespeaker off the podium. The people were hanging themselves.

Let's take a look at this country and its King. The King, who didn't wear a crown, was everything that the Sugarlanders wanted. Thus, he was considered weak by those really in power—he was considered a libertarian. He was figured to be one of what the Sugarlanders idolized in their country, and that was *famous* people. He was ideally placed where he was.

What is a famous person, you ask? That was someone who could walk down a street and people he didn't know the names of would know *his* name. This was very important in this time- and space-frame. Somehow, through a long process of indoctrination, the Sugarlanders looked to these famous people as examples of something missing in them. My understanding of this arcane concept is a bit convoluted, as I'm sure you will understand, because fame, as it was known here, is totally incomprehensible according to any principles of unlimited understanding of which I am aware.

I want you to know something about their king. He was a great man. And there was also another reason why this man was where he was. He was not completely the puppet of those who were anonymous (the faces of the Graymen would *never* appear in the papers, you wouldn't hear anything about them on the box; they remained *totally* anonymous—they chose that, it was the best for business). Their king had within him a great love for God and country and righteousness. What was *God,* you ask? It was an unseen deity that everyone believed in, one that would protect them from burnt lunches and other miserable occurrences which could *ruin their day,* as they called it. God also protected them in their afterlife period, depending upon how much money they invested in their life period for the perpetuation of God's temples. If I appear convoluted here, this is another subject that is *very* arcane to me.

Of course, the Graymen *didn't* believe in God—they simply perpetuated the *belief* in God through the Graymedia so that they could keep everyone in line, so to speak. It was handy for the Grayteam to be able to call upon an unseen deity that would punish the rabble in the streets for any of their thoughts against God and Country and State, and against the *Grayteam.* In accordance with this premise, the Grayteam thought that anyone who believed in God was a superstitious *idiot.* Consequently they also realized that they could utilize that superstition and *their* disbelief to work to their advantage. And they did, grandly, royally, *lavishly!*

This country's King loved God, whatever it was. Their King had a great conscience, for your information. And his understanding of God was a broad stroke, if you will permit me, spreading the colors of all races and creeds across the fertile canvas of the planet. He saw a playful place of joy and love, and children's laughter and dogs barking and chasing sticks, and Sunday picnics near the bandstand, and just plain *down-home* life—that was *God* to him. And ever since this man had been elected to his post, he had prayed every single night for guidance. I know, I've listened.

It was his sincere desire to upgrade his kingdom's war machine, and his desire was righteous. For like the middle-class people—the rabble as the Grayteam would say—he also saw that liberty could be threatened at any time by their mysterious enemies. Therefore, he saw that it was important to build up the strength of his great nation, that it might forever have the armaments to protect its borders, it allies, and its image. The Sugarlanders loved him, and the munitions dealers loved him—he was very naive.

He immediately went to work to reestablish the centurion guards that stood at your door, to keep the mysterious enemy away. It took a lot of cold, hard cash to do that, and the National Clearinghouse was only too willing to lend it—*they* loved him. The munitions makers loved him because he was increasing the number of armaments in this country. And he thought he was doing the right thing, you must understand that.

As his term waned, and he became more aware of what was around him and what was *truly* at work in the Emerald World, the man desperately endeavored to try to change *The Plan*. Still, within his soul, lay an innocent libertarian who was indeed kind and loved his country. Feebly he worked, very diligently endeavoring to keep out foreign investors who were *intentionally* buying up barren farmland in his country, intentionally buying up real estate, intentionally buying up corporations. Why did he try to keep them out? Because the country belonged to the people; not to *other* people, but to *its* people.

And on one dreary, rainy morning, when his full realization came to pass of what *exactly* had been ruling the Emerald World, the King became severely ill. He trusted no one and the Sugarlanders learned that he wouldn't talk to anyone. He couldn't—he had no one to converse with, to whom he could express what he was feeling. He had learned why he was unempowered to make certain decisions. The Brothers Grim.

Even with their faint smiles staring him down, this brave King struggled to bring to the surface, through the Graymedia, the creation of a Sugarlanders' Central Bank. It would be the true bank of the Sugarlanders. He was endeavoring, in his own way, to create his country's own money. It was never as fully investigated as much as his affairs were. And the financial banking wizard that was to help him in this little matter was removed from his post—vaulted, cursed away. The Sugarlanders' Central Bank barely flickered as the vision was laid to rest. Ironically, this King would be one of three who would, in the final analysis, bring about a new Republic in the land. When the end finally came, he would be seen as one of three who had ushered in the new consciousness of unlimited understanding.

In this land they had another game they played, this one with numbers—it was called Votetag. A *vote* was what the Sugarlanders thought gave them participation in their system of government. But somehow they were only allowed to vote for just a few candidates, namely those who the Gray Teammates selected for the posts. So the system, as it was termed, was simply a subterfuge that disguised the Grayteam activities. Whoever the Grayteam tagged as *their* man won the election hands down—*Votetag*. There was a person who came along who was most adept at describing the lay of the land in the written form, in script. Perhaps there was some truth when he wrote, *Politicians aren't born, they are excreted.*

Back to the King, who certainly deserved his post; and perhaps history would remember him as one of the last bastions of freedom that would walk the land. He was endeavoring to hold together from the onslaught of what was bearing down upon his consciousness. He was battling with himself, in the last throes of what was termed *trying to do the right thing,* yet not knowing how to go about it. You can imagine his frustration. He was supposed to be the most powerful man in the Emerald World, yet his hands were tied by the Grayteam, who *owned* the media, who *owned* the centurion guards, who *owned* the King's security force, who *owned* all the money. The King was being thrown screwball after screwball after screwball. No wonder he kept striking out! Perhaps you think this is a fairy tale, this couldn't happen? It did! Yet there is a happy ending to the story. For who's side, you ask?

To try to outsmart the Grayteam, the King desired for the Sugarlander's *In-God-We-Trust* dollar to fall in international value—you remember, the worthless pieces of paper that would make a good fire. It was his hope that the Sugarlanders would not be such a lucrative investment. In the year called nineteen hundred and eighty-seven in their time, in the latter part of the month called January and again in February, there was a meeting of the Grayteam, including their great banker teammates. The heads of all families were present, along with the most powerful delegations from the East. They became more aware of the King's desire, and they began calling in their loans. Hardball.

The Sugarlanders couldn't possibly pay back to the Graymen the debt that was now incurred, that was owed to the National Clearinghouse, which was owned by the Grayteam. Why, the debt had been increasing at the rate of hundreds of millions a minute, as fast as their computers could count it. It was endless debt, owed to the Brothers Grim. Their strategy was to inflate the Sugarlanders' economy through the naiveté of their King, then to pop the balloon, deflating the economy totally, and to scavenge the pieces.

The King squared off against them, and faced them head-on; he was aware of what was occurring. So the Grim ones stated simply what would be called an ultimatum: "Unless you do our bidding by supporting the taxation of your people to render this debt, the moneymakers who have invested heavily in your Stock Papermarket will pull out. We will call all our loans. There will be no more money coming into your country."

What would all that mean? Well, to emphasize their point, the Grayteam gave the Sugarlanders a little taste of it not too long after that meeting. Everyone was playing the Gambling Game in the market that trades paperstock, trades in *rolls* of it. On a day they would call Black Monday, the bottom fell out of it, so to speak. The heavyweights sold and sold and *sold*, and all the lightweights, as they soon found out they were, lost and lost and *lost*. It was the biggest loss *ever* sustained in the Gambling Game. And it was only to show the Sugarlanders that the Grayteam could play hardball if they had to—they flexed their muscles, like little boys on the schoolground.

It only took *one* man, who owned the majority of the paperstocks, to create an absolute crash, and he was one of the people who had threatened the King. The threat sounded a little like this: "You *are* going to pay back these loans. You *are* going to tax your people. You *are* going to cut their wages. You *are* going to put a freeze on purchasing, and your people *will* pay, because if you don't, this is what we *will* do." *Gulp.*

Yet the King was still reticent about tightening the yoke of taxes around the neck of his Sugarlanders—he wasn't budging. Therefore, to press their point further and to scare him out of the batter's box, the Graymedia began a public ridicule campaign. You can imagine what the schoolboys and girls thought about this. Here was supposedly the most respected man in the land being taken to task by the media powerbrokers. Who were those little darlings supposed to believe—their King or the gossip? I suppose they even started taking his pictures off their walls. He was called a lame donkey . . . or was it *duck?* Well, whatever animal it was, he was *openly* made a fool of. And he would learn to duck, because the Grayteam would throw a beanball or two at him . . . *swish, zip,* just to dust him off.

The people who were crafting this Graymedia campaign knew precisely what inning they were playing in. The shadows who were representative of the One World Order were undertaking a very specific party movement. Their siege was in action—the march was on, *no holds barred* and all that. *Duck!* Watch that fastball! *Zip. . . .*

So they took him on, hitting below the belt as they insulted the King, trying to make him look old and decrepit, saying that he couldn't think properly—they were moving in for the kill. Quite to the contrary, he was very wise—the King was holding out. Hurrah for the King! He would not do their bidding, he had burrowed himself completely into his wife's confidence, for he trusted no one, could not talk to anyone, and prayed relentlessly for guidance.

Just to show off how powerful the Grayteam was, and to wake up this wonderful lethargic society that was wallowing in brew and sweets, those who truly controlled the Stock Papermarket did a little number on them. Yes, counted them out. And it was just a little warning, because the Grayteam wanted it to be catastrophic enough so that the public's attention would be centered on their national debt. National Debt—another *insidious* word.

They wound up and threw a dizzy of a pitch—the Stock Paper-market lost a few billion rolls of paper, and everyone panicked for a few days, wallowing in it. The Sugarlanders shouted in the streets,

"Our National Debt is too high. That's the reason the market came tumbling down!" That was *not* the reason why Humpty Dumpty fell off the wall—it was *supposed* to go down. It was perpetrated as just another inning of Grayball.

What do the Graymen care how much *you* lost? They're the ones who printed the money. They don't care if the Sugarlanders' life savings were tied up in penny stocks, or Collective Funds or the XYZ Corporation. Do you think the Graymen are concerned if you lose everything in a wisp of time? No, not at all. Perhaps it's worth a few chuckles over a snifter after dinner on the veranda. They are elitists—they just print more money for themselves. What a game! Are you sure you want to play? Sounds to me like the odds are against you.

On with this grim fairy tale. The Grayteam continued playing Grayball, trying to prove to the masses who were staring into their boxes that everyone had better wake up and do something about this National Debt problem. Why? Because your country is *bankrupt*—the respectable International Bankers are moving in to call their loans. Why do they want to call their loans? Because your country is so shaky, even foreign investors are backing off. So all the people who were playing the papermarket were looking at your King and saying, "Please do something about this national tragedy, posthaste! *I'm* losing money. We *have* to raise taxes to pay down this debt, to prove our country trustworthy again to foreign investors." What a wonderfully strategic manner in which to place in motion what the Grayteam wanted. It was a good pitch.

In order to protect their investments—the investments that were inflated surreptitiously—the Sugarlanders were willing to take on more taxes to pay back a National Debt that would *never* be paid back. And their King, having no one to talk to, feeling *all* the pressure from those who were around him, and discovering almost by mistake the true powerbrokers in the Emerald World, walked around mumbling—"God help us . . . God help us." Wouldn't you, if *you* were being pressed by the Graymedia, that was telling the Sugarlanders and all the Emerald World that *all* this economic disaster was *your* fault? After all, it was "because of the Sugarlanders' *greedy* spending, their National Debt, that was causing the whole *world's* economy to be shaky.''

There were not many countries that were very happy with the Sugarlanders and their economic state during the time who's history I am recounting. What do you think the other countries thought about them? Just what they were told to think. And, sure enough, the King, eventually buckling under the ferocious focus against him announced, ''I will talk about this. Indeed, we will consider this, raising the taxes.''

He did not want to, but they were pressing him hard. And in the top of the eighth inning, the beloved Sugarlanders were to have *unmerciful* taxes placed upon them. The taxes were to serve a dual purpose. Not only would they repay the heinous debt, but they would also thwart power uprisings, for the harder the Sugarlanders had to work, the less chance there was of an uprising. They would be too exhausted to fight.

And the sad Sugarlanders would soon discover that their living standard would not rise anymore. The income-producing status of their labor would no longer be able to increase their wages. They would stagnate at the same level of buying power, year after year after year, a little like slaves. And all the wondrous old Sugarlanders, who had been storing away money in the government—rather, I should say that the government was *taking* it from them—under the guise that they would have a place to live in grace in their later years, would find that their social system of retirement savings was bankrupt as well.

Bankrupt—a very interesting term, I must say! The farmers in Sugarland would continue to be forced into bankruptcy. The middle class, those who supported the elite, and the rabble in the streets, would now take on a further *burdensome* tax, in order to take care of everyone—*everyone!* And that was part of a strategy to break the power momentum potentiality in Sugarland, because the harder you have to work and the lower your buying power, the more docile you're going to become, into the One World Order.

A few years back in the past, before this time, a King was brought to his knees and forced to abdicate his post. There was a tremendous scandal and hullabaloo, all centering around a watering hole near the gateway to this nation's capital. Well, I'll have you know that this disgraced King was guilty of nothing except his own naiveté also. Toward the end of his reign, he endeavored to continue to base the Sugarland's economy on the gold standard. He knew all about the oil prices that were fixed. He knew all about everything that was going on and tried to bring it to public notice. Well, he did achieve public notice, all right. Those who had supported him turned on him; they set him up—for what crime, in truth, did he commit? They struck him out—two fast balls and a roundhouse curve.

You—you who are listening to this message, I haven't painted a very pretty picture of these times for you. And I would be much happier cavorting with you about other celestial stuff, of the Celestial Rainbow within you and all those wonderful things that are at the apex of the human experience.

The Emerald World's *Free*people were not living in the Age of Enlightenment, although some thought they were. They were living in the Age of Tyrants, and had been for nigh a long time. The Grayteam owned the Emerald World. They did not see the Emerald World as being composed of individual freeocracies, and they did not see the countries as *individual* countries—they saw the world without borders. Laws didn't matter to them, because the Grayteam influenced the law; they *were* the law. They *owned* the world, because they controlled the money that ran the Emerald World.

And the land of the free and the home of the brave? It wasn't so free, nor so brave anymore. No one stood up with the backbone and the fervor of libertarians past, to bare their chest and say, *enough!* For what was thirteen families and international bankers against a whole nation of pissed-off people? I borrowed the term because I thought that you would perchance understand it. *Pissed-off*, it means . . . it means, what does it mean?

Why didn't they march? Most of them could not conceive of living without money. Most of them thought of sovereignty only within the limits of their boxed-in freedom of choice. They thought that certain things, such as bearing up under the yoke of unmerciful taxation, increasing indebtedness, lower wages, the tighter yoke—like chickens crammed in the coop—seemed to be normal in life. After all, what else had they ever known? It was accepted, so it was exempt from the challenge of the word *sovereignty*.

Sovereignty—not such a bad word, for sovereignty is absolute liberty from any and all things that own you. There were sovereign people in Sugarland—yes, there were. They had created a life from the land that nurtured them, yet they were really *free* people. Of course, they did not live in style, as it was termed. They did not have personal transportation machines, necessarily. They did not have cloth of silver and gold. They did not have what were termed Persian carpets upon their floors, and they did not eat from silver dishes. But they were *free,* for they earned no income, and survived on what their land produced. They bartered and traded; they had been that way for quite a while. Of course, the Graymedia made fun of them as ignorant people, to be avoided—the meek who wore out-of-style clothes and washed them in a creek.

But for the most part the *Unfree*people of the Land of the Brave could not live without their burgers—ground-up animal flesh that was cooked, seasoned, and eaten for sustenance. They could not conceive of *not* doing business without the bank. They could not conceive of purchasing without the card, because it was chic, it was *in*. The card was about the size of a small, flat rock, and it was offered in exchange for goods and services. The purchase was accounted for by the shop owner or the service giver, and soon further debit markers were exchanged through the bank to honor the debt created—all for convenience and style.

Whose side are you rooting for, the Grayteam's or the Sugarlanders'? If their King could only have the courage to hold out, against all the odds—but would *you* wish to be in his position in the top of the ninth? A hot seat, indeed! You have to try to understand that the people in his country did not know what was going on. They only knew what the pretty faces in the box told them. If their King could have held out, the Grayteam would have declared *war* on this country. The market of paperstock would have been ruined the *very* next day, because *they* controlled its flux. The Grayteam would have pulled out *all* their money from the Sugarland government, and they would have called *all* their loans. For what good is a loan? It is only paper, yes, *paper* dollars—a little like paper dollies.

If the Grayteam had pulled out, the Sugarlanders would have been put into the severest depression they had ever known. And yet, a *total* collapse would have been the grandest opportunity to be freed from the tyrants that controlled and ruled their very lives. For how *will* you stop their rule of the lives of your children, and your children's children? When will freedom declare itself?

As it was seen in this hour, the Sugarlanders were to be taxed unmercifully. And their incomes were to be frozen or lessened. And they would be put painfully under the yoke to take care of a scandalous debt that would *never* be taken care of. That was how it was, before the end came.

What was the aim of the Graymen? Why did they play Grayball? What was it they *wanted?* Wasn't it enough that they owned all the paper money in the Emerald World? Wasn't that enough? Wasn't it enough that they controlled the companies that owned all the black gold in the Emerald World? Do you think the people who wore cloth on their heads owned the black gold? No, they were naive nomads who took out *loans* to develop their oil fields. They owned hot, blowing sand.

Didn't the Graymen have enough? What more could they want? They were destroying the rain forest to create inexpensive housing. Trees that took millenniums to grow, that make oxygen to breathe, were being savaged at the rate of five *thousand* acres a day. Gargantuan, hideous machines were ripping and tearing, and crunching and grinding them into pulp. Could you guess why the rain forest was being destroyed in the Southern Hemisphere of the Emerald World? It was the real estate wheeler-dealers and the bankers and the developers that were financing the clearing of those jungles. Do you think they cared that they were destroying the possibility for atmosphere? They didn't care. It was for greed that leads to power.

What was it they wanted? They wanted absolute power. And absolute power meant taking their ideal of a One World Order to the max. It had changed names from the *Master Race,* but what would a One World Order truly mean? That the whole world, with invisible borders, would be run under the system of what was termed social elitism—the elite would rule them all. To make this more vivid to you, imagine a chicken coop, you being the chickens. The Graymen own and operate the coops. And you just sit there laying your eggs.

What would be the selling point behind this new One World Order? The governing idea was that there would be no more wars. The Graymen would tell all the world's peoples that with One World Government, everyone would be equal. There would be no more enemies—as if there ever were any in the first place. *Yes, they would smile to them through the pretty faces on the box, it would be a world of equality!* All except for the elite, that is, for they would rule all from behind the screens, all the chicks in the coops. And they would tell them, *Humanity will progress without revolution, without war, without pestilence, under a new aristocracy that will proclaim freedom for all!* Sounds like an old soapbox orator I once knew.

In other words, the middle classes of Sugarland, and the races who lived in far-off places, would *indeed* become slaves. And many of them deserved slavery, because they had created the vacuum in which it could occur. They wanted to be told what to do; they wanted someone to make decisions for them; they didn't want to be bothered; they wanted someone to tell them what was going to go on the next day, because they didn't want to be bothered. That is a One World Order—chickens pecking around in a coop.

And of course, a One World Order could only emerge magically if there was *one* World Bank. And if there was one World Bank, why bother with rupees and yen, and markers and dollars. *Why do we have to worry about the flux of the economy?* they would shout at them through the box. *Well, we had to up until this point, but we don't need to any longer. We will issue, rather than the printed paper, a universal card. We will call it the Debit Card.*

Yes, well, you can take this little card and go anywhere in the Emerald World, they would smile at them through the box, singing songs and sipping colorful drinks with hula girls swaying in the background. *Punch in any place you want to punch in.* And everyone took it; who would want to miss a hula?

So the box sold them on the little card, telling them all about it. But there was a little problem with this card—one *small* problem. Everyone who took the card received a number, almost like a tattoo on the back of their wrists. And everything they purchased was known, everywhere they went they were known, *everything* they did was known. At last, they were famous!

Privacy was a glimmer in the past, because without this card, you couldn't purchase or *sell* anything. The common exchange of dollars and markers and yen and gold was done away with. And *everyone* will have a number, and it will be *their* number until the end of their life. And everyone who has this number will have a file. And anyone who steps out of line will be rendered neutral. Neutral, dispassionate, lobotomized, impartial, disinterested; neutral . . . or was it, neutered?

Let's say you go shopping cardless in this card-laden society. At the market you lay down your dollars for bread. They look at your green stuff with contempt, scowling, "We do not take dollars any longer, we only take your card." So you walk to the next baker, all the while smelling the miraculous scent of freshly baked French bread, and the next baker tells you the same thing. And you spend your whole day looking for a loaf of bread, which no one will sell to you, because your dollar is worth *nothing*. So they would go home without bread, for they didn't raise gardens and preserve food. After all, they were *cosmopolitan* Sugarlanders. The only way they could eat the French bread piping hot, dripping in pure, farm butter, was to display the card, or befriend a farmer.

In the card-laden society, your taxation was taken care of, *automatically*—you had nothing to say about it. Your bank accounts and store accounts were taken care of, *automatically*—you had nothing to say about it. And you would never see any payment in exchange for your labor, because the value of your labor was sent electronically from your employer *directly* to your central clearinghouse, your bank. Nobody handed you a paycheck any more. The credits just appeared miraculously.

And every item that you purchased was taken out of your earnings *automatically*—you had nothing to say about it. This was already happening, all around them. And they just nodded and said, "Sounds good, give me the card. It makes me feel important and valuable and wealthy. And it's convenient. I'll take the gold one so that I can think I am *rich.*" And they nodded very dramatically and aristocratically and said, *charge it!* And all the while, those watching behind the screens were just laughing at them. Our favorite casual observer would think this would force the Sugarlanders to resort to computer hacking, for if one could access the mainframe, anything was possible. Instant billionaires!

The Card was sold through great commercials that shimmered on the box, like a crier in the marketplace. Everything was being programmed to be charged on The Card. You could even purchase a home on the card—just charge a home, take two. Charge this, charge that—everything was charged. It was a way to increase the Sugarlanders' awareness of the card slowly—the *ultimate* card, the Debit Card. So they were selling them the way they've always sold things, whether it was a politician or cornflakes, whether it was the idea that they should dive into a war or pass a certain bill. They had always *sold* them, through the papers or through the box. . . . *The ultimate card will render all those things taken care of,* the beautiful faces would smile.

And the amazing intrigue, which was already occurring, was so effective that the majority of those who did business with their banks were *already* wielding the Debit Card. It was just called something else. Those who were infatuated with this card, living off of it, would soon be switched over subtly to *The Card.* And from then on, their life would be automatic.

Yes, the Debit Card's propaganda had already started. Yet there was another little item on the agenda that must come to pass before The Card could be truly implemented. The next inning of Grayball was, in essence, the destruction of the Stock Papermarket.

Hideous, you say? Hardly. Part of The Plan, on schedule. The top of the ninth. The *squeeze* play. Because the Stock Papermarket affected *all* markets, its destruction would automatically signal the glide into the new form of government, the One World Order. For if the Emerald World's economy was an absolute shambles, what would be the choice other than to take *The Card?* Charge a country? Possibly.

When did the total collapse begin? In the month called May the Stock Papermarket began to fall into ruins. What had occurred in just a few moments in time previously, that day the bottom dropped out of the market, was just a lesson aimed at the Sugarland government. It was a wake-up call to the people urging them to start pointing a finger at the *disgraceful* National Debt. It was comical how quickly brotherhood and patriotism flew out the window when it came to the issue of money. At such a time there *are* no brothers; brotherhood is in shambles. And then people can become very hostile before *they* start flying out the window—it had happened before in their economy on a day they called Black Tuesday. Black Monday, Black Tuesday. I wonder what would happen on Black Wednesday?

At the end of what they termed their '80s, the One World Order was in place in various levels throughout the Emerald World. It was the altered self of man, that image, in full bloom. I refer to it as an anti-you, for it truly does not emanate from what was termed the *divineness* within the human being, that righteousness and glory that is within the great self. This thrust was emerging from an image that the horde, the masses, through their evolution of lifetime after lifetime after lifetime, were forced to live up to. That image in repetition always suppressed the divine aspect, which would have allowed the evolution of the human spirit, which would have allowed the manifest destiny of the celestial rainbow to occur in precious man and woman. And in precious child.

Wickedness—there were those in the Emerald World who did believe in what they termed devils and Satan and other bogeymen. But our friend, the casual observer, would know that there were no such demons, only the residue of fear called *wickedness*. Wickedness was by *choice* merely a process of good or bad, expressed in the form of an altered self. Wickedness as it was known here was a natural, emotional state in an altered self.

Now this wickedness—we are not talking about crimes against the state; we are talking about simple crimes that are one and the same, against self and self's reflection upon its neighbor. The altered self *chooses* tyranny and also chooses its victimization. Wickedness lies *by choice* in the image of man and woman for, by choice, they could love rather than hate, by *choice* they could be tolerant rather than intolerant, by choice they could engender what is termed the gentility of the spirit, rather than the unmercifulness of the spirit.

By choice they could *allow* rather than make war. And by choice they chose, inevitably, how they would live in manifested destiny. Wickedness was a choice of each individual; for whether it was through the suppression of one's neighbor, one's lover, what was termed one's husbandman, indeed one's wife, or one's children, to suppress *another* under the guise and aims of your own image *is* a tyranny. And that indeed in the image of the altered self is wickedness. When it happens on a worldwide scale, it is also wicked, by *choice*. The Brothers Grim were in the process of throwing some deceitfully wicked curves. Was there someone on a white horse awaiting in the dugout?

The altered self of a man is very different from his soul/spirit reflection within. Conscience, the *feeling* of righteousness, the feeling termed love, allowance, nurturing, compassion, and tenderness is all within the soul. All those *bountiful* emotions of self-nurturing are suppressed for the glory of the altered self. There was not one Grayman who was not endowed with the God Essence within him— he was not wicked in his soul. His handmaidens—they were not wicked in their souls. They were, by choice, facilitating their image and the lust for power that was the apex of their altered self. It is endless. Frustrating. Grim.

It was not enough that the Grays owned the Emerald World's gold. It was not *enough* that they owned all the fossil fuels under the earth. It was not enough that they destroyed the rain forest for development. It was not enough that they pitted brother against brother for the purposes of greed and lusty, breathless power. But the ultimate ejaculation of ecstasy for their image was to *own* the Emerald World—to be *The Sovereign*. One would, and then wish he hadn't. Aren't you intrigued by all this?

These Graypeople were driven by their heritage. They *had* to fulfill their aims and goals, otherwise they couldn't live. They had birthed themselves in the Emerald World to own it—to them it was *their* world. Literally, their goals were no different from those of the masses they enslaved. Yours are for sovereignty; theirs was for absolute power—the same energy. They *have* to fulfill their visions. It is their destiny—*destiny!* The altered self's ultimate orgasm is *power.* And greed—*greed*—is the way you grab it, grasp it, clench it in your fist. A poor man can soon buy his respect in the twinkling of an eye when he becomes an heir. A rich man can lose everything he thinks he is in the blink of an eye, or a twist of fate.

These Graypeople were forced into this. They hated one another because one of them was that which all of them wanted to be, was number one—Ishna (my term). They *all* wanted to be Number One, so they hated one another and they had violent wars among themselves. And often thousands of Grayteammates died playing over a dispute—they did not care. But *who* was *the* Grayman?

These Graypeople are nearing their ultimate victory march. They have succeeded in their plan, their *long*-range plan, up until this hour. And anyone who stood in their way, they did away with—threw them a beanball, erased them out of the picture. The Grays are aligned and they are obsessed with their goals. What happened? What saved the day for the peaceful ones, the children of the truth—the girls with flowers in their hair, the boys with bright eyes and bushy tails?

The only phenomenon in manifested destiny that would intercede, the only event that could keep the destiny of the Grays from manifesting, was *knowledge*—the Sugarlanders had to *wake up!* There was a prophecy in what they called their Book of Books, in the one book that wasn't tampered with, Revelation—appropriate term. A visionary prophesied in depth about the last days—all the hideous things that would ooze their way to the surface to horrify. Well, if you were what was termed John of Old, and an angel manifested a vision of a computer, a very *giant* computer, blinking at you—humming, wheeling, turning, churning, ominous—and you'd never seen one of these before, wouldn't you rather refer to it as a beast? Yes, of course you would.

This John saw, through a vision of *actual* manifested destiny, what was termed the climax of the very times these people lived in. The Beast fed on a number. The number was *666*. The first *six* meaning the number of man. The second *six* meaning the number of woman. The third *six* meaning the number of child. And what was termed the mark *666* meant a tally of gold. The embossment of the Mark of the Beast means, the beast is embossing the *666* on you through a tally of gold. The preciousness of man, woman, and child would be exchanged for a tally of gold. Embossing . . . a bit like a tattoo on a wrist. Do you remember the imagery?

Those who would take The Card and receive their number, they would be *owned*. They would have given up and allied themselves with the beast. Their bare-bosom liberties and their sunny-day freedoms would be in the ruffian hands of their atheistic, rapist controllers. What happened? When the vacuum became so severe, they had to give up absolute choice and freedom, and then the vacuum collapsed. They were sucked into slavery, not black-skinned slavery but white-collar slavery. The enforcing law of that collapse was *change,* and those who took the card will be changed.

What happened to the inalienable law of The Source when the vacuum of *choice* and *life* no longer existed? And what happened to the glorified human being when its innate, divine right of choice was no longer available? That which was coming, to the horror of all who could think, would deny them the right of absolute choice in freedom. What they had created was an ending of time. Yes, the time flow, life *rolling* forward in freedom, in choice, stopped. Everything that was needed for their immortal souls to evolve, to become broader, immaculate human beings until they have lived as the Light of the Source, stopped. Dead. Grim.

Their destiny was by choice. Their slavery was by *choice,* for it took guts to change. It takes *guts* to go forward into the unknown for the adventure, the game, the *fun* of it. And only in the unknown does one embrace what is termed evolution, indeed *change,* for one cannot evolve without changing. And change is always by choice, by options. That is *natural.* Yes, nature—the all within the all. But when *the choice* no longer exists, when the species is controlled to such an extent that it can no longer evolve, then life as you know it, which *was* the glory of the Godfire evolving as you have expressed it, comes to an end, pure and simple. Full stop. The End of Time. Game called on account of having no options. Stopped. Period!

Why does time stop? What is the purpose of The Source's manifestation in human flesh if it neither toils, nor spins yarn from the backs and bellies of sheep? And what indeed is the use of an anvil on which one could hammer out a horseshoe, a plow that could cut a furrow? What is the use of land and the harvest when there is no freedom to enjoy it. And what is the use of the laughter of children if they will soon be put to the yoke?

There *was* no purpose, no reason for life. What could the purpose be if freedom of choice was collapsed? There was no use for any of it. Time had stopped. It was the bottom of the ninth. And in that moment, they all will hear a great voice echoed from the furthermost star, that emanates through all things that are alive and living. And the voice will roar, "It is *finished!*" And in the reverberation of that voice, before the echo has died out in the universe, will begin Superconsciousness.

. . . *craacklehiss . . . squack . . .* there . . . *craahiss* . . . once was a planet, beautiful it was, emerald green in its color, and the other planets smiled upon it. Its hills were filled with green, and its brooks and streams and lakes and dreams were filled with the laughter of lovers and the bright eyes of mysterious things swimming and multiplying and laughing and living. . . .

The Time: 2100Z
Welcome to Brief 2

To open this brief I want to state conclusively that the time is *now* to reinvigorate the consciousness of Planet Earth, your *ultimate* touchdown point. If it isn't reinvigorated soon, where will you land? Those of you pilots who are attending this brief will be the ones who begin and perpetuate this invigoration.

This is not a war that you will be waging—no one *ever* wins a war, not even the victor. What you will be *waging* is a lifting of the veil of illusion that has hidden from the children what they are, and each of *you* are one of the children. Since you have acquired some skills as aviators, you will be piloting yourself out of the illusion into *Destination Freedom*. In the process, you will lift the veil of illusion for others by being an example, *not* by being a tyrant or a soapbox orator. When everyone *knows* what they are, the consciousness *will* be raised, aye!

The purpose of this Brief, then, is to conquer fear. Let's get into it! You are living, not in turbulent times, but perhaps the grandest times of all. You are nearing the epic age of the times of man. Do you wish to be briefed on the most daring and inconceivable mission?

FRGB CANDIDATES: Yes

FLIGHT INSTRUCTOR: [looking at one candidate] Ask your question.

FRGB CANDIDATE: You have briefed us in your previous book, *Voyage to the New World,* about the Twelve Days of Light. In order to understand its full significance, would you be more explicit as to what is actually going to happen? Are you briefing us for a battle that will take place in the heavens? If so, what are our mission orders? What activities should we be cognizant of?

FLIGHT INSTRUCTOR: You should be aware of activities at many flightlevels. The majority of you will be frightened to death, which is the object of the war.

FRGB CANDIDATE: Do I interpret that to mean that vast segments of the populace will perish?

FLIGHT INSTRUCTOR: If you're frightened to death you will. What else could it mean? [long pause]

Listen very closely to these words. Many just scan my words or listen to bits and pieces from a media presentation of some sort. Listen and *feel* every word in your being so you can interpret them within *your* knowingness.

I have told you all that you are very important, almost to the point of nausea, yours and mine. Most of you do not hear so well, because I have also taught you that the rest of the world does not care if *you* suffer, and they do not really care what you're doing, as long as it does not interfere with what *they're* doing—that is a truth. But tyrants are created because they have a *need* to be powerful, to *exhibit* that power. But they must have something in which to exhibit it—that is why you're important.

Follow me as we take a little time-travel excursion. See if these words jog your Soul memory. There are many ladies and gentlemen in this ready-room, and many people everywhere, who once were under the rule of and imprisoned by a great God; a great and *terrible* God of Wrath. He even admitted He was such and reminded His people daily that He was such, not only through the prophets from the windy deserts but also through absolute demonstration of that power—it was He who destroyed a great city that flourished near the sea, which is now known as "dead."

In order to assure that he was served, so he could exhibit his power, he begat in the world a people of servitude just to acknowledge his greatness. This cadre of worshipers was necessary, because there were others who wouldn't worship this great God and He rid the land of them.

As pilots you are familiar with cause-and-effect relationships—for every cause, so to speak, there is an effect. In order to support this great God's cause, religion was born as the "effect." The effect of religion on this land has been appalling. It has belittled man by taking the God out of him, putting it in the hands of tyrants and despots who have ruled, separated, and warred over the lives of children for eons now.

The majority who listen to these briefings do not believe they are God, so to bring truth here to reverse the roles of continuous programming has been a great undertaking on my part. Due to the *continuous* programming, they are too embroiled in their insecurities and their securities of unhappiness and fame and fortune and all that. They are those who fall prey to a great and terrible God and serve him idealistically, because He will give them a purpose to be—to serve *Him*.

There are those of you who have been *really* reading these words that my scribe has formulated and put to print in this flight-log. Those of you, then, will know how to escape the grasp of this God's truth. Why do you need to know the escape route? Let me take you a flightlevel deeper into this intrigue.

This God is returning from beyond a place called the Pleiades, from a pit that was called the Bottomless Pit—it is called a *black hole* in your understanding. Yet, let's look beyond the perimeter of the black whole. There you will see that it is really a universe whose gravitational pull has become so great, that all the light is being pulled into the core of a single structure. In what is seemingly nothing but blackness, beyond time in the depths inside its perimeter, is a whole civilization of great, *great* intellect.

And so, from the bottomless pit comes forth the great God of Wrath. This God has left this Earth-plane of dimension as He promised, for two thousand years, and He is fulfilling His promise by returning to it. And He has promised to sit upon Sinai and to cleave it in two, and to melt it so that the meltings of it fall onto the plane of Charon, and to develop his kingdom and to devise means for it to move the earth. That is a truth. This great God's prize is the spoils of His teachings, the seeds of His truth that are still here. They are propagated genetically—their truth—very well.

231

And yet what do they become? They are not sovereigns but an enslaved people.

I am a *lover* of you; *all* of you, and all of these enslaved peoples. And as for my legions, they are great; and as for the two great Gods of Mercy that I parley with, they are great in their legions. And what was allowed before shan't be allowed again because you were too ignorant to know better.

In these communications, because I love you greatly, I am endeavoring to teach you of the holiness and sovereignty of you, who *also* are Gods, but who, through cleverly devised processes have been brainwashed and Soulwashed into believing that you are mere instinctual human beings who grovel in the marketplace and become the rabble of rejection and denial.

The Escape Route

The secret of your flightplan of escape lies in your brain—the two-thirds that you were born with, yet which is now dormant, just filling up your skull and holding your hairdo up. Therein is contained the whole unlimited adventure that you are. You use so minute a part of that organ, and yet it had the capacity to be the genius that created all the stars and spewed forth all matter into the universe.

Your brain has the ability to raise the vibratory rate of your body and zap you into another dimension in a flash, and yet look how far you have come in the limitation of the mind—you spend a good part of your existence just battling with gravity, lugging your body around from here to there!

Your brain has been used as a receiver, to teach out of you the God that you *are,* within. This brainwashing has been accomplished by the Deceiver on this plane, as he is called—he has done so openly and acceptably well. Yet, within your brain, as it is powered by your autopilot-Soul, exists the courage to expand into the dimensions of beyond. The courage that is the freedom of hope is hidden there, just waiting to be fired up for blast-off. What are you waiting on? The final destination is near—one day you will turn around and it will be here.

Break Out of the Fear

Why are you so important? Why is what we teach lawless? To entice your mind to open up and return to the memory of one in one—the power of each Godfire Being to be equal to the power of all that is; to break you out of fear. In the days that I marched in your dimension, I was a conqueror. I know what it is to conquer a people who will not fight back. What have I won? Nothing. But if you can know implicitly that you are God and become fearless, and then *love* the fire that is within you and all things—the God *force* that flows through—you shan't be the spoils of war; you will be the Gods that are in control of your destiny.

How far have you flown into *Destination Freedom?* If we ran a sword through and through you, and spilled forth your scarlet river on a snowy, marble floor, knowing straightaway that you will still live is *victory*—that is victory, that is freedom. When you become fearless, so that no matter what anyone does to you, it does not matter, you *have* become God, for nothing can destroy a thought, and you are the thought that has given credence to everything else.

The battleground as it is seen in this hour. From the black hole emerges an outlaw who is right in his truth, and who, according to prophecy and will, is bringing forth a great armada. You will not know from where it comes, for it has the whole range of space to advance forth from.

The armada is not armed with sticks and stones, nor is it armed with little things that drive around and fly around and blow up things—it is not that elementary. The armada is armed with a sting like a scorpion from above, and you cannot hide from it. If you seek a mountain to hide in, it will rend the mountain and find you. And there is no sea deep enough to hide in, for they can part the waters and dry the sand and find you. There is no grave that you can hide in; they will bring forth your bones. You have *nothing* on this plane that will combat their armaments—nothing.

Knowing full well that your toys of war cannot combat that which is coming from above, a colony of thirteen, who are a brotherhood, have taken counsel on your behalf and have devised a gathering—a host has been called forth from beyond the Northern Star. On your behalf, this host will lay siege to the armada of the great God of Wrath. Those days are on the future sunrise. And unto those who look at it, the Twelve Days of Light are the assumed days that are coming, when the whole of the void will be lit.

Now, imagine *billions* of suns radiating all the time, without the turning of the earth on its rotational axis to hide you from the sun. Even where the moon is, there will be light—there will be light all the time, but of greater intensity than what you now experience. The light will emanate from the battle of great ships, for when they spew forth the light and the bombardments from their vessels, they will light the void in doing so. The Twelve Days of Light is a battlefield.

Winners, Losers, Finders, Keepers

The Great Intimidation will occur slowly on your Earth-gameplane, to introduce you to seeing such things in the sky. The *introduction* is already underway; I have manifested openly on this plane entities to prepare you to see that goodness also lies beyond the stars, and it does in greater measure.

This *preflight period* will intimidate your government and all the governments of your world, and perhaps for once they shall join together in an open need to be together, not intimidated by the enemy within, but by the one without. I cannot issue the words to describe the purposeful good which *that* does. So all in all, the Days of Light are very much worthwhile.

Is there a question of who is going to win the fray? I shan't answer that. All I can tell you at this hour is that you are forever energy—*forever*—and you must *know* that, for you can prick yourself simply and you shall bleed. See how delicate you are?

Do not rely upon the body but rely upon the strength within to carry you through, for surely if I take your body from you and split it in two, you will still be. The peace that passeth all understanding shall still be yours. You must *know* that. And listen, if these peoples who once functioned in perfect order can be reminded to do so again, there will be no victory for *who*ever wins. My part here is that I told you so! That is all.

FRGB CANDIDATE: I'm understanding you to say that many of us will die in this process. Am I correct in understanding that?

FLIGHT INSTRUCTOR: Not directly—indirectly.

FRGB CANDIDATE: The physical body.

FLIGHT INSTRUCTOR: Indirectly—because of fright. Fright will cause many to perish, for they will panic and run amok and endanger themselves. Fright will be the greatest slayer of humanity. All in all, you will be a very protected little group of entities. You will see this display openly and a few will be affected by this war indirectly, but no siege will be laid directly on this plane, regardless of the declaration of *any* God's plans otherwise.

FRGB CANDIDATE: What other preparations should ensue?

FLIGHT INSTRUCTOR: Don't live for the day, live for the *now*. If you find shelter and gather up foodstuffs for famine, you are using your intelligence and living. You will still live—don't prepare for war, prepare to *live;* then there is no war. Just be who you are, that is all that is necessary. The elusive Kingdom of Heaven is realized when peace becomes the tranquility of consciousness. That can only be achieved when everyone is happy, living in unresolved joy.

I will tell you this, it did not please me to answer this, your question, because you are already frustrated with your changes on the horizon. I dare say this does not help matters.

FRGB CANDIDATE: [laughter]

FLIGHT INSTRUCTOR: I answered your question, not to frighten you—none of you. If you are frightened of this, get a hold of yourselves. How many deaths does it take for you to die to realize you're going to be born again?

I have communicated with you only to engage enlightenment, to spur contemplative thought and appreciation of what is being done on your behalf. As long as you are the intimidated rabble, the limited man, God *without,* you can easily be overtaken—easily. Tyrants do it all the time to you; your neighbors do it to you consistently.

When you begin to be arrogant and know what you are, and *who* you are, then you do not become so enslaved—you become free. In order to become sovereign God, you must *be* free— *Destination Freedom!* Your mission is to contemplate the power that flows through your being; contemplate what God *means.* And contemplate *why* you haven't used all of your brain-power. Contemplate it, find the reasons why.

God is the simplicity of pure reason, pure knowingness. If you apply to your reasoning the *super*knowingness that you've gained from these pages, you'll reveal all the answers you've ever wanted. Way back when, you were stripped of your dignity and your Godhood. That was all they had to do to enslave the whole of humanity. The illusion, the dreamfog, has been perpetuated *successfully* for eons; that's why you can't think in expansive terms. Just contemplate it; there are answers there.

Now, I did a wonderful thing for your plane when I delivered this message of the great God of Wrath. I manifested for the whole world rings around your planet as heralds of peace so you would see these signs—even recognized by your scientists. This was presented so you could utter, *Yes, what this strange one has spoken is a truth!* It was only created for you to know that I am who I *am,* and what has been communicated to you is purposeful and *is.* If those rings are realities and truth, then there must be some truth to my litany, that you *are* divine. Apply it! That is all.

The mission of this Brief was to conquer fear. You are now prepared for your certification examination. We will meet again at the midnight hour. This Brief is concluded!

Misty morning sunrise. Pale light moves softly across the land-scape. Mind travels into absolute love. Absolute love, a realm without thought where all *is* thought. Into absolute love—where is that Shangri-La? Where is that place of seventy-three-degree warmth that's endless, of hot tubs on mountainsides born in breath-less panoramas, of strawberry nectar wines, of delicate nourish-ment that just is when you think it—fresh succulent, fulfilling.

Where is that place? Where is *Destination Freedom?* Perhaps only in the flightlevels of your mind—perhaps that's the only way you can take yourself time-traveling to myriad adventures in count-less dimensions. Perhaps only in the flightlevels of your mind can you live in absolute freedom. Then you can be free anywhere you are, in any setting you set in, in any country you live in, in the dimension of our minds called planet Earth.

Perhaps you can only exist in absolute love while sailing along in the layers of clouds that are the dimensions of your thought. In absolute love maybe the layer of absolute fear doesn't exist—perhaps you ride the wind, looping around fear, barrel-rolling over it, floating off to the reality of your dreams.

And then again, perhaps not.

Your Final Destination
CLEARED TO THE GREAT BEYOND

———∞———

Freedom
The End of Time

You've time-traveled from a flight student into an FRGB-rated candidate, all according to your flightplan. As your final checkpoints come into view, a rather remarkable milestone appears below you—there is no more pain in living life! Everything has become an isness to you, you know it in totality, and you allow it in Superlove. You're scheduled to blast off into the great beyond, the end of time. Along with Blue Seven, I'll see you on the other side of truth, innocent one.

This time-travel adventure that you've just flown through, can you give me a readback? What was this flightlog all about—the takeoffs and landings; the touch-and-gos; the spin and stall recoveries; plotting a course for far-off, exotic destinations? You've discussed problems and pitfalls with your flight instructor—flying by the book, then flying by instruments, and then flying by instinct. What was it all about?

You've soloed—your shirt was ripped off your back by your buddies and it's blowing in the wind with the windsock. You've learned to take danger out of danger. You've learned your radio calls, and you've been briefed about controlled airspace, or rather, about who is controlling *your* space. Are you ready for the checkride to acquire YOUR FRGB rating? Will you *ace* your written certification exam? Are you ready to fly into uncontrolled airspace?

What *was* this flightlog all about? The first word that it started with is what it's all about. And when you put yourself in the left seat of that cylindrical behemoth, you felt all the G-force, the guilt. When does this flightlog end? It ends at your final destination, when you stop laying *heavies* on *you.*

Simple. Your destination for all these eons has been *FL: Freedom.* Your forever process has been to rid yourself of the G-force. When the guilt of the ages slides away from your control surfaces, you're cleared into any flightlevel you choose, *fearlessly,* in freedom. How do you rid yourself of *all* your guilt? By *superloving* what you are. How do you superlove what you are? By knowing that you didn't originate as a guilt-ridden, Godfire Being—you originated as a *Godfire Being,* period!

The G-force has been a learned trait, taught to you fervently and continuously for millions of years by those who wish to enslave you. *They* know what you truly are; *they* know about all the secrets of the universe. They've been using them against you to keep you in line, to force you *to toe the line,* to enslave you with their doctrines, dogmas, and truths. You know who your enslavers are—*any* person or institution that continues to make you *feel* the G-force.

How do you escape from their enslavement? Not by destroying them, not by hating them, for if you do, *you* become a more grandiose enslaver than they. I know this—I became the greatest bastard there was as I plundered and pillaged, expressing to everyone *my* truth. The way out of your enslavement is to *superlove* those who wish to enslave you. Create your *own* empires of love, create your own economies of love! As the money flows into *your* empires of superlove, all the others will see the folly of *their* empires of enslavement.

Money is the great equalizer—if you *have* it, you're grand no matter what. In the super*tomorrow,* money will be used in love rather than for purposes of enslavement. Money will fall into the hands of those who intend to nourish this planet instead of those who treat it like an unwanted child. And when *that* example is seen by all the enslavers, when that example earns *more* money than all the enslavers, then you shall have your freedom—only then. And only you can *live* it. You who I am speaking to, you *know* who you are!

Fight Fire with Love

You cannot fight fire with fire, that has been seen through all the wars you insist on battling—someone always comes along and *out-fires* you! You *can* fight fire with love, *if* you offer the same rewards received battling fire with fire. Here are the rewards that you will offer to those who have enslaved you:

Joy in knowing that all *your* children are living in freedom and happiness.

Wealth galore for anyone who wants it.

Everyone will share in the responsibility of *their* life—there will be no more need for *saviors* in government, in the press, in business, in religion.

Families will flourish as all will become the *family of man.*

Those who govern will strive for only one reward: the love and respect of those who allow them to govern—*We the people,* remember?

*Super*love will flourish because fear will cease to exist; everyone will know that they live in forever, the fear of death will cease to be anymore.

You will begin traveling with and *without* your body, to myriads of exotic destinations that will make your head spin. You'll be so busy living in that fun and unresolved joy, you won't have any time for your headaches.

The G-force will turn into the Godforce.

Everyone will experience these delights—*everyone,* even those dignified and *proper* people who you think will *make fun* of these announcements. And you should know, they *already* know about all the joys that await you, that's why they've continued to enslave you—they're already experiencing some of the *good cheer.*

Your scientists know all about the worlds in the other dimensions, they know all about the *secret* powers that you've been playing *touch and go* with in this flight manual. They've been using the power against you, but soon they will be using the power *with* you—they will have no choice, it's time to share with *all* the children.

Raise the Backdrop of Forever

This grand illusion that has been played upon you has been played out for a spectacular reason: to show you what you *really* are, to break you out of your sandboxes and place you in the sea of tranquility, so to speak, the place where everything *is*. When you program your autopilot-Soul to this adventureland, you ascend to *FL:Freedom* in Superlove and peace.

What do you think *heaven* is all about? 'Tis not a place where you sit around all day eating popcorn, watching old movies. It *is* a place where you experience, adventure, and explore whatever it is you want to experience, adventure, and explore, in *total* unlimitedness. For if the Godsource is unlimited, do you think he would have created a creature such as you that would be stuck in unlimitedness through all his eons? Why would he do this—to make *himself* look good? Hardly, the Godsource doesn't need to look good to *anyone*—he *is* all and *all* is good.

Do you remember this checkpoint? When you judge *anything,* you judge some aspect of yourself—*that* keeps you limited, that keeps you spinning, that keeps you on the wheel, bouncing off the walls of your fearbox. That is God judging God, a spin-out configuration. You still don't believe you could be FRGB-rated? All your religions define God as omnipresent, *present in all things at all times.* If God is present in all things at all times, then *certainly* He must be present in such a humble creature as *you!* How can you quibble with this statement—even your religions agree with this.

Well then, what are you waiting for to blast off into the grand unknown? Do you need permission? Alright, you *have* permission—it's okay with your mother, she wants you out of the house anyhow; your father is quite excited about it even though he may not *agree* with it; your government would *love* it, they are *exhausted* trying to take care of you, a bit like a worn-out babysitter—you witness their fatigue and confusion every day. So *go for it,* fly out of your doldrums, let's fly into some excitement and fun. Let's rise to the occasion and *be* Godfire Beings!

How? You've read this time-travel adventure, this flight-manual into forever. Use it as a guidebook—keep it with you to refer to as your adventures unfold before you. *Everyone* that you communicate with, come in contact with, know them to be a runner to you, an advisor. Listen carefully to everything they say; listen carefully to *all* your thoughts and reactions—watch for your responsibility, your *respond ability.* Everyone that you touch and go with is a mirror for you—they've been called forth by your autopilot-Soul to instruct you in a procedure that is tricky for you, because the rust has set in.

And when you see the brilliant light of this flight instruction, *don't* rush off to find a soapbox to set up at the corner of First and Main. What do we need with *another* religion? Don't solo so haphazardly—you might crunch a few landings. You don't need to save anyone, the world doesn't need saving—it *needs* to be left alone so it can evolve into the glory that it is.

When you *see the light* and you are quiet about it, you've remained humble. When you see the light and shout about it, someone or something will come along with *more* power than you for the purpose of returning you to humbleness. And this law is as dependable as the Law of Lift: The more obnoxious you are, the more illustrious your humbling.

If you truly superlove yourself, you'll be close-mouthed about your becoming process, *your* flightplans, arrivals, and departures. And if you truly superlove the others who are flying right along on your wing, be closemouthed about *their* flightplans—when you allow them, you *are* superloving them. And contrary to popular opinion, they really *will* correct their own course, they really will learn how to spin-recover on their *own.* You don't need to be the *know-it-all* who saves the day for them—let *them* save their day.

A Support Manual

This flightlog was created to support you while you're fitting the puzzle of your flightplan together. Maybe you've asked yourself these questions:

Where *am* I going? How did I land at *Destination: Nowhere?* What *is* my reality base? What beliefs act on me every moment, creating and influencing my dreamfog? How have I lost sight of what I am? What genius am I capable of? How do I sift through the millions of thoughts that I'm bombarded with each day, to pick and choose the thoughts that make up my perceptions and dreamfog of reality? Who taught me how to sift?

How do I clean up my ship so I *can* fly out beyond my no-where realities into the exotic destinations of *Destination Freedom?* Now that I know I am more than just a body, more than just a mind, what really am I? How can what I really am be augmented in the tomorrows that are here today? And how can I time-warp back to my present-day reality the pictures in my mind, to assist in the unfolding and the evolution of life as we know it on planet Earth?

Now that I *know* what I am, how can I use the FRGB rating I've earned to create the reality in mass of what I am? And how do I do that without devastating the environment of another, my brother?

If you've asked, you've changed, there's movement—you're not like Ogg and Grogg any more. Perhaps it just could be that the reality that you see everyday with your eyes, hear everyday with your ears, breathe in everyday with all your senses, is *not* the only reality there is. Vast dimensions, of which you have not the faintest perceptions, could exist. They've all been hidden away from you by the illusion of your distorted self. The reality illusion that you are familiar with protects its *own* self, hides itself behind fear. The vast dimensions that wait *out there,* are disguised in your imagination.

As you begin to familiarize yourself with *FL: SuperC,* you'll be able to discern between fear and imagination. That breach in *The Wall,* will allow you to uncover *your* knowingness; your FRGB powers begin to unfold. And what is quite comical about this entire *uncovering* process is that you know a *lot* more than you've been letting yourself think you know. The Guilt-force, enforced by fear, is what holds you back; imagination is what shows you the depth of your nature.

As you begin to weigh imagination against *your* dreamfog concepts of what a Godfire Being is, you'll begin to formulate *your* new realities. Why has the age that is moving into view been called an age made up of formless structure? *Your* structure is going to be different from everyone else's structure, your flightplan is completely different from anyone else's.

That's why judgment is such a limitation, why it holds you back, protecting your turf, so to speak. When you judge something, you put it back into that box, that nice, safe place where you examine all things: *Is it a threat to me? What great lengths must I go to, to understand this new experience? How will I define it, how will it fit into my understanding of what reality is?*

Human beings instantaneously place form and structure around anything that is new to them, anything that is a change to them. It is a survival mechanism that allows you to identify, categorize, evaluate, and be safe with anything that comes along. You can be *safe* with it now, because you know how it fits within the boundaries of the fearbox you've placed it in.

The Corner of the Envelope

The FRGBs of tomorrow will be those who don't *need* to judge anything, who don't *need* to lock experiences up in boxes, who are safe with adventures and change simply because those experiences *are,* not because they can be put in a box. Anytime you *need* to put something in a box, you're enslaved to it, you are in *fear* of it; you're throwing away all the hours you've earned flying in the unlimited power of Self.

And any time you need to prove to someone else how grand you are, you're just fooling yourself. An altered ego that is altered *spiritually* is perhaps the most mischievous ego there is. It is also referred to as the religious belief that becomes a fervor. The historical, worldwide devastation and carnage that have been caused by those fervent in their religious beliefs has been appalling.

There is no one whom you need to fool, to impress—it doesn't matter if *your* crystal collection is the finest on the block, nor if *your* religious beliefs are the best and only true ones; that's *old* age. The new-age premises are being expressed by those who could care less about being defined, who live how they want to live as they *honor* all those who they interact with. Perhaps that is what it is to be a God; perhaps that is what a Godfire Being is; possibly *that* is what tomorrow is all about.

The corner of the envelope of *Destination Freedom* has just been discovered. Some of you are poking your nose through The Wall, feeling a glimpse of it. The age of tomorrow, the Light Age, is not a fad. The thrill of the discovery of the grandeur of Self will not fade, it will continue ad infinitum. And through its forever ongoingness, *everyone* will be a part of it. There are no leaders— everyone is his own leader. There are no followers—there is no one leading to follow. There is not just *one* light, all are Godfire-Lights.

Kick in your afterburner by watching everybody *become* what they are; put your consciousness *inside* theirs. Then you can love them, for you *are* them. You will feel all their fears and heartache, you will know all their hopes and dreams, you will love all of their frustrations and let them be what they are.

And if someone one day humbles himself enough to ask you what you're all about, tell him you've discovered what you are, and that it is indeed, quite lovely. The new age needs no heroes, it needs no definitions—once defined it would become the *old* age all over again. There's a flow that emerges within you, a peace that tells you you're right on course; a dignity that allows you to laugh the most raucous of laughs, a joy that lets you lean back in your chair and smile the smile of harmony. You will know it; you will have become in vogue to yourself.

The Release

Where does unresolved joy come from? From the release—the release of self-guilt. Self-guilt cannot be released until you are released from the fear. The fear is almost as bad as *the smell!* The fear of what? You're not frightened of dying—you've died a million deaths. Torture—are you afraid of torture? You'll just ascend from the body when you don't want to experience the pain anymore. Abandonment—you can't be abandoned, you are all things. Who could abandon you? Where would they go?

The fear that everyone is in fear of is the judgement of self *by* self. Who else could judge you, other than you? What else could make you miserable, other than your judgments of you that make you miserable. It is a pretty heavy *heavy* to lay on yourself—after all, it is God judging *God!*

This entire universe that you perceive is an illusion. The illusion is to show you that you are all of it. It is all created from the dreamfogs of your collective mind. It is here for one purpose— to break you out of the judgement of self. That's it. That's all that it's about. History never did happen, it's not happening now; time is happening now, and the now moment is happening now, but the illusion of you is flowering into the specimen of the Fully Realized Godfire Being. (I'm not so hot on abbreviations!)

If I could say it a thousand, million, *billion* times, I would. The fear that everyone is in fear of is the judgement of self by self. The fear that everyone is in fear of is the judgement of self *by* self. The fear that everyone is in fear of is the judgement of self by self. The fear that everyone is in fear of is the judgement of self *by* self. The fear that everyone is in fear of is the judgement of self by self. Let it ring, aye!

In the Garden

Come, fly with me on a time-travel adventure into hyper-thought. Once, when I left your three-dimensional Earth-plane to embrace the unknown God—to look for His face, to hear His voice—I began to realize what His face was and what the sound of His voice was. When I left, I came upon a garden, far from this place.

And the light in the garden was like unto your noonday sun, except that it did not burn, but gently warmed. And the color of this sun was more golden, and everything was pervaded by this golden light—the forest of living things, the emerald grasses swaying in the gentle wind, flowers budding and opening up to the warmth of the glory of this garden. The trees, living ancient beings, enveloped and captured the golden light, swaying in a warm breeze.

I wondered why I was here, but in the moment I had the wonder, I *knew* why I was here. I rounded a bend and came into a meadow of the most spectacular light. And I heard a throb of a melody. It resonated like all of life, from the grasses to the lily, to the trees, to the gentle breeze—all became a chorus of unearthly song and melody. It was they who were alive that gave credence to this melody.

And there I saw The One, sitting on a rock in the middle of the garden, listening—indeed, *listening.* And I contemplated what The One was, so I listened. What was it that It was contemplating? The One, the Is, was listening to a thrush, a beautiful bird, singing a melody. And The One was completely that melody—He was in the mind of the thrush, He was the whole of the garden. And yet, through the reaction of His mind, He gained the beauty of that which He created in an essence of profound understanding.

And I knew, in a moment, that The One and the mystery of man and woman was resolved in that garden. I knew, in that moment, far, far away, why man and woman are tolerated, if you will, by the very light that holds their mass of flesh and blood together.

That which is termed The One, the Is, God, had lived through His most magnificent creation. By *living* through the creation, the

250

action and reaction of God, The One's mind, called Life, was able to reflect and bounce back off the melody of the thrush, to own the beauty of that frequency. My greatest question was aroused in a garden, far away in vibration, by the answer who sat and listened to the thrush.

You Crossed Over at the Midnight Hour

Now, listen very carefully. Humankind is in the midst of its pre-ordained final destination. On 17 July 1987 at the midnight hour, there was an energy shift that occurred on this your Earth-plane. It was of such magnitude, so subtle yet so powerful, that in that hour everything that is called destiny was changed.

And as the clock chimed the hour, it fell in a silent house, yet this energy shift has affected and been impressed upon the lot of you, *all* of humanity—*everywhere!* Those who hunger for their association with their creator heard. The melody did not come in words, the sky did not part, though there is now a light in the heavens that is not diminishing, but it was an energy shift—something beyond relative fact.

This energy has changed forever your future—*forever*. And such is this outpouring—I will tell you whence it comes. It is coming from The One who is standing in the garden. It is coming with all the love and majesty and tenderness that is in forever. All of you are consumed in that vision, for the entirety of the omnipresent is pouring out to *you*. That is what changed.

You are living in the most precarious of times. The prophets who sealed your destiny are now standing on the brink as *Saints* watching. The One in the garden, the *whole* of Its mind, the whole of that which is termed Its love, is pouring out to all of you. Why? Because there are a few who can feel it—they *know*. The birds know; the cattle of the field know; the fish, they know. The animals, in their docility, know. And a few of you know.

You crossed in the night—many of you slumbered, some of you drunk, some of you drugged, and some of you sweetly asleep.

You crossed into the blessed aisles to where the love of The One is pressing you simply to turn and embrace that face, that feeling, that hunger, that spirit, that life. And what is the turning? Is it to look, yes, in the heavens? It might do you a world of good. Is it to search? Indeed. And what is it to turn back to the *I am?* All you have to say is, *I am the essence and the breath of you.*

What is the urgency of this communiqué? Man at this moment has prepared arms to protect his kingdoms, and you are right in the middle of it all. Your choice is to bring back the understanding of the divine man and woman, and not to mock the Godsource by saying, *I am,* or to continue to become diseased, to continue your malice, your hatred, and your unkind and unloving attitude. Your choice is to be what the mystery of man and woman was—to emulate the *essence* of the Godsource as He appeared in His garden to hear the thrush, that the action and reaction could be owned, experienced, loved.

Your teachers have failed you. You cry that you are victims of circumstance yet, you created the circumstance. You wail that you are jailed by your emotions, but *you* jailed them. You cry out that you are the victim of humanity, of technology, of sciences— you accepted them to enhance your *comfort zones.* You wail that your plane is polluted—tolerance is one thing but living truth is quite another. You've become so unfeeling, that you wail for universal love and peace and find despicableness in your brothers— what hypocrisy!

You say you are *Gods*—no, you are man and woman. You yell that you are experiencing a new, expanded consciousness. No, it is only a view from the other side of the box. You insist that you will be saved. Have you ever prayed for those who thought you wouldn't? You label yourselves *New-Age.* In the mind of The One, there was never *new,* there was only life—*new* is the hypocrisy of the old.

There is no new age, there is only you, and that is a living truth. What is it that you have made a pilgrimage to, to learn? What is it that you have been seeking—yet the words fall as empty petals to the ground like a dying flower? You think you are ascending up through seven levels of consciousness in man? There is but one, and that is The One.

A Light That Shines In

You've been endowed with the choice and the free will that has assured your immortality. Immortal? Do you think you're going to die and maybe, or maybe not, fly beyond the grave? No, you're going to the flightlevels of your own restricted consciousness, which *you* created, because, being as divine as you are, nothing else exists unless it is through your perception. So you time-travel to what you can perceive, and yet you are immortals.

There are those of you who have lived to consume their intelligence with only that which exists in front of them. No wonder you cannot hear the voice from within. There are those of you who have been exploited by your teachers and thus you have been betrayed. The One is the living fire in all that you are; there is *more* beyond the grave. And now, with this energy shift, you can live in the knowledge that there is, after all, purpose to this life; action and reaction, the beauty of the flesh, something the angels have not and could not experience.

There are those of you who would rather by choice choose to say, *What folly! This is all there is.* Have you prepared only for the flesh, or are you reunited with the Superlove that will take you into eternity? The *damned* are the hypocrites who speak of brotherly love and love not their brothers; who speak of the glorification of man without The One, because The One is a tacky thing to speak about in these days and times of what is termed perverse intellect. And if God is spoken of at all, He is defined within religious dogma; remember the crusaders, who would kill you to redeem you?

Do you know how it is when you pass by people on the street and never look into their eyes? You just pass by each other like specks of dust in the universe, never noticing the presence of the other? The best place to experience this is New York. Now, don't take me wrong, *I love New York,* but really, when there are twelve thousand people walking down the same sidewalk, it *is* a little difficult to make personal contact. And if someone does, you think he's a mugger, anyhow!

Well, on one of my shuttle flights, I bumped into this stranger. He just had that aura about him, you know, he had it together; there was a peace about him that attracted me. After the flight we exchanged pleasantries and dropped by the cafeteria for tea and crumpets. His card read, *James Summerlund, RNG, MSI*—sounded pretty official to me.

Well, we chitted and chatted and laughed about this and that, (you know how boys are!) and eventually I asked him "How come no problems?" He said he couldn't have any problems—he was a vagabond and always followed where the love flowed. I said that sounded pretty simple, but what about your rules, everyone has rules that they live by—you know the *Golden Rule,* the *Ten Commandments,* the *Good Book,* and all that.

He said he had his set of rules too. I asked him, were they an Eastern philosophy? He said no, they were pretty Western, he thought. I said, they must be *ESTian.* He said, no, they were just *ISian.* I said, they must be *JUNGian.* No, he said they were just *ISian.* "Come on," I said, "tell me!" With a straight face he said, "Okay, well, I live by everything that I learned in kindergarten."

I howled—everyone in the cafeteria turned our way, and I felt like diving under the table. *"In kindergarten,* give me a break," I said. He pulled out this worn crumple of paper and read to me his rules of life:

Rule 1. If you're nice to someone else, they'll be nice to you.
Rule 2. If you hit someone in the face, they'll probably hit you back, and they might be bigger than you.
Rule 3. Wash your hands after you fingerpaint.

Rule 4. During recess, try not to hurt yourself.

Rule 5. Take a nap *every* afternoon.

Rule 6. If you don't feel very good, warm milk and oatmeal cookies help.

Rule 7. Don't take things that aren't yours.

Rule 8. If a girl doesn't want to play with you, be nice to her and leave her alone.

Rule 9. Look both ways before you cross the street.

Rule 10. When sides are chosen to play a game, don't feel too bad if you end up on the wrong side. It's only a game.

"Let me see those," I said. I read them, slowly, thinking about each one, this time not laughing. I smiled, started to copy them down, and then realized I would remember them. "Well, I have to be leaving," I said, "it's nap time! Just kidding, I have to be on the flightline."

We walked out the door together and parted to go our separate ways. We shook hands and I said, "By the way, what do those initials stand for? He said, "Oh, the ones after my name? Well, RNG stands for *Real Nice Guy.* And MSI? That stands for *More Silly Initials!*" I shook my head, laughed, gave him a thumbs-up and said, "I'll see you again sometime. You know where to find me." He smiled, "I'll see *you* again. And you know where to find *me!*"

Unresolved joy, I thought as I walked through the *Authorized Personnel Only* doors to the ready-room. After I read those words in this flightlog, I really wondered about them. What was *unresolved* joy? What could it be? Had I ever felt it? If I had, how could I stay in that space all the time? Was it just a mindset? What switch could I flip to set my mind in it all the time? I suppose this *real nice guy* was a *runner*—I suppose I just bumped into an example of unresolved joy?

Well, on my climb-out that afternoon, looking over the sunset and the blush that it cast over the fields fresh with green, I felt *unresolved joy.* It just hit me like a ton of bricks. I wasn't expecting it, so I knew it wasn't a pseudoenlightening, cosmic experience concocted by my altered ego self. It was real and as simple as grandma's apple pie—I had released myself from self-guilt; I had finally learned when I was judging myself. I finally stopped judging others. I *super*knew what unresolved joy was.

That afternoon, I flew into *FL: Freedom.* A *master?* A master is one who throws his masterswitch to *ON!* A master is one who masters his illusion.

Somewhere Along the Jet Route

Somewhere along the path to the garden, God went out of fashion. Perhaps it was because of the world's religions; perhaps because of their rules, regulations, and rituals. Perhaps it was because no one could describe what God was; perhaps because it has been blasphemy to strive toward that light. I know these truths will make many squirm in their seats—you're angered and embittered and you hate me for talking of this, for you would rather hear all the ways you can glorify yourself, giving credit *only* to you. I will allow your life to give the glory to you.

And there are others of you who don't want to recognize that there is someone watching you, because you have never embraced Superlove, therefore you despise it. Your truth is that in many ways, the only manner in which you *can* glorify yourself is to belittle and destroy, to bear false witness and judgment, to hate those simple souls who live their truth. I will allow your life to give the glory to you, also.

I was nothing—*nothing*—without the essence of the unknown Godsource felt within me. And all my bloody accomplishments were nothing without the purpose of life. You who sit here in flesh and blood with a throbbing heart, I desired you to remember the greatest message of all: that you *are* the Godfire-essence in flesh, that there is a living *fire* within you, and that you are accountable to the omnipresence called life, for that is where you have your purpose in being.

The Last Turning

In preparing for the days to come, in flying through the fires of limited emotions, you've misplaced what it is to turn your face to the living fire of that which created you, the thought that gave birth to the light. In all of this endeavoring to be impeccable man, to have all your dreams manifested, to prepare your covenants of faith, knowing that times are changing, you have instinctively forgotten The One, the Is, who has given you the ability to be who and what you are. Don't you know that in all your hustle and bustle and do-gooding achievement, there exists The One who loves you *immeasurably?* Through Its grace you've been allowed to be.

Woe unto you who do not think beyond your own loins and your own womb, beyond the cosmetic surface of your own features. Why do I say *woe?* Not for the calamities of those who sit in a place where all things are concluded, where there *is* no achievement. I say woe, because you have missed the greatest love of your life, the very essence that I was on fire with in mine.

How important are you? *Everything* is watching you. And The One is holding you dear, waiting for the soul that hears. And what are the choices in these days? Well, if it had been left up to the prophets, you would have reached the holocaust already—already this earth would be a smoking cinder. And if the religions were right, Lucifer would be letting you into his hells to give you everything you ever wanted here on earth, until you want pain just to break the monotony.

If it was within God's or Man's or Woman's irreversible choice, it would have happened already. In other words, there are the most tenuous hours appearing in the future sunrise, because the Superlove and the energy is pouring out from The One for the choice to change, for reality to be understood, for forever to be known.

The Godsource is not angry—He still listens. And He does not despise, as others would have you believe. But because of man, The One's love will reign supreme—it must! And unto the Godsource, the omnipresent Is, the mystery of man is about to unfold. From a destiny that has been set and sealed emerges a voice that is crying from the wilderness—*"Wake up. Embrace the divinity within you. Go back to the earth, go back to the plow. Go back to the water that runs free. Go back and love the garden."* And you are hearing, you are listening—thumbs up!

You Are Not Doomed

You will never be threatened by any insidious weapons that will char that sweet grass into a cinder. No, for though I am despised, though I am called the deceiver, the anti-Christ, the devil, I am still here to convey to you that you are not doomed, that you are superloved for the importance of flesh and blood. Why couldn't the angels ever understand the mystery of man? Because they never *were* man; they never embraced through a pulsing heart an emotion so great and so encompassing that it would lift the hearts and souls of all mankind. You are *that* essence.

I did not come to this most remarkable place once again to create revolution or to create war. I have appeared to tell you what I know about you, to uplift your hearts and your souls, so you can see that you are not wicked, you are *divine*. I came, and only a few recognized me. It was simpler to recognize wickedness than it was to recognize Superlove and truth and the opportunity of that which is everlasting. Could this be the last communiqué? How do you know that this is not the truth?

I will send you a vision; I have already called it forward. The vision is to see the garden back through the eyes of The One, for in the vision all things are known. And this truth will ring through the halls of eternity for you, oh precious human beings, who have never had the opportunity to see through the eyes of The One; who

258

have never had the opportunity to raise your clay bodies up into absolute love. For you, The Ones in the garden.

Sweet, Indeed

My moments with you have been sweet, indeed, for I love you immensely. Watching you grow and bloom as my brothers and sisters, you are *endeared* to the whole of what I am, whatever you think I may be. And where I go, you are not ready to come, but there will arise an hour when you will. You, the Godfire Beings, shall one day, by the will of the Godsource within you, become the next realized Supergods.

I am not a teacher, I am your brother for all times—remember that. It took far-reaching courage to pick up this flightlog, to fly through these pages on the wings of my scribe. It is also the courageous one who takes the sword and masters himself. Wherever you go, wherever you will be, I will be with you always. Learn to *know,* and in superknowingness own unresolved joy in your autopilot-Soul, that your Soul may illuminate the whole of the world. It is your destiny.

Where I go, I carry with me an imprint of you, which I hold dear to my breast, as I would a newborn—I *know* you, I *love* you into the forever wind. You, the infinite mind endeavoring to contemplate itself, know this one thing—that where infinite mind exists, you are certainly there in the sweetest of memory. *You* live on into forever. You *have* earned your wings—the feelings that you feel within you, they will fly you into tomorrow's sunset. I go back home to the garden from where I came. Life is the reality, it is the staging area of the dreaming Gods—may it be forever, and it will.

There Shall Come a Day

There shall come a day where all great nations, large and small, will cease to exist. All will be one nation, filled with Godfire Beings fully realized, Supergods who will herald forth *Starship Earth,* a Super*world.* This Superworld shall exist in a veritable paradise that will nurture its inhabitants, instead of continuing the enslavement of the newborns. That day will come and you shall see it soon, for those who stand with me are affecting the consciousness.

The *horrendous* profit structure you are now under will lift. The pittances you have been thrown to sustain your life will grow into king's ransoms for all the meek who *are* the earth. You will be freed from your creeds, your religions, your *hells,* your damnations, all your fears that keep the *have*-nots having not. You will remember who you are, and not allow it. And you will *not* allow it in love, Superlove for yourself and all that you see.

And you will march in droves to the gates of your prisons, and you will open your doors to freedom. You will live in a paradise that will allow *all* things to be. You will discover all that you are and all that you've created. You will feel awe at the discoveries of your creation. You will give birth to the new seeds of tomorrow. You will cry the tears of yesterday. You will fly with the wind into *Destination Freedom.* You will *never* be alone. You have reached the pinnacle of your destiny.

Turn around and see what you are. Have joy in what you are, for in you exists the paradise of tomorrow.

Sources

The Ramtha Videos
The Human Drama
The Next Step: Superconsciousness